PROGRAMMING PRODUCTIVITY

PROGRAMMING PRODUCTIVITY

Capers Jones

Chairman, Software Productivity Research, Inc.

McGraw-Hill Book Company

New York   St. Louis   San Francisco   Auckland   Bogotá   Hamburg
Johannesburg   London   Madrid   Mexico   Montreal   New Delhi
Panama   Paris   São Paulo   Singapore   Sydney   Tokyo   Toronto

This book was set in Times Roman by The William Byrd Press, Inc.
The editors were Gerald A. Gleason and Joseph F. Murphy;
the production supervisor was Leroy A. Young.
The drawings were done by J & R Services, Inc.
R. R. Donnelley & Sons Company was printer and binder.

PROGRAMMING PRODUCTIVITY

1 2 3 4 5 6 7 8 9 0 D O C D O C 8 9 8 7 6 5

ISBN 0-07-032811-0

Library of Congress Cataloging in Publication Data

Jones, Capers.
    Programming productivity.
    (McGraw-Hill series in software engineering and
technology)
    Includes bibliographies and index.
    1. Computer programming management. 2. Electronic
digital computers—Programming. I. Title. II. Series.
QA76.6.J659 1986   001.64′2′068   85-5194
ISBN 0-07-032811-0

To my loving wife, Eileen

CONTENTS

PREFACE

The computing and software industries are becoming two of the greatest industrial phenomena of all human history. In the space of 30 years, computers and software have joined the automobile industry, the aviation industry, and the telecommunications industry as technical endeavors that will change the way humans live and work. There is evidence that by the end of the century, computers will be standard household appliances and programming will be a basic skill learned in childhood at the same time as reading, writing, and mathematics.

In 1985, the world is still uncertain as to how computers and software can best be absorbed into daily life. In commerce, industry, government, and educational institutions, the impact of computers and software is daily becoming more pervasive, and the benefits of computers are sometimes overshadowed by the problems which have surrounded them.

The major problems have been the high costs of computers and the staffs required to run them and program them. In large industrial and commercial enterprises in 1985, the data processing staffs may sometimes exceed 3% of total corporate employment, and the total expenses often exceed 5% of sales.

Further, attempts to automate critical business activities have not always been successful. Long development periods, outright failures, development cost overruns, high maintenance costs, unfriendly systems, and low quality levels have been so common as to alarm both senior management and end users.

This book is intended to summarize the experiences of the first 30 years of commercial and industrial programming and to point out both the real progress that has occurred and the trends that are likely to take place in the future.

Before any technology can be evaluated, it must be measurable.

Programming has proven to be one of the most difficult human activities to measure or quantify. Chapter 1 covers the major software measurement paradoxes and problems which have concealed true improvements behind spurious results.

Chapter 2 explores the new and emerging sets of measurements that are starting to overcome the historical measurement problems and are actually revealing the true economic productivity of software systems.

Chapter 3 dissects the major variables that have been quantified and are known to be significant factors affecting software productivity and quality. Each variable is shown in isolation.

However, not all of the variables that affect software projects have been quantified with sufficient rigor to state their true impact. Chapter 4 discusses the set of factors that can affect software projects in subtle and intangible ways.

Appreciation is due to J.H. Frame, the former director of IBM's Santa Teresa laboratory and the former ITT vice president of programming, for his support of programming and this research over the last 15 years. Appreciation is also due to T.E. Climis, the vice president of IBM's General Products Division, for his strong personal interest in quality, productivity, and measurements. Special thanks to Bert Albert for his aid in analyzing some of the demographic data and to Bob Kendall for his creative insights. Thanks also to Peter Freeman of the University of California at Irvine, the McGraw-Hill series editor. Special thanks to Gerald Gleason who has been the light at the end of a very long tunnel and to the supportive staff at McGraw-Hill for their help, patience, and advice. Finally, thanks to my wife, Eileen, for her support and assistance in producing this book, to Jackie Shahood who also devoted many tedious hours of her time, and to my mother for her long encouragement over many years.

Capers Jones

PROGRAMMING PRODUCTIVITY

INTRODUCTION

The word "productivity" is surprisingly ambiguous, considering the frequency with which it is used. In discussing software productivity with managers, practitioners, and senior enterprise executives, two common statements capture the essence of today's concerns:

1. The term "software productivity" implies reducing the calendar time required to develop new systems and programs.
2. The term "software productivity" implies lowering the amount of money which enterprises spend for software.

These two statements, repeated hundreds of times in many enterprises, are very revealing of why software productivity is important in modern business. At the individual project level there is an almost universal feeling that software systems take too long to be developed. While at the enterprise level, there is a strong feeling that the total amount of money being spent on software, computers, and staffs has grown to perhaps dangerous proportions.

By contrast, in its conventional economic definition, productivity means to increase the amount of goods or services that can be produced for a given input of labor or expense. The economic definition is cast in positive rather than negative terms, and that fact reveals yet another troublesome aspect of exploring software productivity. In order to deal with economic productivity, it is necessary to have some unit of measure for the yield of the development process, or the goods or services that are being produced. Historically, there has not been a workable definition for software yield, or exactly what is being produced. It is unfortunate that "lines of source code" do not qualify for being either goods or services in the economic sense: They are much too ambiguous to be considered goods and are plainly not workable for services. Several alternatives are being explored as economic yield indicators for software, but none is universally accepted as of 1985.

For the purposes of this book, the word "productivity" is used in the economic sense, and productivity will be discussed in terms of the three parameters of time, cost, and yield. This is an important distinction for software, because the three parameters do not change at the same rates or in the same ways. For example, some of the more effective ways of shortening software development schedules tend to drive up software costs, while some of the methods used to reduce costs tend to lengthen schedules and lower yields.

Programming productivity has become a major international concern, and program quality is soon to be equally significant. Now that computers are used by a majority of the world's business, financial, and industrial organizations, by both civilian governments and military organizations, and by most scientific and academic institutions, problems which once affected only a few large enterprises are now becoming almost universal.

Stated briefly, the issues are these:

1. Computers and programming systems have become vital in operating both high-technology and commercial enterprises and are also vital in government and military organizations.
2. A majority of high-technology products, from aircraft through weapons systems, now require computers and programming for their design and development.
3. A growing percentage of high-technology products now make use of embedded computers, microprograms, and conventional programs in order to operate; and in many cases both safety and reliability depend upon software.
4. Programming systems are now on the critical path to new product development in many corporations and are also on the critical path in new government and military systems.
5. Programming productivity, program quality, and program development schedules are now issues that affect the profits and competitive abilities of corporations, the timing and delivery of new products, the way that enterprises are organized and managed.
6. The consensus of business and industrial management, of government executives, and of military leaders is that programming today is the least professional and most troublesome of all high-technology endeavors. Programming is universally viewed as being too costly, too error-prone, and much too slow. Programming is also viewed as

being largely unmeasured and perhaps unmeasurable, and as being unacceptably low in predictive accuracy for reliability, resources, or schedule duration.

Programming and software engineering managers who work for large corporations or government agencies are aware of the frequent distrust with which their occupation is viewed. In candid discussions with senior executives and operating officers of several major corporations, some of the reasons for this distrust were freely stated: "Programming can't be measured and it can't be controlled" and "programming is always late and the systems are always full of bugs" were typical complaints.While statements such as the above are not universal, they are common enough to make those of us in programming take a careful look at our occupation and question what might be done to place programming at a truly professional level. In order to satisfy the concerns which senior executives have relative to programming and software, there are five fundamental issues that must be resolved:

1. Programming must shorten its development schedules, and reduce the amount of time necessary to drive a new software system through its development cycle.
2. The costs of large software systems must be reduced by a substantial percentage, in order to stay in balance with other enterprise expenses.
3. The rate of growth of programming and data processing staffs must eventually slow down and match the growth rates of the entire enterprise.
4. Software must become predictable within a reasonable margin of error, such as plus or minus 15%, when making estimates of schedules, productivity, and quality.
5. Software systems must achieve quality and reliability levels substantially better than current norms, in order for senior executives to feel relatively secure when planning warranty and maintenance strategies.

The purpose of this book is to explore these five fundamental issues and discuss the underlying factors that affect them.

For a task such as programming to be predictable, it must first be measurable. A close analysis of contemporary programming metrics reveals some mathematical paradoxes that have distorted the true results of programming's history and concealed significant progress. Units of measure such as lines of code have intrinsic deficiencies that must be overcome before they can be used safely.

When these paradoxes and mathematical misconceptions are removed, then accurate programming estimates become a great deal easier.

It is now technically possible to develop estimating methods that will come within plus or minus 15% of reality 90% of the time. This exceeds the criterion established by Boehm, who stated that a good software estimate should "come within plus or minus 20% of reality 70% of the time."

The second fundamental issue, to actually improve software productivity and quality and reducing development schedules, is a challenging technical issue, but significant recent progress has occurred and much more is anticipated. Currently in 1985, leading-edge programming projects are achieving quality gains of an order of magnitude relative to 1975 averages, with schedule reductions in excess of 75% occurring at the same time. In the sense of yield, software staffs in leading-edge enterprises are capable of delivering almost 10 times the functionality per unit of labor as industry averages of a few years ago.

When reviewing the projects that are already achieving high levels of productivity and quality, it is seen that certain technologies have been pragmatically effective, and the attributes of these technologies can be identified.

In terms of successful technologies, five general classes stand out as having significant impacts: (1) technologies which lower defect rates and hence minimize the largest cost element of programming; (2) technologies which minimize paperwork, which is the second largest cost element of programming systems; (3) technologies which enhance communication and coordination among the departments and locations involved in large system development; (4) technologies which utilize broad and accurate measurements from historical projects as planning and estimating inputs for future projects; and (5) technologies which substitute standard reusable designs and reusable modules for unique hand-coded functions.

In spite of the current problems and uncertainties associated with computer programming and software development, the prognosis is very favorable. A new science of programming is emerging that should be able to take a place beside engineering, medicine, mathematics, and other professional disciplines as a field that benefits and augments the human condition.

THE PROBLEMS AND PARADOXES OF
MEASURING SOFTWARE

Scientific progress in every field has been heavily dependent upon the ability to take accurate measurements. While it is true that Heisenberg's uncertainty principle questions the ability to measure accurately at the subatomic level, progress in all of the sciences that deal with macro phenomena has been significantly obliged to progress in measurement for progress in the science itself. To a surprising degree, Fahrenheit's invention of the mercury thermometer, Harrison's invention of the chronometer, and the invention of instruments to measure pressure, voltage, speed, the force of gravity, and other natural phenomena have been important precursors to new scientific concepts and sounder theories. For example, Kepler's discovery of the elliptical orbits of the planets was due to the accuracy of the astronomical measurements of Tycho Brahe.

The measurement of programming has been the weakest link in the whole science of software engineering. When the common metrics used for programming are explored under controlled situations, we discover three major mathematical paradoxes that have completely distorted the history of programming and concealed significant true progress. The paradoxes are:

1. Lines-of-code measures penalize high-level languages and often move in the wrong direction as productivity improves.
2. Cost-per-defect measures penalize high-quality programs and always move in the wrong direction as quality improves.

3. Ratios established for programming subactivities such as design, coding, integration, or testing often move in unexpected directions in response to unanticipated factors.

In addition to these major paradoxes, a number of other measurement problems must be overcome for programming to achieve the level of a science. The six most significant problems have been:

1. Failure to define the counting rules for source code statements or lines of code has introduced. errors of more than an order of magnitude into many published reports on both productivity and quality.
2. Failure to define the scope of effort actually included in productivity analyses has introduced errors of more than two orders of magnitude in many published reports on productivity.
3. Peripheral and support activities for programming projects (i.e. documentation, management, training, and travel) have been under-reported and largely unmeasured. In some cases, there are not even any metrics defined for the activities.
4. There has been a blurring together of the concepts of economic productivity (i.e. goods or services produced per unit of labor and expense) and common productivity (i.e. finishing a task as rapidly as possible). This has caused significant misunderstandings and has caused many measurement reports to focus mainly on code development, rather than on economic factors such as products delivered.
5. Some of the most significant factors that affect quality directly, and productivity indirectly, are still intangible and hard to quantify and are significantly underreported. For example, the physical office environment is seldom evaluated as a productivity factor.
6. The two elements of programming maintenance are the addition of new functions to existing programs and the repair of defects in existing programs. These two concepts have been blurred together, with the result that the costs of the two separate activities are not clearly distinguished.

Of all the issues that must be dealt with for programming to become a science, measurement is the most fundamental and the most important. Each of the major problems must be clearly understood for progress to occur. When they are understood, then it is possible to consider measurements that will be accurate and reliable. Chapter 1 takes each of the measurement problems in turn, and Chapter 2 discusses possible measurement improvements.

THE PARADOX OF LINES OF CODE AS A PRODUCTIVITY INDICATOR

Since the programming industry began, the single most widespread assumption about productivity has been that improving software productivity means augmenting the ability to write lines of source code at a faster rate.

Another assumption has been that high-level languages improve software productivity. However, if productivity is measured in terms of lines of source code produced per unit of time, then the most significant paradox in the programming industry is encountered: High-level languages will tend to cause lines-of-code production rates to get smaller rather than larger. This retrograde movement is directly proportional to the level of the language, and the highest-level languages will have the lowest production rates when a complete development cycle is measured.

Failure to understand this paradox, and failure to deal with it when estimating, is the largest known problem in measurement and estimating in the software engineering world. The paradox can be illustrated by three examples involving functionally identical programs that are written in Assembler language, in PL/I, and in APL respectively. In these three examples, the functions delivered to end users are the same. The Assembler language version of the program took 100,000 source code statements, the PL/I version took 25,000, and the APL version took 10,000. Assume that programming labor costs are constant at $5000 per person month.

Observe in Table 1-1 the impact of the paradox. While economic productivity improves significantly and total costs decline from $1,000,000 to only $400,000, cost per source line goes up 400% and lines of code per programmer-month decline from 500 for assembler language to only 125 lines per programmer month for APL. (These three examples are simplified to show results in whole numbers, but real-life examples are discussed later.)

The reasons for the paradox are because many of the activities of programming development, such as documentation, are not really affected by the programming language used. When a typical large software project is analyzed, over half of the total effort will go to tasks that are not affected by the choice of programming language.

This paradox is based upon a classic industrial phenomenon. When a manufacturing process has a high level of fixed costs and there is a decline in the number of units produced, the cost per unit will go up. Programming development also has a significant amount of costs that are either fixed or at any rate inelastic and not affected by source languages. When projects written in high-level languages are compared to projects written

Table 1-1 The paradox of lines of code as a productivity indicator

	Assembler	PL/I	APL
Source lines	100,000	25,000	10,000
Activity (person-months)			
Requirements	10	10	10
Design	30	30	30
Coding	115	25	10
Documentation	20	20	20
Integration/testing	25	15	10
Total person-months	200	100	80
Total cost	$1,000,000	250	125
Lines of source code per person-month	500	250	125
Cost per source line	$10	$20	$40

in Assembler language, these fixed or inelastic costs become increasingly significant, and they drive up the cost per source line and drive down the lines of code per unit of time.

This paradox also highlights a major issue: the lack of a clear distinction between economic productivity and common productivity. In standard economic theory, productivity is defined as the amount of goods or services produced per unit of labor or expense. For programming, economic productivity would mean the functions delivered to users per unit of labor or expense. A line of source code is neither goods nor services and hence it is not an economic unit of measure.

The lines-of-code paradox is made more troublesome by the fact that high-level languages actually do improve coding speed. Note in the assembler language example that coding alone proceeded at a rate of 870 lines per month, while the PL/I and APL versions proceeded at a slightly faster rate of 1000 lines per month. Yet this increase is overshadowed by the non-coding tasks that are always part of programming development and which have a tendency to act like fixed costs when an entire development cycle is analyzed.

When the paradoxical problems with source lines are initially encountered, it might be thought that switching over to object lines or bytes of memory would avoid the situation. However, object code metrics have another problem that is almost as severe. Measurements based on object code tend to penalize optimizing compilers and to achieve their highest rates for the least compact efforts.

For example, if the average Assembler language instruction takes 5

Table 1-2 The paradox of lines of source code as a quality indicator

	Assembler	PL/I	APL
Source lines	100,000	25,000	10,000
Defect source			
Requirements	500	500	500
Design	1,500	1,500	1,500
Coding	4,000	1,000	500
Documentation	1,000	1,000	1,000
Total defects	7,000	4,000	3,500
Defects per 1,000 lines of code	70	160	350

bytes to execute, then the 100,000 source-statement program shown in Table 1-1 would consist of 500,000 bytes. If the PL/I example in Table 1-1 were compiled on a checkout compiler, rather than an optimizing compiler, then each source instruction might expand to 40 bytes, and hence the 25,000 source-line program would result in 1,000,000 bytes. On the other hand, an optimizing compiler might take the same source code as input, and result in only 25 bytes per instruction, for a total of 625,000 bytes. In neither case are the results directly comparable to the original assembler language program, and so comparisons would be unreliable.

The paradox that true improvements are masked when expessed in terms of lines of code also affects quality, if all defect types are included. Table 1-2 gives examples of the kinds of defect counts that might be anticipated in the assembler language, PL/I, and APL examples shown in Table 1-1.

Note that in spite of a significant reduction in total defects, and an eight-fold decrease in coding defects, the defect count normalized to defects per 1000 lines of code heavily penalizes high-level languages. The reason is that for most large programming systems, errors outside the code are more significant than errors within the code.

The impact of the paradox of lines of code has caused three major problems for the programming community. These have been especially critical in commercial and governmental programming, where costs, schedules, and quality are often determined by contractual and marketing considerations. The problems are:

1. The paradox has been a major factor in estimating errors, since many managers assume that switching from a given language to a higher-level language will cause an increase in lines of code produced per time unit when in fact it causes a decrease. Estimates made without consideration for the paradox are immediately off the scale, and projects will be much more costly than anticipated.

2. When productivity or quality comparisons are made between projects written in different languages, the paradox always penalizes the higher-level language and conceals significant true gains in productivity.

3. When measurements are made at the enterprise level, such as corporate productivity and quality metrics programs, the paradox sometimes causes management to think that productivity or quality has declined, when in fact migration from lower-level to higher-level languages has brought about an increase in economic productivity and in actual quality.

As an example, if an enterprise produces an average of 100 new programs per year, and all of them are written in Assembler language, then it is not improbable for the average code production rate to be in the vicinity of 3,000 lines of source code per person year. However, if the 100 programs were in languages such as COBOL or PASCAL then the average annual production rate would not be much above 2,500 lines per person year, counting all activities and staff members in both cases.

To summarize, lines of code per unit of time is the most widespread unit of measure in the programming industry, but the paradox based on this metric is simultaneously the greatest single measurement problem. Both productivity and quality measures are affected, and the basis of the concern is that true economic productivity and true program quality can improve at the same time that measures of apparent productivity or quality based on lines of code move backward and appear to get worse.

Once the mathematical paradox associated with trying to use lines of source code as a productivity indicator is understood, then we can compensate for it. As discussed in Chapter 2, several ways have been developed to do this. Although it is now possible to use lines-of-code metrics without excessive distortion, the paradoxical results from incorrect and uncompensated historical usage have damaged the credibility of this metric to the point where it is unlikely that it will ever be fully credible again.

From the standpoint of economic theory, lines of code are not economic measures, and a basic deficiency of the software engineering domain is that no fully satisfactory economic measure exists for programming. Attempts to create economic metrics for programming are discussed in Chapter 2.

THE PARADOX OF COST PER DEFECT AS A PRODUCTIVITY INDICATOR

One of the most widely repeated aphorisms of the software community is "it costs up to 100 times as much to fix a bug during maintenance as it

Table 1-3 The paradox of cost per defect as a productivity measurement within a software development cycle

	Number of defects	Fixed costs	Variable costs	Total costs	Cost per defect
Reviews	200	$ 5,000	$20,000	$25,000	$ 125
Testing	40	$ 5,000	$10,000	$15,000	$ 375
Production	10	$ 5,000	$ 5,000	$10,000	$1,000
Total	250	$15,000	$35,000	$50,000	$ 200

does during development.'' This statement, as it is commonly used, is incorrect and has no basis in fact. Here too a fundamental rule of industrial production has not been recognized. Cost per defect is always lowest where the number of defects found is greatest, and always highest where the number of defects found is least. Since the number of bugs found during development is usually much greater than the number of bugs found during production, the cost per defect will always be higher during production. Indeed, for the few zero-defect programs being created, which still have some maintenance effort associated with them, cost per defect can reach infinity. This is because of the fixed and inelastic costs associated with defect removal. The situation is analagous to the classic industrial phenomenon of a manufacturing environment with fixed costs. If the number of units declines, the cost per unit must go up.

To illustrate the point, Table 1-3 shows the typical results of defect removal for an application program developed and used within a single location. Assume programming labor costs are constant at $5000 per person-month.

What occurs is that the fixed costs associated with preparation, training, and readiness become increasingly significant as the variable costs decline, and this artificially drives up the cost per defect and leads to erroneous conclusions. The major error introduced by cost per defect is failure to recognize that even high-quality, zero-defect software will have substantial costs associated with preparation and execution of defect removal activities, even though repair costs may be zero.

The major paradox associated with cost per defect is that as program quality improves, cost per defect will rise steadily until it reaches infinity for a zero-defect program, and hence this metric penalizes quality and rewards errors.

The cost per defect paradox has a mathematical reason for existing, and does not reflect the actual work of finding and repairing faults. It is due to the common method of calculating cost per defect by simply dividing the total defect removal expenses by the total number of defects removed. This method ignores the fixed and inelastic costs of preparation and execution, which will still be incurred even for zero-defect programs.

Table 1-4 The paradox of cost per defect as a productivity measurement for high-quality programs

Activity	Low-quality COBOL program	High-quality COBOL program
Design review preparation	$ 5,000	$ 5,000
Design review execution	$ 5,000	$ 5,000
Defect repair	$ 30,000	$ 2,500
Test case preparation	$ 5,000	$ 5,000
Test case execution	$ 5,000	$ 5,000
Defect repair	$ 50,000	$ 2,500
Total removal costs	$100,000	$30,000
Defects removed	500	50
Cost per defect	$ 200	$ 600

The cost per defect paradox, incidentally, also occurs in fields outside of programming, such as computer hardware repair, but its significance is less understood for software than for other activities.

There are three independent sources of expense in removing defects:

1. Preparation expenses, such as writing test cases
2. Execution expenses, such as running test cases
3. Repair expenses, such as fixing bugs and recompiling

Of these three, only the third is directly related to the number of bugs present in a programming system. Table 1-4 gives an example of the paradox. In the first case a low-quality program with 500 defects is shown, and in the second a comparatively modern program with only 50 defects is shown. Both examples assume COBOL as the programming language.

Note that although total defect removal costs for the high-quality program were 70% below those of the low-quality program, the cost per defect is greater by 200%. Clearly, something is wrong with a metric that penalizes quality.

However, once the paradox of cost per defect is understood, time and motion studies reveal true variations in defect removal efforts as a function of quality. As program quality improves in real life, both the number of simple bugs and the number of severe bugs are reduced at a faster rate than the mid-range defects. Thus the defects encountered in high-quality programs, on the average, actually do take more effort to repair than the defects encountered in low-quality programs. Since this point is counter-intuitive, Table 1-5 may help to clarify it.

In low-quality software, the enormous numbers of relatively simple bugs tend to mask the more serious bugs, when cost per defect is used to

Table 1-5 Defect repair costs in high- and low-quality software

Time to repair	Defects in low-quality COBOL program	Defects in high-quality COBOL program
One week (serious defects)	4	0
One day (moderate defects)	46	10
One hour (minor defects)	450	40
Total defects	500	50
Total repair time (hours)	978	120
Average hours per defect	1.956	2.4

assess productivity. To understand the economics of defect removal, it is necessary to analyze preparation time, execution time, and defect repair times separately. However, only a few reports such as those of Fagan [1] and the author [2] have dealt with the fine structures of defect removal.

To summarize, if overall defect removal costs are merely divided by total defects found, then cost per defect will always be greatest where the number of defects found is least. This is a purely mathematical paradox, and is based on the well known industrial phenomenon that in a manufacturing process with fixed costs, any decline in the number of units will raise the cost per unit. The fine structure of defect removal has been masked by the use of cost per defect, and it includes fixed costs such as preparation, inelastic costs such as execution, and variable costs such as repairs.

THE PARADOX OF PERCENTAGES AS PRODUCTIVITY INDICATORS

One of the commonest methods in the programming industry for expressing the relative costs of programming activities is the use of percentages or ratios, such as the historical rule of thumb for assembler language programs that design will take 20% of a software development cycle, coding will take 30%, integration and testing will take 50%; or the modern rule of thumb for high-level-language programs that design will take 40%, coding will take 35%, and integration and testing will take 25%; or the hypermodern rule of thumb for spreadsheet programs that design will take 5%, coding will take 90%, and validation will take 5%.

Unfortunately, ratios and percentages have paradoxical aspects which cause them to be very inaccurate and unreliable. The ratio-and-percentage paradox is a subset of the line-of-code paradox, and the first problem with using percentages is that they break down completely when programs in different languages are being compared. To illustrate this

Table 1-6 The paradox of percentages of productivity indicators

| | Assembler language | | COBOL language | |
	Effort (months)	Percentage	Effort (months)	Percentage
Activity				
Requirements	5	3.33%	5	5%
Design	10	6.66%	10	10%
Coding	50	33.33%	20	20%
Documentation	30	20.00%	30	30%
Integration	15	10.00%	10	10%
Test	30	20.00%	20	20%
Management	10	6.66%	5	5%
Total	150	100.00%	100	100%

problem, Table 1-6 presents a case with two functionally identical programs of which the first was written in Assembler language and required 30,000 source lines, while the second was written in COBOL and took 10,000 source lines.

Note that of the seven activities shown, three took exactly the same amount of time in both examples, but the percentages differ. Even more significant, integration differed by 5 months between the two examples and testing differed by 10 months for a total variance of 15 months. Yet the percentages for integration and testing are exactly the same in both programs.

There are many other phenomena that can cause ratios and percentages to vary widely from one program to another, and the general conclusion is that percentages invariably are misleading. Some of the other factors that cause ratio or percentage changes in otherwise similar programs are:

1. Programs involving multiple development locations will have significantly different ratios from single-site programs.
2. Programs involving new tools or insufficient tools will have significantly different ratios from programs developed with a well-formed tool set.
3. Programs that are novel or of a kind with which the staff personnel have no experience will have significantly different ratios from programs that are of a familiar type.

To demonstrate some of the cautions that surround ratios and percentages, it should be noted that coding, the heart of the software discipline, may vary from a high of 95% of all development effort for small personal spreadsheet programs to a low of less than 25% of all development effort for large government contract programs with significant documentation requirements, independent verification and validation, and other ancillary tasks.

Percentages and ratios are hazardous and unreliable, and their common usage for software projects is one of the reasons for estimating and planning errors.

VARIATIONS IN DEFINING LINES OF CODE

The next measurement problem to be discussed is not paradoxical in that the results do not move backwards or in counter-intuitive directions as progress is made. However, the range of variation from inconsistent definitions of lines of code can yield apparent differences in both productivity and quality of more than five to one.

Although the phrase "lines of code" is used daily by almost all commercial, industrial, and governmental programming enterprises, there is no universally agreed-to definition for exactly what a line of code really is. There are 11 major variations in two sets that must be considered, plus the special case of how to count deleted code. Following are the 11 variations:

Variations in Software Line-Counting Methods

Set 1: Line-counting variations at the program level

1. Count only executable lines
2. Count executable lines plus data definitions
3. Count executable lines, data definitions, and comments
4. Count executable lines, data definitions, comments, and Job Control Language
5. Count lines as physical lines on an input screen
6. Count lines as terminated by logical delimiters.

Set 2: Line-counting variations at the project level

1. Count only new lines
2. Count new lines and changed lines
3. Count new lines, changed lines, and reused lines
4. Count all delivered lines plus temporary scaffold code
5. Count all delivered lines, temporary code, and support code

Line-Counting Variations at the Program Level

There is a range of as much as 5 to 1 between the most diffuse counting technique and the most compact. Since few authors bother to define the line-counting rules they used, much of the world software productivity literature has an uncertainty of perhaps 500% attributable to line counting variations—plainly an unsatisfactory condition.

As an example, a single BASIC program analyzed by the author consisted, in round numbers, of 900 executable statements, 400 data definitions, and 100 remarks or commentary statements. The average number of executable statements per physical line was 2.5. Counted in the most compact way, the program might appear to consist of 360 physical executable lines. Counted in the most diffuse way, it might appear to consist of 1500 total statements.

Method 1, in which only executable lines are counted, is seldom used since it obviously excludes the important factors associated with data declarations.

Method 2, in which executable lines and data definitions are both counted, but comments or job control language are not, is used in some of the productivity studies published by the IBM Corporation [3] and hence is fairly common among IBM customers. Method 2 is used throughout this book as the standard method.

Method 3, in which executable lines, data definitions, and comments counted is the method used by Boehm [4] in his book "Software Engineering Economics" and hence is widely known.

Method 4, or counting everything including comments, is perhaps the simplest to use, since compiler output can often be scanned quickly for this result. However, since commentary lines are viewed as easy to write, there is a distrust of this method among productivity researchers.

Methods 5 and 6 deal with whether lines will be counted as physical records such as card images or as logical statements terminated by programming delimiters. Following is an example of two BASIC language statements on the same physical line. They simply interrogate a micro-computer's built-in calendar for month and day:

$$M\$=left\$ (D\$, 2): DA\$=MID\$ (D\$, 3, 2)$$

In method 5, the above example would count as a single line. In method 6, the portion to the left of the colon, which deals with months, would count as one line while the portion to the right, which deals with days, would count as a second line. In his book on Software Engineering Economics, Boehm [4] used method 5, while the data in this book uses method 6.

The distinction between Boehm's method of counting code and the methods of other authors illustrates the generally hazy status of software measurements today. There are no current standards, and each research-er selects the technique that seems most appropriate. Since Boehm uses methods 3 and 5, while this book uses methods 2 and 6, the two books would show the same programs as having different sizes. For programs written in assembler language and restricted to a single physical line per statement, Boehm's method, which includes comments, should yield sizes about 15% larger than the method used here. However, for programs in BASIC or other languages featuring multistatement lines, Boehm's method of counting physical lines rather than logical lines would yield sizes that are smaller by as much as 75%. Needless to say, when productivity researchers can define the size of the same program in ways that differ by several hundred percent, there is clearly a need for future standardization.

Line-Counting Variations at the Project Level

In the early days of programming, almost all programs were new, and all of the code was uniquely developed for each application. In this environment, it was appropriate to consider only new code production rates. Since developed code and delivered code were essentially identical, it was normal to measure development with a unit of measure such as lines of code.

But as the industry matures, more and more programming is done to add functions to existing systems. This is starting to trigger a subtle but profound change in both measurement and philosophy. What is important to productivity is not how fast a program can be developed, but how fast the program functions can be delivered. This change from emphasizing development to emphasizing delivery is paving the way to new kinds of economic studies, in which the value of reusable code, standard designs, and purchased software are considered.

If measurement switches from development to delivery, and reused code is considered in the productivity measurements, then enormous productivity rates can be encountered. Depending upon the quantity of reused code, productivity rates of over 25,000 lines of code per person-year are not uncommon, with peaks of more than 100,000 lines of code per person-year occasionally happening. Indeed, it is now technically possible to develop some new applications that consist entirely of reused code, with no unique hand-coded modules being developed at all.

Although the situation is still new, leading-edge enterprises are beginning to focus on the deliverable outputs of a programming development cycle, and not simply the hand-coded unique code. This is a step toward evaluating economic software productivity, although only a small step in that direction.

The other line-counting variations listed in Set 2 above are also concerns in industrial and commercial programming organizations. It frequently happens that during programming development a large amount of temporary or scaffold code will be developed for testing purposes and then discarded when the program is complete. A question arises, should this temporary code be considered for productivity purposes? Most enterprises do not include temporary code in their productivity metrics, although a few projects may count temporary code separately for calibration purposes.

It may be necessary to develop tools and support packages before a new program can be completed. Should these tools be viewed as independent programs and measured separately, or should their development be considered as part of the effort for the program they support?

From a technical point of view, the tool and support programs would be better dealt with as independent programs and measured separately. However, it may sometimes happen that for contractual purposes, the expense of tool development will be added to the expense of developing the primary application covered by the contract.

The Special Case of Deleted Code

Deleted code is technically the most difficult aspect of programming to measure. It is not uncommon for real-time programming systems to have considerable efforts devoted to pruning, or carefully going over the code to improve speed or reduce memory utilization.

Obviously, any metric that equates productivity gains with developing more lines of code per time unit will come to grief when the activity being measured is the deletion of lines of code.

Perhaps the commonest way of dealing with this situation is to simply ignore the deleted code. This of course drives down the productivity rate, but since performance tuning and code compression are difficult tasks, that reduction should be expected and planned for.

The lack of standard line-counting methods for programming makes productivity and quality research difficult, but it does not make it impossible. However, one factor comes close to making the research impossible, or at least the results unusable, and that is to publish a study on programming productivity or quality without stating the line-counting method used. This is a relatively common occurrence, unfortunately, and it means that much of the literature on software engineering productivity cannot be used for serious research, because the definitions either are not included or are not sufficient to understand what was being measured. Since the possible variations span a range of over 5 to 1, there is no way that the omissions can simply be ignored.

Many of the industry wide statistical studies of programming show scatter diagrams that vary over enormous ranges for apparently very similar programs. It is not commonly recognized, but the wide variations in reported productivity often reflect only the anomolies in measurement techniques and not true differences in a real-life productivity.

Table 1-7 Variations in apparent productivity attributable to variations in counting new, reused, and base code

Lines counted	Case 1	Case 2	Case 3
New code only	1,000	1,000	1,000
Reusable code	—	5,000	5,000
Base code	—	—	9,000
Total code counted	1,000	6,000	15,000
Lines per month	333	2,000	5,000

Combinations and Permutations of Line-Counting Techniques

The major variations in counting lines of code often occur together. Assume that 1000 lines of new code will be joined to 5000 lines of reusable code from a module library, and that this code will be added to an existing base program of 9000 lines, so that a total program of 15,000 lines of source code is delivered to users. Assume that the new code took 3 months of effort. Table 1-7 shows the ranges in apparent productivity that can result from these combinations.

Variations in counting at the project level are often joined to variations at the program level. In Table 1-8, the same program is shown with variations in defining lines, plus the inclusion of 1000 lines of temporary code which is not delivered.

In Tables 1-7 and 1-8 the apparent productivity for the same program, changing only the methods for how lines of code are counted, varies from a low of 333 to a high of 7,666 lines of code per month!

Table 1-8 Variations in apparent productivity attributable to variations in defining lines of source code

	Executable lines only	Executable lines plus data definitions	All lines	All lines plus temporary code
Lines counted				
New code only	500	1,000	2,000	5,000
Reusable code	3,000	6,000	8,000	8,000
Base code	5,000	9,000	10,000	10,000
Apparent size	8,500	15,000	20,000	23,000
Lines per month	2,833	5,000	6,666	7,666

LINE-COUNTING STANDARDIZATION

There are no standard counting methods for lines of source code in the industry currently. However, for any kind of productivity or quality studies to be decipherable or roughly comparable, it is necessary to know the counting rules under which the author developed and analyzed the data. The counting rules under which the examples in this book were developed are:

1. Executable statements (commands, verbs, and functions), data definitions, and labels are considered to be the elements of a line of code.
2. Comments or remarks are not counted, nor is job control language (JCL) if it occurs.
3. Reused code extracted from a module or macro library is counted each time it occurs in mainline code.
4. Base code to which new functions are to be added is counted if the new version will replace the existing base code and become part of the new delivered program.
5. Base code to which new functions are to be added is not counted if the original version will continue to be used, and is not a part of the new delivered program.
6. Lines are terminated by logical delimiters, not by the physical appearance of a line. Each statement within a multi-statement physical line counts as a separate line.
7. Deleted or removed code is not counted.
8. Temporary code is not counted.
9. Tools and support programs developed to aid a primary software package are not counted as part of the effort for the primary software package.

The emphasis of these counting rules is on programs as delivered to end users, rather than on the development of code. That is, by including macros, reusable code, and under some conditions, base code from previous versions of a program, the measures are aimed at assessing what users receive and not what programmers do. This is a significant change in point of view, but it is necessary to make this change in order to come to grips with the economics of software.

APPARENT PRODUCTIVITY VARIATIONS DUE TO SCOPE OF EFFORT

Once the fundamental paradoxes and uncertainties of dealing with lines of code have been overcome, a new and equally significant problem appears in the area of what human activities should be included in productivity measurements.

The widespread failure in the software literature to report exactly which activities were included in measurements and over what time span the measurements were taken has introduced potential uncertainties that in extreme cases can span more than two orders of magnitude. Table 1-9 shows the range of possible variation in measuring a single programming project in a single enterprise. Assume that the project consists of 50,000 lines of COBOL source code and that it will be delivered and installed by development personnel at 100 user locations.

The variation in apparent productivity of nearly two orders of magnitude is symptomatic of the fact that the software engineering literature has blurred together three different concepts of productivity without considering their various implications. The three are:

1. Personal productivity
2. Project productivity
3. Enterprise productivity

The first and oldest productivity concept is that of the personal productivity of an individual programmer. This concept was started by

Table 1-9 Apparent software productivity variations due to inconsistencies in defining scope of staff activities

Software activities included	Apparent productivity included in lines of source code per person-year
Coding only, measured for 1 day with the results converted to an annual rate	25,000
Module design, coding, and unit test measured for 1 month	12,000
Design, code, desk checking, and unit test measured for a complete project assignment	6,000
Activity of one programmer measured for 1 year, including breaks between projects and non-coding activities such as training	4,000
Requirements, design, code, desk checking, all reviews, integration, all testing, quality assurance, internal and external documentation, and management for the program	2,500
Requirements, design, code, desk checking, all reviews, integration, all testing, quality assurance, internal and external documentation, management, on-site delivery support to 100 customers, and customer training to use the program	750
Total software effort by an enterprise for one year, including cancelled projects, all development, all enhancements, and all maintenance	250

programmers themselves in the days when programming was done partly in machine language and partly in assembler language, and writing lines of code rapidly was such a difficult feat that those who could do it felt a justifiable pride in their accomplishment. Although historically the oldest, personal productivity is not a very satisfactory measurement method.

In the second productivity concept, project productivity, the concern is not just coding, but the entire development cycle, ranging from requirements through delivery and sometimes out through maintenance. Although project productivity is still commonly measured in terms of lines of code, much of the work is no longer coding, and activities such as documentation, quality assurance, and management must be considered.

The third, and emerging, productivity concept is that of productivity at the enterprise level, or economic productivity. Since economic productivity deals with goods and services produced per unit of labor and expense, productivity at the enterprise level deals with factors such as the costs of canceled projects, maintenance, capital equipment purchases, travel expenses, hiring and training expenses, real estate, and many other functions that were not historically considered aspects of programming productivity since they spanned many projects and were not "owned" by any single programming group. Yet enterprise productivity is in many ways the most important topic of the productivity domain. Improving productivity at the enterprise level implies knowledge of cost elements such as hiring, relocation, project transfers, cancelled projects, and many others. A much broader scope of measurement and analysis is required to deal with enterprise productivity than to deal with personal and project productivity.

Measurement of Peripheral and Support Activities

The desirability of considering economic and enterprise productivity brings up the point that modern programming spans a much broader range of activities than coding alone. Indeed, for very large systems such as an operating system or a military system, only about a fourth of the personnel involved may do any coding at all. Following are discussions of the major peripheral and support activities that should be measured at the project and enterprise level.

Documentation. While small programming projects may have comparatively little documentation, the documentation requirements for large programming systems sometimes elevate documentation costs to the greatest single expense element. For example, an analysis of the documentation of a large telecommunication system revealed a total of more than 100 different kinds of documents produced and more than 60,000 total pages, with an overall total in excess of 30,000,000 words. This was an average of 120 English words per line of source code.

While this was a fairly large system, the documentation produced was actually not unusually verbose. Large government and military systems may sometimes create over 125 kinds of documents, more than 250,000 total pages, and more than 125,000,000 English words, and may average more than 200 English words for every line in the delivered system.

Yet in spite of the very high costs associated with paperwork and software documentation, very few enterprises have measured this activity at all.

Defect removal. For medium to large programming systems, defect removal costs are usually the most expensive single activity, when all forms of defect removal from desk checking through reviews and testing are summed. Yet very few enterprises measure this cost, and a 1985 survey by Applied Computer Research [5] found fewer than 14% of the respondents measured software quality or defect removal.

In a large programming system of a relatively normal kind developed by designers and programmers of average skills, perhaps 30% of the total development effort is spent on defect removal activities: desk checking, reviews, inspections, tests, and of course repairing the bugs that are discovered. With so much effort and cost involved with defect removal, it should be a high-priority measurement item.

Travel and communication. The great majority of programming systems developed in the world are produced at only a single development location and have virtually no travel or communication costs. However, for programming systems that are developed among multiple locations, and especially for those developed among international locations, travel and communication will be one of the top three expense elements and may sometimes be the most expensive. One major software system, whose development involved five European locations and one U.S. location, required more than 3000 trips, and the cost of travel and hotels actually exceeded the cost of coding.

Hiring and relocation. Because the turnover and voluntary attrition rate among programmers is in the vicinity of 12% in the United States, most programming organizations have relatively high recruiting and relocation costs. By the time agency fees, furniture moves, mortgage assistance, and other costs are totaled, as well as the expense of training new hires in company policies and methods, from $25,000 to $75,000 per professional can be expended.

Capital equipment. It is interesting to note that the organizations at the leading edge in terms of productivity often average more than one terminal per programmer, accompanied by ample computing power and subsecond response time. One of the major issues in programming is to quantify just exactly what impacts capital expenditures have on programming productivity. Yet this factor is seldom measured or quantified at the project level, and many companies do not even have a convenient way of linking capital purchases to individual projects.

Quality assurance. Within large corporations that have formal quality assurance organizations, the resources devoted to this activity range from less than 1% to the high of approximately 10% which IBM applies to marketed commercial systems. Quality assurance has developed some very interesting measurement techniques long used for hardware. Yet very few software projects make use of concepts such as "cost of quality" or the other quality assurance metrics of significance.

Training and education. It is not widely recognized, but the number of staff instructors and educational personnel in the set of Fortune 500 companies in the United States approximates the total faculty size of all U.S. universities. In terms of student-days, it is possible that the private, in-house training programs of major corporations approach the combined computer science departments of U.S. academic institutions.

For a number of corporations, technical training is a major commitment, and targets such as 10 to 20 days of training per staff member per year are not uncommon.

Although the evidence is not conclusive, Lutz suggests a correlation between staff technical training and software productivity [6]. It appears that some correlation may exist between staff education and productivity, since those organizations which encourage education and professional activities, such as IBM, DEC, and Bell Labs, appear to be among the leading-edge organizations in terms of economic productivity.

Integration. While small application programs and microcomputer software may have no integration expenses at all, large systems may find 15% of the total development time and effort are associated with integration, or the tasks of getting the separate pieces of a large programming system to work together simultaneously.

Canceled projects. Very few enterprises include canceled projects in their productivity measures. Yet the overall impact of such projects can be very high. Within two large corporations, between 20% to 30% of all projects larger than 100,000 source statements were not completed and were canceled before delivery.

Measurement and tracking. Productivity and quality measurement is itself a significant cost element for those enterprises which do it. Within three large corporations, the number of full-time professional personnel engaged in measurement activities ranged from 1% to 3% of the total number of software professionals. When part-time and intermittent workers were considered, such as project managers or staff workers that supply data, productivity and quality measurements approached 7% of all development effort.

VARIATIONS IN SCOPE OF EFFORT AND IN LINE COUNTING

Variations in scope of effort are often compounded with variations in counting lines of source code, and this lead to uncertainties of astonishing magnitude. For example, the programming system discussed in the second column of Table 1-8, which consisted of 1000 new lines of source code and 5000 lines of reusable code added to a base program of 9000 lines of code, might have its productivity assessed by including (1) only the time required to do the coding; (2) the time to do mainline development work from requirements through delivery; or (3) the efforts of the entire staff, including quality assurance, documentation, management, and the like. Table 1-10 shows the range of possible uncertainty, expressed in lines of code per person-year, that can occur from using different scope-of-effort and line-counting rules.

In the absence of a standard way of looking at productivity, any one of the combinations might be cited, although some are less likely than others. In many enterprises today, the programmers themselves might consider row A, column 1 as the best productivity indicator; the project manager might choose row B, column 2; and the corporate controller might think that row A, column 3 was the most appropriate measure. However, from the point of view of the functions received by end users, row C, column 1 comes closest to matching what was delivered.

It can easily be seen we cannot take at face value any productivity claim that does not include a description of how lines of code are counted and which activities are included in the productivity analysis. The moral

Table 1-10 Range of apparent productivity caused by simultaneous variations in defining source lines and defining scope of effort

Case 1: Code measured	Lines of source code per person-year		
	Case 2: Coding only	Case 3: Mainline effort	All staff on project
A. Only new code	6,000	2,000	1,000
B. New and reused code	30,000	10,000	5,000
C. All code + base	90,000	30,000	15,000

of the story is that even if no measurement is fully satisfactory, at least we should fully describe the one we use.

MEASUREMENT METHODS OF NONCODING ACTIVITIES

Since considerably less than half of the effort on large programming systems is devoted to coding, another question arises: What kinds of measurements exist for the noncoding activities? Productivity has three different meanings that should be, but often are not, considered in the context of measurements:

1. Productivity in the sense of speed
2. Productivity in the sense of cost
3. Productivity in the sense of yield

When attempting to improve the productivity of a given activity, is it more important to speed up the activity or to lower its cost? Since the metrics and technologies that relate to speed are not necessarily the same as the ones that relate to cost or to yield, this distinction can lead to very different conclusions. Table 1-11 cites the common software measures for speed, cost, and yield:

Table 1-11 Common software speed, cost, and yield measurements

	Speed	Cost	Yield
Activity			
Management	None	Dollars	None
Initial proposal	None	Dollars	None
Planning	None	Dollars	None
Requirements	None	Dollars	None
Education	None	Dollars	Student-days
Budgeting	None	Dollars	None
Functional design	Pages/time	Dollars	Pages/function
Internal design	Pages/time	Dollars	Pages/function
Documentation	Pages/time	Dollars	Pages/function
Screen displays	Screens/time	Dollars	Screens
Coding	Lines/time	Dollars	Lines/function
Design reviews	Pages/time	Dollars	Defects
Code inspections	Code/time	Dollars	Defects
Testing	Tests/time	Dollars	Defects
Defect repairs	Repairs/time	Dollars	Repairs
Quality assurance	None	Dollars	None
Travel	None	Dollars	None
Installation	None	Dollars	None
Maintenance	Changes/time	Dollars	Changes
Slack time	None	Dollars	None

Table 1-11 highlights the significant weaknesses of the current measurements available for programming productivity. Of the 20 activities listed in Table 1-11, more than half have no common measures of either speed or yield.

This lack of measures for speed and yield has introduced subtle distortions into the overall understanding of software productivity. For example, the lack of full-life-cycle speed measures has caused undue emphasis on the few activities, such as coding, that do have common speed measures. The lack of common yield measures has slowed down the economic analysis of software.

Only for costs are there relatively stable measures; this is one of the reasons why the cost of software production is much better understood in 1985 than either speed or yield.

THE MISSING ECONOMIC MEASURES OF SOFTWARE PRODUCTIVITY

The overwhelming historical emphasis on lines of code has been the central theme of most programming measurement studies. However, as programming becomes a mature discipline, other alternatives are being explored.

Economic productivity is defined as goods or services produced per unit of labor or expense. When programming is analyzed in terms of this definition, a significant problem occurs: What, exactly, are the services which a program performs, or how can a program be viewed as "goods"?

There is currently no really satisfactory economic definition of what services programs perform, although the work of Albrecht in defining functions is approaching such a definition, as seen in Chapter 2.

Although software and programming lack absolute productivity measures that are effective, and they lack economic productivity measures, it is possible to deal with productivity in a relative fashion. For example, suppose that a small manufacturing company developed an order-entry system in 1975 with a new and inexperienced staff of personnel and no particular use of structured programming methods. At that time, the system took 12 calendar months and 150 person months to develop. In 1985, the company is ready to replace the system with a new version, but this time the personnel are experienced and full use is made of the structured programming methods. The new system is functionally equivalent to the old, but now it is completed in only 6 calendar months requiring only 50 person-months for development. From this type of analysis, it may be seen that economic productivity improved significantly: Identical functions are produced in only half of the calendar time, with only one-third of the resources. This kind of analysis does not yield absolute productivity measures, but it provides helpful information about significant trends and improvements.

Note that if the two projects were compared by means of hazardous metrics such as lines of code, the improvements would not be so visible. Indeed, if the company's early system were written in Assembler language and took 30,000 source statements and its new system were written in COBOL and took only 10,000 source statements, they both would have identical productivity rates of 200 lines of code per person-month!

MISAPPLICATION OF STATISTICAL METHODS TO PROGRAMMING

A physician's knowledge that the average life expectancy of a U.S. male is 67.2 years and that of a U.S. female is 72.3 years is of almost no value in diagnosing the condition of any given patient.

Unfortunately, the software engineering literature is much more heavily weighted with articles that attempt to derive average values rather than explore the reasons for the wide standard deviations that occur. Since many of the statistical studies are based on project data that did not define either line-counting rules or the scope of activities included, software statistical analyses are sometimes performed on raw data containing errors approaching two orders of magnitude.

What is even more unfortunate is that the average values are often presented in such a fashion that readers are led to believe that they can apply those averages as predictive indicators for estimating new projects.

Statistical studies have a place in programming, just as statistical epidemiological studies have a place in medicine. However, medical practitioners do not as a rule use statistical methods for either diagnosis or treatment, except as background data against which anomalies such as high blood pressure, excessive triglyceride levels, or white-cell counts may be compared.

Since many of the published statistical studies in software engineering deal with only a few variables, such as total development time or total development effort, their value as predictive instruments is very low. When these problems are all compounded together, the results can range from being mildly in error to being dangerously misleading.

For example, many large-scale statistical studies of programming result in scatter diagrams whose deviations are so broad as to be almost inexplicable, unless it is realized that the source data was not corrected for either line-counting methods or scope of effort; i.e. potential errors of two orders of magnitude lurk in the raw data on which many statistical studies have been made.

However, the most serious shortcoming of many statistical analyses is that the statistical papers tend to deal exclusively with "how much" and often ignore "why."

THE METRICS OF PROGRAMMING QUALITY

Considering the importance of quality to programming's end users and the fact that defect removal is one of the top expense elements of all programming systems, the measurement of the key factors affecting quality is surprisingly underreported in the literature. Even the relatively thorough studies of Endres [7] and Weiss [8] have gaps, as do the studies of Myers [9] on testing; Dunn [10] on defect removal; Deutsch [11] and Kopetz [12] on verification, validation, and reliability; and Musa [13] on reliability. Boehm's monumental volume, *Software Engineering Economics*, already mentioned provides one of the best summaries of the available defect and quality data, but even here critical topics such as the linkage between quality and reliability are not fully discussed.

The word "quality" has many definitions and many ambiguities associated with it. For practical day-to-day purposes, a high-quality programming system can be considered one without defects that would cause the system to stop completely or to produce unacceptable results. Unless this definition is viewed as fundamental, then quality considerations of other factors such as extensibility, maintainability, and so on, have very little significance.

The measurement of quality in its fundamental meaning requires the ability to quantify these variables:

1. The number of defects in the programming work products
2. The defect removal efficiency of reviews, inspections, tests, and other methods of eliminating errors
3. The "bad-fix" rate, or the quantity of new defects that are introduced while fixing previous defects
4. The origins of defects, in terms of whether they stem from requirements, design, code, or some other source
5. The distribution of defects through the modules of large programming systems to isolate error-prone modules
6. The graded severity of defects, ranging from insignificant to catastrophic
7. The number of invalid defect reports, or problems that upon investigation turn out to be user mistakes or faults external to the program
8. The probability that a given defect will be encountered by more than one user of the program

None of these eight key factors have been studied to the depth which the situation warrants, and one of the most important (factor 2, or defect removal efficiency) has scarcely been dealt with at all.

In its simplest and most elementary form, the quality of a programming system is a function of the number of mistakes made by the designers and developers minus the defect removal efficiency of the reviews, tests, and defect removal steps used to eliminate faults. Both the number of defects and the defect removal efficiencies are tangible and finite and lend themselves to metrical analysis.

For example, a study by the author [14] indicated that large programming systems written in Assembler language often had in excess of 50 defects per 1000 source code statements, and the defect removal efficiency of all reviews, inspections, and tests summed together was less than 85%. That left in the vicinity of 7.5 defects per 1000 source lines still latent in the program at delivery to users, and this was a critical factor during maintenance.

The study also indicated that the removal efficiency of testing was much lower than expected, with unit testing of individual modules or small programs by the programmers themselves sometimes finding fewer than 25% of the defects and even major, large-scale testing prior to delivery seldom finding more than 75% of the errors that were actually present.

Defect removal efficiency is a key factor in programming, and it should be well understood. Defect removal efficiency is defined by the following formula:

$$\frac{\text{Defects found by removal operation}}{\text{Defects present at removal operation}} = \text{removal efficiency}$$

While the formula itself is simple, it is not easy to find out how many defects were present at the time of any given removal operation. Pragmatically, the efficiency of a given removal activity such as unit testing cannot be determined until somewhat later, after the defects found subsequently are totaled. IBM adopted an internal measure that evaluated all defects found during development and compared that quantity to the set of all defects found in the first year of customer usage after delivery.

There is a more immediate method that is more talked about than actually practised. A known quantity of defects is artificially injected into a program before a defect removal operation begins, and the efficiency of the removal operation is calculated based upon the percentage of known bugs which are found. Although this method has worked reasonably well, there is no way of being sure that the "tame" bugs that were artificially injected are close enough to "wild" bugs for the results to be meaningful.

In many of the large programming systems thus studied it has turned out that defects are not smoothly or randomly distributed through all of the code, but rather the defects tend to "clump" in a small number of modules now termed "error-prone modules." In the case of IBM's Information Management System (IMS), only 31 modules out of the total of 425 contained 57% of all of the defects in the entire product. The distribution of defects among the modules of a large system is a very significant measurement opportunity, although one not widely utilized.

After defect removal efficiency, the second most important variable in the domain of quality is the distribution of faults, so that error-prone modules can be identified and eliminated. This means that defects should be measured down to the module level. Related measures should look for the origin of the defects, since a surprisingly large proportion of error-prone modules are not actually due to coding errors. One of the commonest reasons for error-prone modules is lack of test coverage or even any testing at all, which is often caused by failure to design the modules and enter their characteristics into the specifications turned over to test groups. In other words, some code is never tested because test personnel don't know that it has been added.

One measure, already discussed, that should either be avoided completely or used with extreme caution is cost per defect, since the paradoxes associated with this metric destroy its validity and usually lead to confusion and mistakes.

THE METRICS OF PROGRAMMING MAINTENANCE

Of all programming activities, the field of maintenance is perhaps the most poorly covered by the software engineering literature, and it is the one for which the least reliable measurement information is available. Most of the information on maintenance is either subjective and anecdotal, such as the widely quoted claim that "maintenance costs are equal to 70% of life-cycle costs," or so narrow and incomplete as to be almost useless. Of the almost 250 periodicals on software topics, only one is devoted exclusively to maintenance: Zvegintzov's "Software Maintenance News" [15]. Less than a dozen books on maintenance currently exist, with those of Martin [16] and Parikh [17] being perhaps the most widely known.

The definition of the term "maintenance" is so ambiguous that it covers everything from pure defect repairs through the development of major functional extensions.

In this book, the word "maintenance" is defined as meaning the effort devoted to repairing defects in a programming system after the system has been delivered to its users. New features, functional enhancements, or code changes made to satisfy new user requirements are excluded from this definition, and will be discussed separately as enhancements.

For internal projects, not marketed to outside customers, maintenance is often handled informally by development personnel as the need arises. Unless the program is installed at many locations, this kind of maintenance is usually not very costly and seldom totals more than 10% of development expenses.

However, when programs are marketed to outside customers, maintenance becomes a different situation. Unfortunately, few studies have been published on the most significant cost elements of commercial maintenance. The key maintenance cost factors for commercial software are discussed below.

1. *Delivery support.* When a programming system is delivered to its users, it can either be simply mailed or picked up, which is the case with microcomputer software, or it can be installed on the user's computer system by field engineers representing the organization that developed and marketed the program. This on-site installation is such an expensive activity that for programs with more than a few hundred customers, this method of installation can actually cost more than all development activities summed together. The key metrics for delivery support are the number of customer locations, the effort expended, and travel costs to widely dispersed customer locations.

2. *Field Service.* Once a program has been delivered and installed and the field engineers have departed, the next maintenance task to consider is: What happens when problems occur? For microcomputer software, the customer will usually telephone or visit the dealer, or there may be a hot line available from the software development organization. However, the larger computer manufacturers, such as CDC, IBM, DEC, and so on, have field personnel who go to the customer's premises and assist in finding bugs and installing repairs. This kind of field service is very expensive, and for large systems with more than a few hundred customers, it can cost more than all of the development expenses put together. It is even more costly if the customers are widely scattered geographically, so that air fare and hotel accomodations are part of the maintenance costs. The key metrics for field service are the number of defects found, the effort spent on field service, and travel costs for widely dispersed customers.

3. *Central Maintenance.* Many commercial software houses and some microcomputer manufacturers, such as Tandy Radio Shack, Commodore, and so on, have maintenance facilities staffed by programmers or systems engineers. They receive letters and telephone calls from

customers who experience problems; they respond to those problems, develop fixes, and then distribute the fixes by mail, networking, or publication. Major computer manufacturers such as IBM may even have 24-hour maintenance locations in order to provide instant responses to customer problems. This kind of maintenance, too, is very costly, although because of the lack of travel expenses, it is the least expensive of the three major maintenance classes. Central maintenance of a program will usually not exceed 25% of the development costs, unless the program is released in a very hazardous and error-prone condition. The key metrics for central maintenance are the numbers of defects encountered and the overhead costs of operating the facility.

To illustrate the costs of delivery support, central maintenance and field service versus the costs of software development, Table 1-12 shows the approximate effort in terms of person-months to maintain a 100,000-source-statement COBOL program for 1 year after initial delivery, assuming 1, 10, 100, and 1000 users, respectively:

Table 1-12 Person-months of maintenance effort as a function of the number of users of a software system

	Person-months of effort			
	1 User	10 Users	100 Users	1000 Users
Activity				
Development	600	600	600	600
Delivery support	1	10	50	250
Central maintenance	2	5	10	50
Field service	2	20	75	700
Total effort	605	635	735	1600

Table 1-12 illustrates why high-volume commercial software producers are interested in both metrics and technologies that address all aspects of maintenance.

There is another aspect of maintenance that is also underreported in the literature: the cumulative maintenance expenses of large enterprises with sizable inventories or portfolios of systems and programs in production. A medium- to large-sized manufacturing organization, a state government agency, or large city data center will typically have an inventory that ranges from 500 to more than 3000 application programs that are run on either periodic or as-needed basis. Alhough no single program in the inventory may require more than slight intermittent maintenance, the cumulative maintenance bill for the entire inventory can be very expensive. The annual portfolio maintenance costs reported by

Applied Computer Research in their 1984 survey typically ranged from 30% to 40% of the total development budget, although "maintenance" in this case included enhancements as well as defect repairs.

Because new programs tend to enter the inventory at a slightly faster rate than old programs are retired, the usual trend is for the inventory of operational applications to grow with time. Indeed, very large organizations such as major manufacturing companies, large banks, telecommunications companies, computer manufacturers, and government agencies may have inventories that exceed 20,000 separate programs and 50,000,000 lines of source code.

One of the best "treatments" of the typical growth in programming inventories is that of Gibson and Nolan [18], whose observations on the stages of data processing growth in organizations from the first tentative steps through sophisticated applications are very thought-provoking.

The software inventories of medium-and large-sized enterprises will vary with the nature of their business, but a typical pattern for a medium-sized manufacturing enterprise is expressed in Table 1-13.

A significant weakness of software measurements over much of the history of programming has been the paucity of useful metrics that have been applied to the inventories or portfolios of software in the aggregate.

However, when aggregate measures are applied, the results are often interesting. The basic parameters of software inventories include:

1. The total number of applications
2. The sizes and size ranges of the applications
3. The rate at which new applications enter the inventory
4. The rate at which old applications leave the inventory
5. The defect repairs against the inventory
6. The enhancements against the inventory
7. The staff or workers doing development

Table 1-13 Typical software inventory of a medium-sized manufacturing enterprise

	Number of programs or systems	Size of inventory (source lines)
Software type		
Accounting/finance	125	250,000
Engineering/design	50	500,000
Human resources	20	150,000
Manufacturing	125	750,000
Marketing/sales	130	250,000
Systems software	125	3,000,000
End-user tools	25	100,000
Total	600	5,000,000

8. The staff or workers doing enhancements
9. The staff or workers doing maintenance (defect repairs)

A mathematical model by the author, based on the pattern of development, enhancement, and maintenance within a large multinational corporation, indicated that at the enterprise level, pure development productivity gains would be ineffective unless coupled with quality gains. The faster new code entered production status, the greater the maintenance and enhancement costs. These efforts would grow so rapidly that either development personnel would be drawn into maintenance, or the overall programming staff would have to increase by more than 15% a year to meet the growing load. In either case, the results would be economically catastrophic in the long run. This kind of analysis, of productivity at the portfolio and enterprise level factoring in the balance among development, enhancements, and maintenance, is the direction that contemporary productivity research is now taking.

In summary, there are six major variables affecting maintenance at the project and corporate levels which must be clearly understood to avoid confusion.

1. Is the program to be installed on the user's premises by systems engineers as part of the distribution of the program?
2. How many users are there for the program? And especially in how many separate geographic locations will the program be installed, from which fault reports may be sent in?
3. What is the number of defects in the program? This variable interacts with variable 2, because some defects will be encountered by many users of the program and hence trigger multiple fault reports for the same problem.
4. Will defects reported by customers lead to the dispatch of field service personnel to explore the problems on the customer's premises?
5. What tools and support systems are available for reporting defects from the field, searching for common problems, and distributing fixes back to customers?
6. What is the cumulative inventory of software packages that must be maintained by an enterprise? At the corporate or government level, this variable is a critical factor in determining overall maintenance expenses.

Maintenance is now a major worldwide programming activity, and as the industry matures, by the end of the century we may find that more programmers will be performing maintenance than development. In order to deal with maintenance at a scientific and professional level, it is necessary to replace the anecdotal and mistaken assertions about maintenance with reports based on serious studies.

Also, maintenance at the corporate or government agency level, where thousands of applications and millions of lines of source may be involved, is a field of research distinct from that of maintenance of a single program. The notable differences in metrics, costs, tools, and staffing between maintaining a single program and maintaining a portfolio of many programs deserves much more research.

THE METRICS OF FUNCTIONAL ENHANCEMENTS

Because programming is a new industry whose age spans only some 30 years, most professional programmers believe that the primary work of the occupation is the design and development of new systems, starting with requirements and concluding with delivery. Certainly the software engineering literature encourages such a belief, since a visit to a major computer science bookstore such as the McGraw-Hill retail outlet in Manhattan will turn up more than two hundred titles in print dealing with new program development and its methods.

However, as the software industry matures and moves toward the end of the 20th century, something unexpected is happening. Many programmers find themselves working on enhancements to existing systems rather than doing new development. For example, of the approximately 15,000 professional programmers in the IBM corporation in 1983, it is probable that 10,000 are working on adding features and extensions to the existing operating systems and major application programs such as IMS, CICS, and the like.

The unexpected change from new development work to functional enhancements is causing several unanticipated problems to occur. One of the most severe problems is that since enhancements are usually lower in technical interest to programming personnel than new development, enterprises locked into significant amounts of enhancement work may find low morale and high turnover rates. Even IBM, which traditionally has one of the lowest attrition rates in the industry among its programming staff, is finding that programmers working on enhancements to existing systems may leave in significant numbers, compared to the historical turnover of those working on new projects.

From the point of view of measurement and estimating, the unexpected change from new development to functional enhancements may be disastrous, because the ratios and cost elements for working on existing code are very different from those involved in new code. Unfortunately, a review by the author of more than 50 books on programming methodolo-

gies revealed almost no citations dealing with the productivity of functional enhancements, except a few minor references in the context of
maintenance. Only the pioneering study of Belady and Lehman [19]
comes directly to grips with the topic.

The work of functional enhancements to existing software systems is
underreported in the software engineering curriculums also, and very few
courses exist in which this kind of programming is even discussed, much
less taught effectively.

The major difference between new development and enhancement
work is the enormous impact that the base system has on key activities.
For example, while a new system might start with exploring users'
requirements and then move into design, an enhancement project will
often force the users' requirements to fit into existing data and structural
constraints, and much of the design effort will be devoted to exploring the
current programs to find out how and where new features can be added
and what their impact will be on existing functions.

The tasks of making functional enhancements to existing systems can
be likened to the architectural work of adding a new room to an existing
building. The design will be severely constrained by the existing structure, and both the architect and the builders must take care not to weaken
the existing structure when the additions are made. Although the costs of
the new room will usually be lower than the costs of constructing an
entirely new building, the costs per square foot may be much higher
because of the need to remove existing walls, reroute plumbing and
electrical circuits, and take special care to avoid disrupting the current
site.

When the major tasks of enhancing an existing system are compared
to the tasks of developing a new system, as in Table 1-14, it may be seen
that notable differences exist in the constraints if new development is
taken as the normal mode of operation.

From the point of view of measurement and estimating, the work of
enhancing an existing system tends to be much more costly than new
development work for the tasks of coding, integration, and testing, and
especially for defect repairs if the base system is not well structured and
very stable. Table 1-15 gives a side-by-side comparison of the schedule
and effort to develop a new 10,000-line COBOL program with the effort
required to add 10,000 lines of COBOL enhancements to an existing
50,000-line COBOL system. Assume that the existing program is of
average quality and relatively well structured and that both the new
project and the enhancement are for equivalent functions and use
identical technologies and personnel of equal skill levels. The results are
generalized from data studied by the author on several large enhancements within IBM.

The side-by-side comparison indicates that the impact of base code

**Table 1-14 Constraints on enhancements
to existing programs**

	Constraints on enhancement
Activity	
Requirements	Constrained
Design	Constrained
Coding	Severely constrained
Documentation	Normal
Integration	Severely constrained
Testing	Severely constrained
Defect repairs	Severely constrained
Attributes	
Quality	Often lower
Schedules	Often longer
Productivity	Often lower

* Constraints on new development are taken as normal.

tends to make coding, integration, testing, and defect repairs much more significant tasks in enhancment work than in new development, while documentation is essentially unchanged and requirements and design are affected slightly. Indeed, requirements and design effort for enhancements may sometimes be lower than for a new development project of

Table 1-15 Schedule and effort comparison of new development and enhancement work for 10,000 COBOL source lines

	10K new program	10K enhancement to 50K base program
Schedules (calendar months)		
Requirements	2.83	3.36
Design	3.89	4.61
Coding	3.49	4.80
Integration and testing	3.75	5.97
Total	13.96	18.74
Overlapped	10.20	13.68
Effort (person-months)		
Requirements	3.95	4.70
Design	6.13	7.00
Internal documentation	6.90	6.90
External documentation	14.77	14.77
Coding	19.68	28.81
Integration and testing	10.48	16.81
Defect repairs	18.46	31.35
Management	7.43	9.48
Total	87.80	119.82

equivalent size. This is due to the fact that both users and developers know the base system quite well.

However, a strong caution is needed that ratios and cost-estimating techniques based on new development work will be totally misleading and unreliable when transferred to enhancement projects. This is one of the reasons why almost all interactive estimating systems either do not work for enhancements or use very different algorithms for dealing with enhancements to existing systems.

Failure to come to grips with enhancements is also one of the reasons why the software engineering literature cannot simply be accepted at face value. Many of the large-scale statistical studies include enhancement work side by side with new development work, and the authors of the studies do not distinguish between the two different kinds of programming.

A final problem concerning enhancement work is the way that it is usually lumped together with the tasks of defect repairs or maintenance. The only thing that enhancements have in common with maintenance, in the sense of fixing postdelivery bugs, is that they both change existing software. In many enterprises, such as IBM, the enhancements are funded differently, are carried out by different organizations, and are logically distinct from the defect repair tasks. The current practice in software engineering of lumping maintenance and enhancements together is unfortunate, since it distorts both activities and only leads to confusion and mistakes in estimating.

SUMMARY OF SOFTWARE MEASUREMENT PROBLEMS

Software measurement has been the weakest link in the chain of technologies comprising software engineering. The common metrics applied to software projects, such as lines of code per unit of time and cost per defect, are subject to such dangerous and misleading mathematical paradox that the understanding of software economics has been delayed. Not only are the common metrics paradoxical, but lack of any standard definitions for those metrics has introduced potential errors in excess of two orders of magnitude into the software productivity literature.

In addition to the numerical aspects of software measurement, the industry has also blurred nine different concepts together without full realization of their significance:

1. Measures of time
2. Measures of cost
3. Measures of yield

4. Development projects
5. Enhancement projects
6. Maintenance projects
7. Personal productivity
8. Project productivity
9. Enterprise productivity

In the philosophy of Zen Buddhism, emptiness is the source of creativity; before a cup can be filled, it must first be empty. Before a new science of software measurement can be created, it is first necessary to eliminate the paradoxes and ambiguities of the historical software metrics which have obscured the true economic and productivity trends of the software engineering domain.

As of 1985, it can finally be said that the problems of software metrics have been explored and mapped; even if the problems have not yet been solved. From this point on, new metrics can be developed that are free of the distortions and paradoxes which have been so troublesome in the past. While software engineering may not yet be a true science, the steps are moving in that direction.

REFERENCES

1. Fagan, M.E.; "Design and Code Inspections to Reduce Errors in Program Development"; *IBM Systems Journal*, Vol. 15, No. 3, 1976; pp. 182–211.
2. Jones, C.; "Program Quality and Programmer Productivity"; TR 02.764; IBM Corporation; San Jose, CA; January 1977. (Also included in Jones, C.; *Programming Productivity, Issues for the Eighties*; IEEE Press; Silver Spring, MD; Cat. No. EHO 186-7; 1981; pp. 130–161.)
3. Jones, T.C.; "Measuring Programming Quality and Productivity"; *IBM Systems Journal*, Vol. 17, No. 1, 1978; pp 39–63.
4. Boehm, B.W.; Software Engineering Economics; Prentice-Hall, Inc.; Englewood Cliffs, NJ; 1981.
5. *Survey of Productivity in Systems Development*; Applied Computer Research; Phoenix, AZ; 1984; pp. 6–8.
6. Lutz, T.; *Foundation for Growth—Productivity and Quality in Application Development*; Nolan, Norton and Company; Lexington, MA; 1984.
7. Endres, A.; "An Analysis of Errors and Their Causes in Systems Programs"; *IEEE Transactions on Software Engineering*; June 1975; pp. 140–149.
8. Weiss, D.M.; "Evaluating Software Development by Error Analysis—The Data from the Architecture Research Facility"; *The Journal of Systems and Software*, Vol. 1, 1979; pp. 57–70.
9. Myers, G.J.; *The Art of Software Testing*; Wiley; New York; 1979.
10. Dunn, R.; *Software Defect Removal*; McGraw-Hill; New York; 1984.
11. Deutsch, M.S.; *Software Verification and Validation—Realistic Project Approaches*; Prentice-Hall; Englewood Cliffs, NJ; 1982.
12. Kopetz, H.; *Software Reliability*; Springer-Verlag; New York; 1979.
13. Musa, J.; "Software Reliability Measurement"; *The Journal of Systems and Software* 1; 1980; pp 223–241.

14. Jones, T.C.; "Prevention and Removal of Programming Defects"; *Electrical Communication—The Technical Journal of ITT*, Vol. 57, No. 4, 1983; pp. 295–300.
15. Zvegintzov, N.; *Software Maintenance News*; The Software Maintenance Association; 141 St. Marks Place, Staten Island, New York.; published monthly.
16. Martin, J. and McClure, C.; *Software Maintenance—The Problem and Its Solution*; Prentice-Hall; Englewood Cliffs, NJ; 1983.
17. Parikh, G.; *Techniques of Program and System Maintenance*; Ethnotech; Lincoln, NB; 1980.
18. Gibson, C.F. and Nolan, R.L.; "Managing the Four Stages of DP Growth"; *Harvard Business Review*, January-February 1974.
19. Belady, L. and Lehman, M.M.; "A Model of Large Program Development"; *IBM Systems Journal*, Vol. 15, No. 3, 1976; pp. 225–252.

TWO

THE SEARCH FOR A SCIENCE OF MEASUREMENT

The essence of scientific progress is dissatisfaction with the current theories that attempt to explain natural phenomena. As Kuhn points out in his book *The Structure of Scientific Revolutions* (1), normal science has an agreed view or paradigm with which scientists work with until the evidence against it becomes overwhelming, and then there is a fairly abrupt change to another agreed view.

For programming measurements, almost everyone is dissatisfied with lines of code; but thus far there is no commonly agreed replacement for this metric. The jumping-off place for most of the alternatives to lines of code is always dissatisfaction with that unit of measure, but unfortunately no fully satisfactory alternatives have yet come to light.

The current research into measurement alternatives to dealing with "raw" lines of source code can be divided into five major categories:

1. Attempts to minimize the current problems with lines of code by compensating for the mathematical paradoxes and inconsistent definitions that have been so troublesome in the past.
2. Attempts to go beyond lines of code by exploring the separate functional and data aspects of code. Notable in this school of thought is a method termed "software science" created by the late Dr. Maurice Halstead (36).

3. Attempts to look at the structural complexity as well as the size of programs, by examining branching patterns, data flow patterns, nesting, recursiveness, and other deeper structural elements. Notable in this school of thought are the complexity metrics of Thomas McCabe (24).
4. Attempts to eliminate lines of code altogether and to deal with the underlying functions which the programs carry out, independent of the languages in which the programs are written. Notable in this school of thought is the function point method of A.J. Albrecht (32).
5. Attempts to go beyond the conventional definitions of programming and deal with the economic issues of software rather than simply with lines of code.

Each of the five schools has developed some valuable insights and made progress in its respective domain, but it cannot be said that the fundamental measurement problems have yet been solved.

• While the attempts to isolate and identify the problems of lines of code have been successful, they have found that this measure cannot be used as a normalization method without some form of relatively complex mathematical compensation.

• The attempts to explore the separate data and functional portions of code using the methods of software science have yielded interesting and valuable observations, but the overall results are clouded with ambiguity and some of the concepts are not truly scientific, in the sense that they are not derived from the observable facts but are intuitive assertions for which no real evidence exists.

• The attempts to measure complexity have yielded very good techniques for analyzing the pragmatic complexity of code, but there are no results to date as to why code is complex or whether the complexity is even necessary.

• The attempts to depart from lines of code and deal directly with functions have had some early successes, but this method has its own sources of ambiguity and thus far does not cover the entire software engineering domain.

• The attempts to deal with programming productivity in an economic fashion are only starting to emerge from the shadow of the paradoxical lines-of-code method and have not yet produced any notable results, although the prognosis for economic productivity studies is good.

In sum, the state of the art of programming measurement in 1985 is that the problems are now better known than at any time in the past, but solutions that might overcome those problems are not yet fully developed.

OVERCOMING THE PROBLEMS OF LINES-OF-CODE METRICS

The first step in overcoming the problems of lines of code is simply to catalog the problems and quantify their impacts under controlled circumstances. As discussed in Chapter 1, the problems with lines of code come in several varieties, of which the most significant are:

1. The lack of standard line-counting definitions can cause apparent variances of about an order of magnitude in measuring any given program.
2. The lack of standard scope-of-effort guidelines as to what activities should be included in the overall measurement of programming productivity can cause apparent variations of about two orders of magnitude in measuring any given program.
3. When a programming productivity analysis includes a reasonably complete set of activities and especially those activities that are not affected by the choice of source language, high-level languages will show a paradoxical reduction in lines of code per unit of time compared to low-level languages. The magnitude of the reduction is roughly proportional to the level of the language.
4. Estimates based on lines of code per unit of time tend to be erratic and unreliable, especially when they include activities such as requirements, design, and slack time, which are highly independent of source languages.
5. The historical concentration on lines of code has led to severe underreporting of those aspects of programming that are not related to coding, such as travel, document production, slack time, and the like.
6. For menu-driven generators, graphics-based languages, spreadsheets, query languages, and the general set of fourth-generation languages, lines of code does not really apply.

In spite of the historical problems with this method, by using careful procedures to overcome the mathematical paradoxes, by devoting some effort to validating raw data, and by publishing the line-counting rules together with the results, it is possible to use lines of code in meaningful ways for the first three generations of programming languages. Fourth-generation languages tend to go beyond the capabilities of lines-of-code metrics, while graphics-based fifth-generation languages are in a domain where even linguistic and psychological principles have not yet been worked out.

The Origin of Lines-of-Code Metrics

Von Neumann computers, which in 1985 are still the only major type of general-purpose computers in use, are built on the concept of a common memory for both instructions and data, coupled with registers to keep track of exactly where a program is executing at any moment. The shared memory for both instructions and data requires very careful management of storage locations within the computer, since a wrong address in a program instruction causes the computer to attempt to execute an instruction at a place where no instruction exists, thus stopping the computer completely.

As Goldstine points out in *The Computer from Pascal to Von Neumann* (2), in the early days of computing, from 1944 through the early 1950s, programming was done in machine language. Since this was usually a binary representation, a simple multiplication of two numbers might look like the following:

111111000101001000000100100111100000001010010101

In addition to being essentially unreadable and even unrecognizable, the use of actual addresses for data and instruction sequences made programming very difficult and made any kind of code insertion after the program was written a time-consuming activity, since all addresses had to be recalculated by hand.

The first assembler languages were created to offer two major advantages to programmers: (1) symbolic operation codes, in languages which humans could understand; and (2) symbolic addresses, or "labels," so that human beings did not have to keep recalculating the locations of all instructions and data. This second improvement was the most significant, since address calculation was an enormously difficult activity.

Thus, instead of the machine language multiplication string of binary 1s and 0s, it became possible to multiply two numbers using statements that resemble the following:

MP HOURS, RATE

where MP is the operation code for multiply and HOURS and RATE are the symbolic names for computer memory locations that contain the numbers to be multiplied. The set of codes intended for human consumption are termed "source codes" and the final machine language version of the program is called "object code." One source code statement triggers the execution of only one object code instruction in the computer, which is an important factor in determining the "level" of a language.

It was customary in Assembler languages to write each instruction on a separate line of a coding pad, in longhand. Therefore, the phrase "a line of code" was more or less an accurate description, and each line was physically and logically separate and unique from all other lines in a program.

In Assembler language, any individual instruction might have from one to five distinct parts:

1. A symbolic label (used to flag significant starting points)
2. An operation code (used to cause the computer to act)
3. One or two addresses (used to locate data or instructions)
4. A comment (used to tell other programmers what was occurring)
5. A unique serial number (used for sequencing purposes)

Thus, even in the earliest days of computing, a line of code was subject to variation, although in early Assembler languages, the variations were not yet extreme.

Because lines of code as just described contained an operation code which caused the computer to take some action, such as moving data, branching to another location, addition, and the like, they are termed "executable" lines. However, programming has always had to deal with data as well as functions.

In Assembler languages, data could either be entered directly as what was termed a "literal," such as 3.14592, or it could be derived from a calculation or read into the computer from an external source. In any case, it was necessary for programmers to assign memory locations to hold the data their programs were going to utilize.

Thus another kind of line of code exists, which does not contain an operation code but merely reserves memory locations and gives a label to the locations so that the program can access them. For example, a set of memory locations might be set aside to hold the variable "hours worked each day" by means of an Assembler language instruction that might look like this:

HOURS DS CL4

In such an instruction HOURS is the label, DS is the code for Define Storage, and CL4 means that 4 bytes of memory are to be reserved.

In a typical Assembler language application program, such as an accounts payable program, perhaps 70% of the program's lines of code would be executable instructions and 30% would be data storage instructions, subject to fairly wide variations that depended on the nature of the application.

The Development of Multistatement Programming Lines

Early Assembler languages had a fairly rigorous and fixed format, in which labels could only occupy certain locations and operation code another set of fixed locations, and the same was true for addresses or operands. Since each line of code was written separately on a coding pad and punched into its own tab card for reading into a computer, when someone spoke of a line of code there was a fairly clear conception of what was being discussed.

However, it was soon noted that lines of code were usually rather short and seldom occupied a complete 80-column card. The next step away from fixed-format Assembler languages were what was termed "free-form" Assembler languages, where multiple statements were allowed on any given line of a coding pad, with the statements being separated from one another by what was called a "delimiter" that notified the Assembler processor that one statement had stopped and another was beginning. Typical delimiters were (and still are) colons and semicolons.

This change introduced the first major source of confusion into the use of lines of code for productivity purposes, since it was now unclear whether to count the physical line or the separate logical statements on a physical line. Early Assemblers only gave automatic counts of physical lines, so it was expedient to use this method, since any attempt to count logical statements meant that manual examination would be required.

The Development of Macro Assembler Languages

In the early basic Assembler languages, each statement written on a coding pad by a programmer would trigger the execution of only one machine instruction, or "object instruction," as it is called.

It soon became obvious that repetitious strings of commonly used source instructions could be bundled together and assigned a name that programmers could use in their programs. For example, all of the instructions needed to calculate the square root of a number could be written down and given a name such as SQRT. These collections of many individual source code statements could be inserted into a program simply by using their assigned name and supplying the values which the calculations needed.

Macro Assemblers, as they are called, created a major problem in defining lines of code for productivity purposes. No longer was there a one-to-one relationship between the source code written by a programmer and the executable instructions in the assembled object code. Not only that, but in many cases the macro definition, such as the square-root-extraction code, was not even written by the programmer who was using it. From this point on, lines of code have been ambiguous and difficult to use as productivity normalization methods.

The Development of High-Level Languages

Macro Assembler languages differed from basic Assembler languages in that commonly used sets of instructions were bundled together by experienced programmers and made accessable by assigning them unique names. Other programmers could use these bundled instructions by using the name as though it were an operation code. Indeed, these macroinstruction names were sometimes called "pseudo operation codes" because they had the effect of making the computer do something, even though the action might be beyond the computer's basic instruction set.

High-level languages are based on the concept of lumping commonly used instruction sets together and assigning them unique names. However, in high-level languages, the functions which these collections of individual machine instructions perform are not defined by individual programmers: they are part of the definition of the language itself.

This is simultaneously the reason for the power of high-level languages and why there are over two hundred of them. Except for basic arithmetic operations, reading and writing, and a few other essential activities, programming languages are aimed at specific kinds of problems, and their lumped collections of machine instructions are targeted for convenience in facilitating certain kinds of applications.

Thus, FORTRAN has convenient statements for mathematical operations, COBOL has convenient statements for business applications, and many special-purpose languages exist that have convenient statements for application areas that range from architecture through zoology.

Because these languages are especially targeted for certain kinds of problems, two languages of the same numeric level are usually not equal for all applications.

The level concept refers to how many machine instructions a given source statement will cause to be executed. Although both individual programming styles and the efficiencies of the compilers which convert source language statements into executable statements vary widely, some of the common programming languages can be roughly classified as to their levels. Table 2-1 gives the approximation.

Because languages tend to be optimized for certain kinds of applications, the numeric level of the language is not the only factor to consider when selecting appropriate languages.

As mentioned earlier, programming deals not only with functions and executable statements but also with data and with defining the kind of

Table 2-1 Approximate levels of selected software languages relative to basic Assembler language

Language	Ratio of source statements to executable statements		
Assembler	1	to	1
Macro Assembler	1	to	1.5
C	1	to	2.5
ALGOL	1	to	3
CHILL	1	to	3
COBOL	1	to	3
FORTRAN	1	to	3
JOVIAL	1	to	3
Pascal	1	to	3.5
RPG	1	to	4
PL/I	1	to	4
MODULA-2	1	to	4.5
Ada	1	to	4.5
PROLOG	1	to	5
LISP	1	to	5
FORTH	1	to	5
BASIC	1	to	5
LOGO	1	to	6
Fourth-generation database	1	to	8
STRATEGEM	1	to	9
APL	1	to	10
OBJECTIVE-C	1	to	12
SMALLTALK	1	to	15
Query languages	1	to	20
Spreadsheet languages	1	to	50

data that is being processed, such as whether it is character-string data like English text or numeric data of various kinds.

Most of the improvements introduced by high-level languages are in the area of consolidating useful functional collections of machine instructions and giving them a single name for use in programs.

Because language level has increased more rapidly on the functional side than on the data definition side, the relative proportions of executable instructions and data definitions in modern high-level-language programs is now skewed toward the data side.

For example, it was mentioned that in Assembler language, a typical application program might consist of 70% executable statements and 30% data definition statements. In a language such as COBOL, the ratio might be 60% executable statements and 40% data definitions for the same application, because COBOL has a more powerful set of executable functions; but the data definition method is not that different from Assembler. If the same program were written in BASIC, then there might be a 50/50 split between executable statements and statements that deal with data; but for a modern spreadsheet language such as VisiCalc, with very powerful functional capabilities, the data portions may outnumber the calculations and formulas by 3 or 4 to 1 in terms of the volume of information used.

One of the most interesting forms of research into programming language utility has been the frequency studies of various kinds of instructions, such as the pioneering work of Elshoff (3) on PL/I programs.

When the evolution of programming languages is traced from the vantage point of measurements, it may be seen that there is a correlation between the level or power of a language and the ambiguity of the language in terms of how easy or difficult it is to count lines of code within the language. Assembler language is comparatively unambiguous but is also comparatively weak in functional capabilities. COBOL, FORTRAN, PL/I and the other so-called third-generation languages are more powerful than Assembler language but are also more difficult to measure and more ambiguous in terms of productivity.

This trend continues with increasing power of a language, with fourth-generation languages being in some cases still unmeasurable if lines of code is the metrical unit selected.For the emerging fifth generation of graphics-based languages, the phrase "lines of code" will have no real meaning.

As of 1985, languages whose levels range up to about 15 times the power of Assembler can be at least roughly evaluated in terms of lines of code. Above that level, the languages tend to be so powerful and so amorphous in structure that lines-of-code measurements become very impractical. Thus for languages in the class of spreadsheets, graphics "icons," database query languages, fourth-generation languages, and the like, lines-of-code measures are no longer meaningful and some other technique must substitute.

The field of psycholinguistics begins to overlap the domain of programming measurements for these ultra-high-level nonprocedural languages, and it is of interest to consider the linguistic aspects of the 10 major language classes used for software to see what measurement problems might be noted, using the language classification system developed by the author (4).

Category 1: Unrestricted natural language. Programming languages are derived in part from natural language, and so it is of interest to consider the measurement aspects of natural languages.

Natural language, such as English, is sometimes cited in the software literature as being a very high level language but this is not the case. As pointed out previously by the author (5), it usually takes an average of from 7 to 20 English words to specify the meaning of a single line of

Assembler language source code, thus making natural language substantially lower in power than any other language used in the software domain.

There is a comparatively rich science of measurement associated with natural languages, and the frequency with which nouns, verbs, adjectives, and adverbs occur in natural language text has been studied for several centuries. When natural language descriptions of software systems are studied, the sources of ambiguity are clear: Undefined adverbs and adjectives such as "user-friendly" and "high-speed performance" are the primary sources of confusion, while the basic nouns and verbs are not as troublesome. The ambiguity of adverbs and adjectives, coupled with the fact that natural language grammar is very rich in constructs (such as the past tense and the progressive passive) which are difficult to process via a computer, makes natural language a poor choice for programming. Given the fact that the sources of ambiguity of natural language have been known for over a century, it is surprising that natural language is sometimes considered a candidate for a future programming language.

Category 2: Natural language with restricted syntax and semantics. Because of the ambiguous adjectives and adverbs of natural language text and the very rich grammatical aspects of natural language, the first successful attempts to use a derivative of natural language for software consisted of massive removals of the offending elements: The vocabulary was stripped down to a basic set of predefined verbs, with nouns being rigorously defined as data elements. The syntax or grammar was stripped down to the present tense and the imperative mood, with the result that perhaps 95% of English syntax and 98% of the English vocabulary were eliminated. What was left over became the COBOL programming language; there are also a host of pseudocodes and structured English languages for specification purposes. A COBOL program is essentially a subset of English with the syntax and semantics cut down to basics, as can be seen by this brief COBOL illustration:

```
PROCEDURE DIVISION
CALCULATE.
        MULTIPLY PRINCIPAL BY RATE GIVING YEARLY-
        INTEREST
        ADD YEARLY-INTEREST TO PRINCIPAL
        ADD 1 TO STARTING YEAR.
        IF STARTING-YEAR IS EQUAL TO 1984, THEN PRINT-
        ANSWER.
```

Languages in Category 2 are relatively easy to measure, assuming that some care is taken in defining the verbs and nouns.

Category 3: Natural language with augmented symbology. Symbol systems for written communication fall into three broad classes: (1) those whose symbols represent sounds, (2) those whose symbols represent concepts or ideas, and (3) hybrid systems where both sounds and concepts are represented. The more powerful programming languages fall into the hybrid class, as do mathematical notation, Boolean logical notations, and most other communication methods for scientific topics.

As a general rule, the hybrid languages use the sound-based symbols to present background information and the equivalent of nouns and use the concept-based symbols for algorithms and the equivalent of verbs. Typical concept-based symbols used in mathematics and programming include the following:

The assignment statement	=
Mathematical operators	+ — * /
Logical operators	> < >= <=
Brackets and braces	[ ] ( )

Following is a short PL/I expression to illustrate the hybrid nature of Category 3 languages:

```
DO I = 1 TO 20
    DO J = 1 TO 20
        PUT LIST (I*(I>J));
    END;
END;
```

As may be seen, some of the symbology (i.e. DO and END) represent sounds, while the rest (i.e. =, *, and >) represent concepts. From the point of view of measurement, Category 3 languages are substantially more challenging than Category 2, because of the various ways the symbols can be evaluated and because of the need to establish precedence rules. However, these problems are not insurmountable.

From the point of view of human perception, Category 3 languages with hybrid symbology tend to be difficult to scan and interpret quickly. Ordinary natural languages have developed spontaneous mechanisms to limit the complexity of spoken and written statements in order to fit the capacity of human temporary memories. Hybrid languages, especially those using parentheses and nested parentheses as in the above PL/I example, go far beyond the normal capacity of average human temporary memories and hence are very difficult to read or interpret. This of course is one of the reasons why programming can be so difficult.

Category 4: Natural language with predefined verbs and nouns. One of the more interesting varieties of languages used for software appears in the area of database applications and database query languages. In Category 4, all nouns are predefined in a data dictionary and all verbs are predefined as well. The result is a class of languages where any valid expression can immediately be performed. Following is a generalized example of a Category 4 language:

START:
>ACCESS THE PERSONNEL-MASTER-FILE;
>SEARCH ATTRITIONS FROM JANUARY THROUGH DECEMBER 1984;
>SORT ATTRITIONS FROM HIGH TO LOW;
>USE REPORT-FORMAT-2;
>SEND REPORT TO SMITH, JENKINS, WILLIAMS;
STOP.

Languages in Category 4 are relatively straightforward in terms of measurement, although those varieties which allow mathematical and logical notation (i.e. $<$, $>$, $+$, and $-$) can be as difficult as languages in Category 3.

Category 5: Menu-driven questions with restricted responses. Category 5 is the domain of ordinary menu-driven systems, where a software system displays a set of questions together with all possible valid answers, and the user selects the appropriate response. Following is a short example of Category 5, in the form of a typical menu-driven system:

Processor: PLEASE TYPE IN THE NUMBER OF THE ACTIVI-
>TY YOU ARE INTERESTED IN:
>1. SEARCHING THE AUTHOR INDEX
>2. SEARCHING THE TITLE INDEX
>3. SEARCHING THE KOWC INDEX
User: 2

Category 5 is sometimes used as a mechanism for driving application or program generators as well as conventional information systems, and it presents a major challenge to measurement. While it is simple enough to measure the number and kinds of user responses, the interpretation of the results of such measurement remains ambiguous and elusive.

Category 6: Menu-driven questions with unrestricted responses. Category 6 is the domain of very sophisticated interactive software systems that can interpret unrestricted natural language. This category is in transition under the impact of new research in artificial intelligence, and it may become very widely used in the future. Following is an example of a typical Category 6 dialog, taken from an actual system:

Processor: PLEASE ENTER YOUR QUESTION.
User: WHICH SKYHAWKS LOGGED LESS THAN 10 HOURS?

Processor: PLEASE ENTER A SPECIFIC TIME PERIOD.
User: BETWEEN JANUARY 1 AND JULY 1, 1984.

Since Category 6 languages can be used to activate program generators and perform end-user query functions, they raise exceptionally difficult challenges from a measurement point of view. While the individual responses can easily be measured, two different people attempting the same task, or the same person doing the same task at different times, might well use widely different statements.

Category 7: Menu-driven questions with nonlanguage responses. Category 7 is a specialized domain in which a software processor evaluates not only the explicit response given by the user but also certain nonlinguistic aspects of the response such as how long it took the user to answer.

Category 7 processing techniques are sometimes used in computer-aided instruction (CAI) situations: If a student hesitates or takes too long in responding, the software system is programmed to then give a different set of answers than if the student responded quickly, on the assumption that the student is having trouble.

Category 7 techniques also have more exotic applications in military and defense systems, but they are not widely used for software development.

Category 8: Matrix languages with positional syntax and semantics. This is a transitional category between text and graphics languages; it is the home of various matrices such as decision tables, spreadsheets, and to a certain degree relational databases. Figure 2-1 gives an example of a limited-entry decision table to illustrate this category.

	1	2	3	4	5	6	
Quantity-Ordered ≥ Discount-Quantity	Y	N	Y	Y	N	Y	ELSE
Wholesale	Y	–	N	Y	–	N	
Quantity-Ordered ≤ Quantity-on-Hand	Y	Y	Y	N	N	N	
Bill at Discount-Rate	X	–	–	X	–	–	–
Bill at Regular-Rate	–	X	X	–	X	X	–
Ship Quantity-Ordered	X	X	X	–	–	–	–
Ship Quantity-on-Hand	–	–	–	X	X	X	–
Backorder Quantity-Ordered less Quantity-on-Hand	–	–	–	X	X	X	–
Investigate Error	–	–	–	–	–	–	X

Figure 2-1 Example of a Category 8 language; sample of a decision table.

Category 8 languages are often used as adjuncts to software specifications, and several decision-table compilers have been produced which can yield executable programs in a variety of languages from decision-table inputs.

Category 8 languages cannot be measured satisfactorily in 1985. While it is possible to measure the textual information and some of the geometric information, such as the number of cells, one aspect of this language class is difficult to quantify. The same symbol can have totally different meanings depending upon where it resides on the matrix. In the Figure 2-1, the letters Y and N mean different things in every cell where they appear.

Although it is dissapointing to say so, the lack of satisfactory metrical techniques for dealing with hybrid geometric and character-string information is making productivity analysis of these powerful language classes very difficult.

Category 9: Free-form graphics with natural language inclusions. Category 9 is the home of flowcharts, HIPO (Hierarchical Input, Process, and

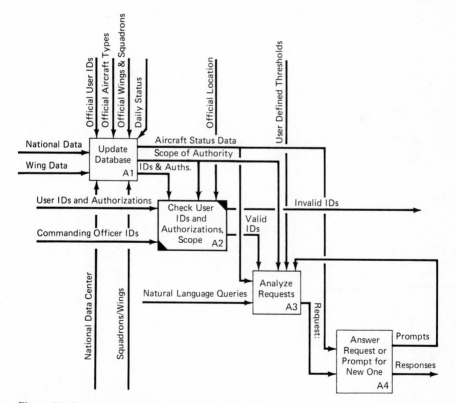

Figure 2-2 Example of a Category 9 language.

Output) diagrams, bubble diagrams, and perhaps 40 other semi-graphical languages for expressing software concepts. Figure 2-2 gives an example of a typical Category 9 language to illustrate the concept; in this case it is a structured analysis diagram in the SADT (Structured Analysis and Design Technique) language developed by Ross (6).

Languages in Category 9 are seldom if ever used for actual coding or programming, and so the measurement of their information content is seldom attempted. The commonest geometric shapes in this category are rectangles, circles, squares, and diamonds. However, these geometric structures are used primarily as containers for text and have very little meaning divorced from the words or symbols which they contain. The arrows have limited meaning in expressing control flow and, in some cases, the kinds of information being transferred.

From the point of view of human factors, these languages give a decided clarity to the geometric aspects of software systems. However, the arbitrary, almost random placement of the geometric structures would make computerized editing or processing, other than simply creating the diagrams under human control, somewhat difficult.

In sum, Category 9 languages are seldom measured or quantified, and no agreed or standard metrics have yet been applied to this class.

Category 10: Derived graphics with natural language inclusions. Category 10 differs from Category 9 in that the geometric shapes convey meaning independently of the text that they contain. In order to do this, the

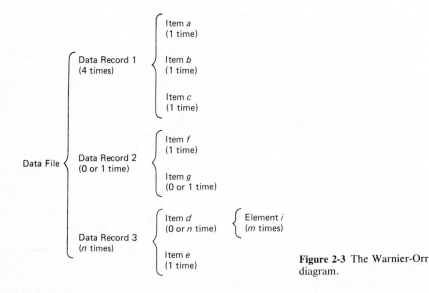

Figure 2-3 The Warnier-Orr diagram.

geometric shapes must be derived from an underlying science that lends itself to graphical representation. The structured programming theorems, set theory, and network theory are the three sciences which have been most fruitful in leading to Category 10 languages, and actual languages have been derived from all three of them. Nassi-Shneiderman charts (7) from the structured programming theorems and Warnier-Orr diagrams (8) from set theory are shown in Figures 2-3 and 2-4 giving examples of two of these languages.

The significant aspect of Category 10 is that the derivation of the geometric shapes from underlying sciences provides enough rigor so that these languages can actually be compiled, to produce executable programs. Although in 1985 graphics compilers are still laboratory prototypes rather than commercial products, they do exist, and they pave the way to what might be termed fifth generation languages.

In 1985, the measurement of compilable graphics languages is still in its infancy. However, for languages based on the structured programming theorems such as Nassi-Shneiderman charts, it is possible to evaluate the structure using a variety of relatively standard techniques. For languages based on set theory and network theory, measurements are also achievable. Needless to say, lines-of-code measurements are not suitable metrics for compilable graphics languages.

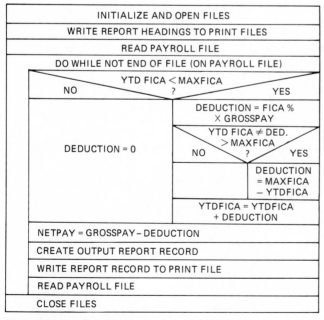

Figure 2-4 The Nassi-Shneiderman chart.

Measurement of Symbol Systems and Communication Methods

The measurement of programming languages is actually only a minor subset of a major issue: the measurement of the information content of symbol systems and communication methods. Although programmers and software engineers are often criticized for lack of suitable measures for software, when the problem is analyzed carefully it may be seen that the fundamental reason for measurement problems in software is that there are no valid linguistic or psychological metrics for symbol systems other than natural language and certain ideograms. When the communication method includes graphics, tables, matrices, or other kinds of visual information, there are no currently available metrics from either psychology or linguistics that may be used.

The need for such metrics can easily be shown. The results of an informal analysis of the kinds of symbols and communication methods used in articles about software in major professional journals (*IEEE Transactions on Software Engineering, IBM Systems Journal, Communications of the ACM,* and *Scientific American*) are shown in Table 2-2:

Table 2-2: Symbols and communication methods used by software periodicals to describe programming systems

Communication method	Frequency
Graphics	2.2 per 1000 words
Percentage of pages with graphics	35%
Tables	3.0 per 1000 words
Mathematical and logical symbols	60 per 1000 words
Type sizes	6-, 8-, 12-, 16-point
Type styles	Normal, italic, boldface
Special features	Superscripts, subscripts, equations, greek alphabetic symbols

While linguists often analyze textual communication and psychologists sometimes analyze graphic communication, there is almost a complete lack of studies that attempt to analyze hybrid communication in which graphics and text together convey the messages.

It is ironic that software engineering and programming, long criticized for lack of effective measurements, may become the originators of an entirely new science that couples both linguistics and psychology to study the most effective ways of conveying complex, abstract ideas from human to human and from human to machine. This emerging discipline, which is not yet a true science but may become one, might provisionally be called "conceptual symbology," or the study of all symbol systems used to represent intellectual concepts. As may be seen, this science would be a superset of conventional linguistics, with a strong basis in perceptual psychology.

Some of the pioneers of this emerging discipline include Curtis, whose *Human Factors in Software Development* (10) is a compendium of much of the current research; Shneiderman (11), who is coinventor of one of the graphics languages capable of direct compilation and a longtime researcher into hybrid communication methods; and Sheppard, Kruesi, and Curtis (12), whose pragmatic experiments in the perception of graphics versus text for software have been influential.

Although software engineers have been more active than conventional linguists in exploring enriched symbol systems and hybrid communication methods, linguistics has not been totally passive in this regard. Skemp put together a special issue of the journal *Visible Language* (13) on the symbolism of mathematics which summarizes linguistic research dealing with symbol systems outside the domain of natural language.

Avoiding the Hazards of Lines-of-Code Metrics

Generally speaking, there are two common purposes for which lines of code are counted: (1) to assess productivity or quality, and (2) to estimate new projects.

Overcoming the hazards of lines of code for assessing productivity essentially means to recognize the mathematical paradox that will cause production of lines of code per unit of time to get smaller as language levels get higher.

This means that it is not possible to make direct productivity comparisons between programs written in different languages without the results being significantly in error, assuming that the levels of the languages are significantly different.

Perhaps the first method for normalizing different languages is to use basic Assembler language as unit of measure and convert the true size of any program being analyzed into "equivalent assembler"; that is, multiply the number of source statements by the nominal level of the language. For example, if a COBOL program actually has 1000 source statements, and COBOL is considered to have a level 3 times higher than Assembler, then the number of equivalent assembler statements to do the same program would be 3000.

This method is statistically unsound and obviously somewhat subjective and unreliable, but at least it causes productivity or quality results to move in the expected direction, whereas uncompensated counts of actual code will not.

One of the major reasons for estimating errors in the entire programming industry is failure to compensate for the mathematical paradoxes associated with lines of code. Since many of the rules of thumb about productivity, such as the anticipated rates of 200 to 300 lines of source code per programmer-month, were originally derived from Assembler language programs, all estimates made for high-level-language programs using these rules of thumb will be catastrophically off the mark.

Managers become mentally trapped by the conflicting notions of productivity into the following disastrous syllogism: "If we've been averaging 200 lines of code per month with Assembler, and a high-level language will improve productivity by 50%, I'll estimate 300 lines of code per month for our new job." Unfortunately, because of the mathematical paradox, the new job will yield only about 150 lines of code per month, thus exposing the unfortunate manager to a 100% budget overrun!

In order to use lines of code as even a rough estimating method and avoid absolute disaster, it is necessary to base the productivity assumptions on each language individually, or at least on languages with the same numeric levels. Table 2-3 gives the total effort required to develop approximately equal functions in some of the major current programming languages, based on analysis by the author. In Table 2-3, structured programming and experienced development personnel are assumed, the complexity of the data being processed is fairly simple, and a standard programming environment with individual workstations or terminals and relatively good support is assumed.

The tasks shown are for a complete development cycle and all major associated work, including requirements, design, professional documentation, design reviews and code inspections, coding, quality assurance, integration, full testing, and management. Installation and postinstallation maintenance are not included.

Table 2-3 starts with a program in basic Assembler language, which is assumed to be 10,000 source statements in size, using executable statements and data definitions but excluding commentary lines and job control language. The programming is done by a single group at a single location so travel costs are not part of the total effort. The only value

Table 2-3 Effort required to produce programs containing equal functions in different source languages

Language	Size (lines)	Development (person-months)	Lines of code per person-year
Assembler	10,000	40	3,000
Macro Assembler	6,666	28	2,856
C	5,000	22	2,727
COBOL	3,333	16	2,500
Pascal	2,500	13	2,307
Ada	2,222	12	2,222
BASIC	2,000	11	2,181

Table 2-4 Effort required to produce a constant amount of source code in selected programming languages

Language	Size (lines)	Development (person-months)	Lines of code per person-year
Assembler	10,000	40	3000
Macro Assembler	10,000	42	2857
C	10,000	44	2727
COBOL	10,000	48	2500
Pascal	10,000	51	2354
Ada	10,000	52	2308
BASIC	10,000	53	2264

which changes is the level of the language. Note in Table 2-3 that as economic productivity improves, lines of code per person-year paradoxically moves lower and lower, as the noncoding parts of the development cycle become increasingly significant.

Table 2-3 clearly illustrates how deceptive and misleading lines-of-code measures can be: As economic productivity improves by almost 4 to 1, lines of code per person-year decline by almost 1.5 to 1.

It is also revealing to look at the effort required to produce an identical amount of code in different languages, since the paradoxical effects of language level manifest themselves here also. Table 2-4 gives the development effort needed to produce 10,000 source code statements in the same languages and using the same sets of development activities shown in Table 2-3.

It is important to realize that the actual coding time does not increase at all as a function of language, and indeed it tends to go down slightly as the level of the language goes up. What happens is that the functions within the program are increasing rapidly, and hence the noncoding parts of the development cycle, such as the documentation, tend to increase. For example, a user's guide for a 10,000-line basic Assembler language program would probably total 80 to 100 pages of text. But the functions embodied in 10,000 COBOL statements would be so much greater that the user's guide for a 10,000-statement COBOL program would almost certainly exceed 200 pages.

In order to use lines of code for measurements or estimating with reasonable success, two fundamental rules must be observed:

1. High-level languages will have characteristic rates of code production that are inversely proportional to the level of the language.
2. The tasks and activities not directly affected by source language (i.e. documentation) are increasingly significant as language levels go up.

Distinguishing the Effects of Programming Languages

For estimating accuracy, it is necessary to divide the overall group of programming development activities into three distinct sets: those that are totally independent of programming language choice, those that are directly impacted by programming language, and those in which the impact is indirect or partial. Following are some representative activities of the three sets:

1. Activities independent of programming languages
   - Customer requirements
   - External functional specifications
   - Design reviews of externals
   - Customer education in externals
   - User's guides
   - Hiring and staffing
   - Travel and meetings
   - Business-phase reviews
   - The quantity and kind of data to be processed
2. Activities directly affected by programming languages
   - Internal design
   - Maintenance documentation
   - Maintenance training
   - Coding
   - Code inspections
   - Testing
   - Correctness proofs
   - Repairs of coding defects
3. Activities indirectly affected by programming languages
   - Management
   - Configuration control
   - Integration
   - Installation at customer sites
   - Quality assurance
   - Repairs of maintenance defects
   - The selection and use of databases and dictionaries

Activities in the first set are the primary cause of the mathematical paradox relative to lines of code per unit of time because these activities are totally independent of the source language selected. As the level of the source language gets higher and higher, the impact of these activities becomes an increasingly significant percentage of total development effort.

Activities in the second set are directly affected by source languages, and estimating output in terms of lines of code per unit of time is fairly regular and predictable, although each language level will have a characteristic rate.

Activities in the third set are the most difficult to evaluate for estimating purposes, because so many different factors come together to affect them. The source language, the available tools, the kind of contract, and many other factors must be dealt with simultaneously.

SUMMARY OF LINES-OF-CODE PRACTICES

The use of lines of code as a productivity measure has been a great source of historical trouble to the programming industry. It has concealed true improvements in economic productivity and has been a major factor in errors in cost estimating.

Attempts to overcome the problems and paradoxes inherent in lines-of-code measures have been partly successful. If great accuracy is not required, it is possible to use lines of code in a day-to-day fashion to achieve useful results for languages through the third generation, i.e. languages whose power ranges up to about 15 times that of Assembler. Beyond the third generation, languages no longer lend themselves to lines-of-code techniques. However, it is necessary to take the following precautions:

1. Understand the nature of the mathematical paradoxes that accompany lines of code when used for high-level language.
2. Establish line-counting rules that are satisfactory to your organization.
3. Establish scope-of-effort standards for activities to include in your project accounting.
4. Publish your line-counting rules and your scope-of-effort definitions with all productivity reports, or your results will be unusable.
5. Make a clear distinction between measures of time, of cost, and of yield.
6. Make a clear distinction between personal productivity, project productivity, and enterprise productivity.

The problems of lines of code are many and severe, but the concept is so deeply embedded in the programming industry that it cannot be quickly replaced.

MEASURING PROGRAMMING OPERATORS
AND OPERANDS

Some of the earliest attempts to depart from lines of code measures and move toward something else have stemmed from the pioneering work of the late Dr. Maurice Halstead of Purdue University, whose analysis of the separate functional statements and data definitions within programs has created a large new body of literature (36).

Unfortunately, the name "software science" has been applied to this work, which upon close analysis is not entirely scientific in the usual sense of the word. The ambiguity of operators and operands is not greatly different from the problems of counting lines of code, and some of the assertions in the software science literature are intuitions rather than scientific observations.

The initial origins of software science are traced by Fitzsimmons and Love (14) back to 1972, when Halstead began an empirical study of algorithms to test the hypothesis that a count of operators (verbal expressions) and operands (nouns or data expressions) in a program might be correlated to the number of bugs in the algorithms. This study was fruitful and caused Halstead to continue with his research.

In Halstead's software science, programs are viewed as being constructed entirely of two atomic particles, operators and operands. "Operators" are the functional statements within the program: arithmetic statements such as + or -, statements to move or read data, and the associated punctuation marks that terminate such statements. "Operands" are the constants and variables that the program uses as data: 3.141592, PAYRATE, and the like.

The basis of software science consists of four fundamental measures that attempt to come to grips both with the quantities of operators and operands used and with their uniqueness. To give an example based on English text, the four software science measures may be likened to counting the total number of nouns and verbs in a novel and then counting the frequency with which the various nouns and verbs are used.

The four basic software science metrics are:

n1	The number of unique operators (verbs) used
n2	The number of unique operands (nouns) used
N1	The total number of times operators are used
N2	The total number of times operands are used

Before going further, it should be noted that the same practical counting difficulties which hamper use of lines of code also hamper taking measures of operators and operands. Indeed, because software science deals with parentheses, punctuation marks, and other subelements of lines of code, the range of variability in how operators and operands can be counted can actually exceed lines-of-code counts. Also, the variations in counting at the project level and the scope of effort variations are just as severe with software science as they are with conventional lines-of-code measures.

From the four basic measures, software science derives a large set of supplemental measures. One of the clearest discussions of the derivative software science measures is that of Christensen, Fitsos, and Smith (15) which covers both the metrics themselves and the possible sources of ambiguity associated with the measures. Many other authors have not dealt with this.

The first derived measure in the software science repertory is the "vocabulary" of a program, or the sum of the unique operators and unique operands. The word "vocabulary" in software science approximates its normal definition as the set of unique words used by a writer or speaker. The formula for a program's vocabulary is:

Vocabulary (n) = unique operators (n1) + unique operands (n2)

The second derived measure in software science is the "length" of a program, or the total sum of all occurrences of operators and operands. The word "length" in software science is used in about the same way as ordinary English might use it in discussing the length of a novel in terms of the total number of words it contains. The formula for a program's length is:

Length (N) = total operators (N1) + total operands (N2)

Up through the length derivation, software science consists primarily of a different way of looking at lines of code, in which the functional and data elements are treated separately. However, from the point of view of linguistics, it is unfortunate that Halstead and his followers chose to deal only with operators and operands rather than with a richer set of constructs. For example, in many programming languages such as Pascal, in which data is defined as being of various types such as decimal, binary, and so forth, programming statements that resemble adjectives and adverbs occur, as well as nouns and verbs. By artificially forcing all programming constructs into either the set of operators or the set of operands, software science is creating a minor subset of linguistics that does not lend itself to the powerful analytic methods of modern structural linguistics.

The departure from conventional linguistic science, or at least the failure to use its findings, begins to manifest itself in the first of the predictive theorems of software science: estimated length.

Halstead noted what was for programming at the time an exciting discovery: that the length of a program is proportional to its vocabulary.

Translated into the terms of English text, Halstead noted that long novels often use a wider variety of words than do short stories.

The departure from conventional linguistic science, or at least the failure to use its findings, begins to manifest itself in the first of the predictive theorems of software science: estimated length.

Halstead noted what was for programming at the time an exciting discovery: that the length of a program is proportional to its vocabulary. Translated into the terms of English text, Halstead noted that long novels often use a wider variety of words than do short stories.

For natural languages, such as English, German, and Mandarin Chinese, the linguist George Zipf had published similar findings in 1935 (16), and subsequent research had demonstrated that the phenomenon of a relationship between vocabulary size and the length of a text passage is statistically expected and often occurs. Indeed, the mathematician and discoverer of fractals, Benoit Mandelbrot, had noted that if a string consisting of a finite set of alphabetic symbols is divided at random intervals by blank spaces, the frequency with which short "words" occurs is much greater than for longer ones, because of nothing more than probability. Also, the number of different long "words" rises as a function of length. Thus the software science derivation of estimated length turns out to be true for unordered random symbols that are randomly divided, as well as for programming languages and natural languages.

However, these findings were not widely known among the software science community, and the discovery of the vocabulary-to-length relationship and its subsequent confirmation for a variety of programming languages were viewed as significant. This confirmation of what was a statistically normal situation was unfortunately viewed as proof that software science was on the path to major discoveries, and it tended to give credence to later assertions that were not as well justified.

On the other hand, some of the software science findings are in fact leading to new insights about programming. In an attempt to explore the relative proportions of operators (verbal statements) and operands (nouns) in 992 Assembler language programs and 490 PL/S programs, Fitsos of IBM (17) noted that the operand, or data portion, was much greater than the operator, or functional portion, especially for the relatively high-level PL/S programs. Since it has been noted earlier in this chapter that for high-level languages, functions become much more compact than do data definitions, this finding was predictable, but its confirmation is of value, because it gives programming language technologists a new goal: to improve the way that programmers deal with data in future generations of languages.

The next software science metric to be discussed, and the last based on quantifiable observations, is Halstead's volume metric, or V. The volume of a program is essentially the number of characters it takes to encode it. To make a parallel to natural language, an English translation of a Chinese poem would have a higher volume than the original brushstroke representation; in the original Chinese each symbol represents a word or concept, while in English, each letter represents only a sound. A short Chinese poem counted by the author contained 18 brushstroke ideograms, but the English translation contained 30 words and a total of 163 letters and punctuation marks.

In a similar fashion, an algorithm encoded in a high-level language such as APL requires fewer characters than the same algorithm encoded in Assembler language.

The software science formula for Volume is:

$$\text{Volume (V)} = N \log 2\ n$$

While lines of code, program length, and program volume are somewhat different conceptually, they are all used as size measures for programs, and all share more or less the same problems and sources of ambiguity.

The four basic software science metrics (unique operators and operands and total operators and operands) are relatively straightforward, as are the three basic derived measures (vocabulary, length, and volume).

The software science analyses based on these seven observations have been useful and have led to some interesting findings on the relative proportions of data definitions and functional statements in different programming languages. However, from this point on, the software science theorems begin to depart from the canons of the ordinary scientific method and enter a realm that is closer to intuitive metaphysics than it is to what is conventionally termed "science."

The first of the purely subjective assertions of software science is the concept of "difficulty," or D as it appears in various formulas. Continuing in alphabetic sequence are "effort," or E and "intelligence content," or I. While the notions implicit in these concepts are sometimes interesting, they are purely subjective and not in any real sense derived from objective data. Indeed, the statistical deficiencies of most studies dealing with D, E, and I are so severe as to make the results meaningless.

To the credit of Halstead and his followers, the software science analysis of programs is an interesting departure from conventional lines-of-code measurement, and the distinction between the functional and data aspects of programs is starting to highlight the importance of data in programming languages. But on the negative side, the failure of software science to include structural linguistic findings and its arbitrary division of program elements into only the two subsets of operators and operands appear to be major limitations that will cause software science to eventually become a technological dead end, somewhat like the pre-Newtonian conceptions of gravity.

To be more effective, the software science methodology should perhaps have been based on a richer set of linguistic concepts than only operators and operands or verbs and nouns. Also, given this dichotomy which includes only operators and operands, Halstead's software science cannot be effective in the analysis of fourth- and fifth-generation languages, hybrid graphics languages, or any of the powerful emerging symbologies for software.

MEASURING PROGRAMMING COMPLEXITY

To both professional programmers and those who program only for their own entertainment, programming is subjectively viewed as being one of the most complex of all human activities, and programming's high complexity level is cited as a major reason for low productivity, long schedules, and low quality.

This brings up both general and specific questions:

1. What does "complexity" mean to the human mind?
2. How can programming's complexity be measured?
3. How can programming's complexity be reduced?

Measuring programming complexity breaks down into two logically distinct tasks: (1) measuring the complexity of the problem, i.e. the functions and data to be programmed; and (2) measuring the complexity of the solution to the problem, i.e. the code itself.

Measuring the Complexity of the Problem

The general human perception that a problem is simple or complex goes beyond the scope of this book, although significant research is being accomplished in the field. The current findings are what might be expected from intuition: experts find easy tasks which amateurs and novices find to be very complex. One of the most convenient fields of study for complexity is chess problems, because of the plentiful supplies of both amateurs and experts and the relative ease with which complexity can be established, varied, and validated.

As Larkin and associates (18) point out, one of the distinguishing features that separates chess masters from novices is the ease with which they remember and analyze board positions. In experiments where a typical midgame chess position with 25 pieces in play is shown for 5 seconds, a master can reconstruct the position with about 90% accuracy, while a novice seldom exceeds 25%.

However, when the experiment switches to 25 chess pieces in a random configuration, not based on real-life game situations, the performance of chess masters and chess novices is equal. The conclusion is that chess masters recognize patterns and that cognitive processing is not based on 25 separate pieces, but rather on the overall configuration into which they fit.

A similar kind of situation seems to prevail in programming, where Curtis, Sheppard, and Milliman (19) note that experienced programmers confronted with sample programs for review tend to be aware of the overall patterns that occur for things like loop control, while novices tend to view each instruction separately.

Larger programming studies have noted that programs that are in areas familiar to the development team, such as compilers developed by compilation experts, are typically developed at a faster rate and with fewer problems than programs which have a higher novelty content and deal with aspects that are unfamiliar to the team. The assumption is that the familiar patterns are the cause of the higher productivity—a reasonable assertion.

The problem of general human perceptions of complexity involves questions not fully answered by cognitive psychologists, dealing with perceptual methods for graphic and textual materials, with temporary and permanent memories, and with physiological and even biochemical issues.

However, in the more limited context of programming design and specifications, program code, and user documentation, there is some evidence that the way a problem is first envisioned will exert a substantial influence on productivity and quality during development.

There are two common ways of envisioning a software system or a program: One can start by thinking of the functions which the system will perform, or one can start by thinking of the data which the system will process.

For information systems and applications programs, Jackson (20), Warnier (21), and Orr (22) assert that a data-analytic approach is the most effective view and that a function-analytic approach tends to bog down in ambiguity. The justification for their assertions is that information systems primarily are created to provide data and information to human beings, and unless the information needs of the human users are the place of origin of the system, late changes in requirements will severely affect the structure of the system. In other words, the data complexity of these systems is high, while the processing complexity is low.

For scientific, real-time, avionics, telecommunications, process control, and certain other software system types, the starting point for system design is usually the functions which the system will perform. For these systems, the input/output and data portions are relatively well known and constrained, while the algorithms and processing complexities are the source of difficulty.

Measuring the Complexity of the Solution

Program code is a final output of a long and only partially explored series of analytic steps that begins with what users think of as their requirements, or at least with what program designers think of as users' requirements. While the technology for measuring the complexity of code is reaching maturity, it must be pointed out that whether or not the code has to be complex is not yet known. Indeed, in a study based on reprogramming error-prone modules (23), Jones pointed out that much of the complexity in the original modules appeared to be accidental rather than necessary and was due either to haste or inexperience or both.

The most widely known complexity measurements in the software engineering literature currently are those of Thomas McCabe, and his methodology is commonly termed either "McCabe complexity measures" (24) or "cyclomatic complexity."

McCabe's complexity measurement procedure is to graph the flow of control of a program, as shown in Figure 2-5, which is taken from Pressman's example (25).

The McCabe technique is to count the number of regions in the resulting graph, where "regions" are defined as the surrounding outside area of the graph and all enclosed or bounded domains. Thus in Figure 2-5, there are five regions in all, and hence the McCabe complexity measure would be 5.

McCabe has noted certain correlations between the complexity number and the real-life subjective difficulty of a piece of software:

Modules or programs with a complexity number of less than 5 are usually considered simple.

Modules or programs with a complexity number greater than 5 but less than 10 are usually considered well structured and stable.

In programs or modules with a complexity number of 20 or higher there appears to be a direct correlation between the number and subjective complexity.

Programs or modules scoring higher than 50 are often error-prone and viewed as extremely troublesome.

In practical terms, the McCabe complexity metrics predict that as the number of branches in a program goes up, the complexity also goes up, and by implication, the number of bugs and errors should go up also.

Sheppard, Curtis, Milliman, and Love (26) provide experimental

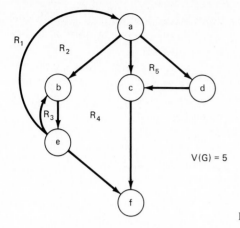

V(G) = 5

Figure 2-5 Control flow graph complexity.

evidence that this is so, and indeed the McCabe complexity measure has been one of the most successful trouble indicators or "bug predictors" yet discovered.

However, in spite of the success of McCabe's complexity measure, it only covers code-branching situations in finished programs and has no direct way of dealing with the complexity of the original problem. Neither does the McCabe method come to grips with data complexity. The McCabe technique is a very good start and has some excellent practical results, but there are still more unexplored than explored areas of complexity.

Measuring Data Complexity

As noted earlier, modern high-level programming languages tend to be at much higher levels of functional than data-handling capability. Indeed, the equivalent of high-level languages for dealing with data are the external databases and data dictionaries that are outside the scope of the languages themselves.

Data complexity is not as easily studied via controlled experiment as is functional complexity, because some of the aspects of data complexity are large-scale file structures where perhaps hundreds of data elements can potentially interact.

However, attempts to come to grips with data complexity have been relatively fruitful and indeed have resulted in a major subdiscipline of software engineering: the data-analytic design methods; as already noted, Jackson, Warnier, and Orr being the best-known methods in the field.

The data-analytic design methods collectively assert that much of a program's complexity is really due to the complexity of the data which it must process. Jackson, Warnier, and Orr go beyond this observation to the recommendation that the structure of a programming system should actually be based on the structure of its data rather than upon arbitrary decomposition methods that are based on functions.

The Jackson, Warnier, and Orr methods have one other significant attribute. When a program is being designed and planned, there are two separate ends to consider: the inputs which the program will accept and the outputs which the program will generate.

The Warnier and Orr methods make the very significant claim that both design and measurement should be driven by the outputs, not by the inputs. Pragmatically, in systems where the inputs are considered first, two major problems may occur because the outputs have not yet been determined:

1. There is a tendency to collect much more input data than the problem really needs.
2. There is a probability that some vital input may be accidentally left out.

As Figure 2-6 illustrates, there are quite a wide variety of ways of approaching the software design task.

The topic of data complexity overlaps the larger topics of database and data dictionary design, which are outside the scope of this chapter.

One of the topics of debate in the software engineering literature is that of the pros and cons of "data typing," or whether programming languages should require explicit definitions of the "types" of data used (i.e. integer, character, Boolean, etc.) and permit only those functions that are appropriate to its type to be executed on a data element.

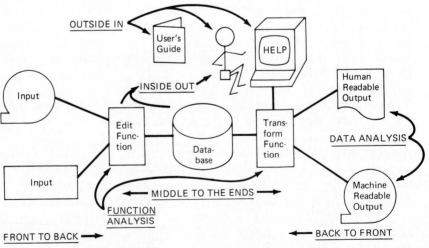

Figure 2-6 Illustration of architectures.

Some programming languages, such as Pascal and Microsoft BASIC, are termed "strongly typed," because they require that data be explicitly declared as to type, or at any rate they assign strictly enforced types to all data. Other languages, such as BLISS and BCPL, are termed "typeless," because they are insensitive to what kind of data is being addressed for any given function, and they will try to execute the function even if such action is irrational: for example, they will attempt to add a numeric field to a character field.

Gannon (27) described a small but interesting experiment which demonstrated that typed languages requiring explicit identification of data types seemed to produce programs with fewer data errors than untyped languages; but a single experiment is not conclusive.

Burding, Becker, and Gould (28) explored the interesting and important topic of how the human mind holds and organizes data, i.e. whether it is stored in terms of a hierarchy, a network, a list, or something else. Their study was inconclusive, but since it was published in 1977, it lacked some of the modern hypotheses, such as that of Pietsch (29) that data is stored in the human mind holographically and accessed by means of Fourier transforms.

The analysis of data complexity is still a very young discipline, one which will soon be undergoing rapid change as the next generation of high-volume data storage devices allow images, graphics, and voice records to become part of databases and to exist side by side with alphabetic and numeric information.

MEASURING PROGRAMMING FUNCTIONS

Programming is an important activity today and the worldwide number of professional programmers is in excess of 3,250,000, as noted by Jones (30); the number of current applications in existence no doubt exceeds a million; and the number of lines of source code in the world is in the billions. But it is not a law of nature that this situation will continue forever.

Already many functions that once would have been viewed as purely in the domain of programming are starting to be implemented in very large scale integration (VLSI), in microcode, from standard reusable modules, or in some fashion other than conventional line-by-line programming. The possibility that today's programming languages may change significantly enhances the desirability of measuring functions directly rather than measuring the program, which really is only one out of many possible ways for embodying those functions.

In an interesting observation, Kendall (31) points out that electromechanical tab-card devices that preceded electronic computers—sorters, collaters, and the like—embodied a general set of "functions" from which a wide variety of business applications were constructed. As Kendall observes, the basic functions needed for either a computer program or any other large-scale manipulation of business data are relatively small and finite: Reading and writing data, selecting subfields within records, merging files, sorting, basic arithmetic operations, updating records, converting from one format to another, and linking these separate functions together into larger procedures are sufficient to create almost any current business application. If a few additional functions are added for graphics capabilities, Kendall proposes that a set of fewer than 50 generalized functional modules might be placed in a single VLSI chip to carry out virtually all of today's programming tasks. Indeed, Kendall observes that multiple versions of these standard functions could be iterated many times on the VLSI chip, thus allowing parallel processing to take place, with some of the redundant functions also serving as backups in case of failure. Kendall argues that such an architecture would minimize or eliminate conventional programming and also couple super-computer speeds with around-the-clock reliability. The result of Kendall's architecture would be something other than a general-purpose computer, but for a set of well-defined and finite operations, the costs, performance, and reliability would be over an order of magnitude better than today's general-purpose computers and software applications.

Kendall also observes that to truly optimize the data processing function, and indeed go beyond today's capabilities, such a computer would be linked to an integrated database and data dictionary with very low storage costs. In Kendall's view, many of the problems and limitations of today's computing environment are historical legacies from the recent past, when data storage was very expensive. Current low-cost storage, and the even less expensive storage methods soon to arrive, will allow all changes and updates to a file or database to simply be accumulated and time-stamped, so that not only the current values of data but all past values are available along with knowledge of the applications that made modifications. In Kendall's architecture, many database problems simply disappear, and many new and currently unavailable features become possible.

Whether or not Kendall's observations will be implemented in the near future, they raise the valid point that what is important about programming is not lines of code but the underlying functions which the program contains.

Current Experiments in Measuring Functions

In 1979, Albrecht of IBM (37) presented the results of an interesting measurement experiment that completely avoided the use of lines of code and yet was highly successfull both in revealing productivity trends and in isolating the technologies that were responsible for those trends. Also, unlike conventional lines-of-code metrics, Albrecht's technique was not paradoxical when dealing with programs written in high-level languages; it successfully captured the significant productivity gains which high-level languages can yield, but which are concealed by use of lines-of-code measures.

Albrecht worked in IBM's data processing services organization, which produced contract programs written in a variety of languages, as the customers' needs indicated. In Albrecht's first attempts to explore productivity, he encountered the same paradoxical situations described earlier in this chapter, and so he began to search for a more revealing measurement technique.

What Albrecht arrived at was a technique called "function points," although that is something of a misnomer because the technique does not deal with functions explicitly, and it also overlaps into the area of data measurement. In Albrecht's method, the following weighted items are evaluated:

- Number of inputs, multiplied by 4
- Number of outputs, multiplied by 5
- Number of inquiries, multiplied by 4
- Number of master files, multiplied by 10
- Number of interfaces, multiplied by 7

The result, for any given application, is a dimensionless number which Albrecht calls a "function point." In other words, function points are somewhat analogous to Dow Jones averages for the stock market: an abstract and synthetic but practically useful indicator of performance.

Albrecht states that the raw function-point total can be modified subjectively for other factors, such as high complexity or on-line processing, with a permissable maximum range of plus or minus 25% for the subjective modifications. Although the method is empirical and partly subjective, the results have been interesting enough for the technique to attract other researchers, including Gannon (33) and Behrens (34). Indeed, both IBM and GUIDE, the association of IBM's commercial customers, have started major research projects dealing with function points.

Albrecht originally discussed a total of 22 projects completed over a 5-year period, during which the development technologies and the programming languages were studied and improved. With the function-point measurement technique, the productivity gain was reported to be about 3 to 1. The following factors were cited as the chief causes of the improvements: the use of structured programming, the use of high-level languages, the use of on-line development, and the use of a programming development library.

The same projects analyzed in terms of lines of code per unit of time revealed ambiguous results, which Albrecht correctly pointed out were due to the failure of the lines-of-code metric to reveal true productivity gains when applied to high-level languages.

Although the function-point methodology itself has sources of ambiguity, such as the uncertainty in just how to count inputs, outputs, data files, and inquiries, it is becoming widely used for information systems and application programs. The function-point method is not widely used for real-time systems, military systems, or other kinds of software where algorithmic complexity is high and data complexity is low.

Viewed objectively, the function-point method can be seen to be substantially incomplete, since it lacks any effective quantification for the structural aspects of software, such as branching, loops, recursive calls, and the like. This gap in the standard Albrecht function-point method has led to a growing interest in hybridizing Albrecht's work with other metrics. Since the McCabe complexity metrics cover the gap in Albrecht's methodology, several interesting but not yet completed experiments are under way which attempt to couple the Albrecht method with aspects of the McCabe method. Symons (35) in particular is developing a hybrid form of measurement that joins the Albrecht and McCabe concepts, with the McCabe structural complexity technique substituting for the highly subjective Albrecht complexity factors.

The Albrecht methodology is potentially valuable for several reasons, of which perhaps the most important is the ability to use Albrecht function points as a size predictor to estimate how many lines of source code will be needed in any arbitrarily chosen language. This work is originally based on the analysis of Behrens, who noted that it took an average of 65 PL/I source statements and 100 COBOL source code statements to code one Albrecht function point.

Table 2-5 gives the approximate number of source code statements, using executable lines and data declarations but not comment lines or job control language, that might be required to implement one Albrecht function point. The margin of error in Table 2-5 is fairly high, and Behrens himself noted a range of as much as plus or minus 50% for COBOL programs, due to uncertain causes. However, even with a high margin of error, the possibility of using a metric that can be applied during requirements and design to predict code size during development is a path worth serious exploration.

Table 2-5, it may be noted, is essentially the reciprocal of Table 2-1, in which the level of the language is divided into the number of Assembler language source statements to produce the results shown. Table 2-5 has not been validated for all languages and should be regarded as only a

Table 2-5 Approximate number of source statements required to code one Albrecht function point in selected languages

Language	Source statements per function point
Assembler	320
Macro Assembler	213
C	150
ALGOL	106
CHILL	106
COBOL	106
FORTRAN	106
JOVIAL	106
Pascal	91
RPG	80
PL/I	80
MODULA-2	71
Ada	71
PROLOG	64
LISP	64
FORTH	64
BASIC	64
LOGO	53
Fourth-generation database	40
STRATEGEM	35
APL	32
OBJECTIVE-C	26
SMALLTALK	21
Query languages	16
Spreadsheet languages	6

starting point for analysis. However, for the languages which have been explored (Assembler, COBOL, PL/I, BASIC, Pascal, and several spreadsheet languages) it has been surprisingly useful.

To summarize the function-point results to date, the technique has been exceptionally fruitful in triggering new concepts and fresh research, and its potential to estimate lines-of-code sizes makes it a candidate for serious continued study. However, the function-point method also has gaps and sources of ambiguities of its own.

HYBRID MEASUREMENTS OF FUNCTIONS, COMPLEXITY, AND DATA

Three more or less independent streams of research are beginning to overlap and coalesce: measures of functions, measures of complexity, and measures of data. Although no single hybrid technique has been fully developed as of 1985, the possibility exists that the Albrecht function-point technique might fruitfully be joined to the McCabe complexity technique to create a synergism that is stronger than either method alone. This is an obvious coupling, since the most visible weakness of the Albrecht technique is in the area of structural complexity, which is the primary strength of the McCabe technique.

The remaining element, or data complexity, is not as far along in 1985 in terms of measurement possibilities. However, the Warnier-Orr data-analytic methods may turn out to provide a basis for coming to grips with data complexity.

What suggests itself is the software equivalent of a "standard cost unit," which would consist of programs with predetermined Albrecht and McCabe values. For example, a program with one input, one output, one data file, one inquiry, and one interface would have an Albrecht function-point total of 30. If this same program were well structured, it would have a McCabe complexity total of 5. If it were possible to add a similar data complexity value, then programs could be evaluated in terms of all three aspects, with potentially valuable results.

APPROACHING ECONOMIC PRODUCTIVITY

Because of the historical emphasis on lines of code in the programming literature, actual studies of economic productivity are almost nonexistent in the programming field.

Economic productivity is generally defined as goods or services produced per unit of labor or expense. However, this definition is taken from the early days of manufacturing durable goods, and it is not entirely suitable for intangible products such as computer programs.

In terms of goods or services, programming systems are generally developed for one or more of the following three reasons:

1. To speed up processes that were formerly done manually
2. To provide access to large volumes of information
3. To perform functions that cannot be done manually (i.e. real-time programs)

Only in the first case can a numerical value be easily applied, by comparing the costs of the manual activity with the costs of the automated activity. In other words, economics itself does not deal with certain classes of products, which include software systems.

Programs that manipulate large volumes of data, such as the many commercially available database management programs, can have their costs quantified, but the value to a potential user is based on the perceived value of the information to be utilized.

The ability of computers and programs to perform tasks which human beings cannot perform at all (i.e. real-time target tracking from radar inputs, kprime-number-based cryptanalysis, medical tomography, etc.) is the most difficult topic of all from the standpoint of economic analysis. In some cases, the functions have never been previously performed in all human history, and so it is not easy to assess their true value.

However, economic productivity is usually an issue for only three main reasons:

1. Are we doing as well as our competition?
2. Are we getting better as time passes?
3. Are we doing as well as we could be doing?

The first question is of course an important one for commercial enterprises, since if you are not doing as well as your competition that will affect the future of your enterprise in perhaps unpleasant ways. This question is of great significance to companies that market software, since their revenues are directly involved.

The second question is the one that comes up most often in the programming and software engineering literature, but usually the answer is couched in terms of lines of code per unit of time and so economic productivity is not considered.

The third question is not asked often, but it is the most interesting of all, since it leads to subsidiary questions about the state of the art and the limits of productivity. In most enterprises, however, there is a tacit feeling that probing too deeply into this question is an implied criticism of management, since if you are not doing as well as you could be doing, someone is likely to get blamed for it.

Economic productivity overlaps the field of financial analysis, where enterprises are measured on certain key indicators that reflect their health or lack of health. For example, earnings per share, inventory turnover ration, and debt-to-equity ration are relatively common financial measures.

Economic productivity for programming systems can be approached by abandoning lines of code as a unit and switching over to ratios that compare current performance against some key indicator, such as a standard baseline. The standard baseline indicator is an assumption about how much a program would cost and how long it would take at a fixed level of technology—for example, unstructured assembly language developed using methods common in 1960. Current performace can then be compared against the baseline to ascertain the levels of productivity in a rough economic sense.

In order to approach economic productivity, we must explore some of the aspects of large-scale software trends over time, including the following:

1. Number of software staff employees as a percentage of total enterprise employees.
2. Annual computing and software expenses as a percentage of total enterprise expense.
3. Rates of growth of software staffs and expenses over time.
4. Number of users of data processing or software systems, with trends over time.
5. Data processing and software costs per user, with trends over time.
6. Numbers of batch and on-line applications in the active program library, with trends over time.
7. Number of terminals and personal computers per employee in the enterprise, with trends over time. (By 1990 certain high-technology enterprises should have more computers than they have paid employees.)
8. Volumes of data used by applications and systems, in terms of both databases and other file structures, with trends over time.
9. Volumes of data per employee of the enterprise, with trends over time.

While there are many other possible measures, this set gives a sample of the kinds of significant questions which can pave the way to future explorations of economic software productivity.

There is one other aspect of economic productivity that should be illustrated: trends in productivity over time. Table 2-6 illustrates three versions of the same system as they might appear if they were developed at 10-year intervals, using the prevailing technologies of the day: unstructured Assembly language in 1964, unstructured COBOL in 1974, and highly structured methods and coding practices in 1984:

From an inspection of Table 2-6, several points become apparent:

1. Neither cost per line nor lines per month are economic indicators. Indeed, they conceal the true economic picture, which is that the 1984 version took only 33% of the effort and only 50% of the time of the 1964 version.
2. Inflation is tending to move at a somewhat faster rate than productivity has been increasing, so total dollar costs for equivalent functions have not declined.
3. By working backward from the output, it is apparent that if 280 person-months were required to develop 30,000 lines of Assembler source code and its accompanying documentation in 1964, the same 280 person-months would yield some 90,000 equivalent Assembler

Table 2-6 Productivity for systems with identical functions, developed at 10-year intervals

	Case 1	Case 2	Case 3
Year	1964	1974	1984
Size (lines)	30,000	10,000	10,000
Language	Assembler	COBOL	COBOL
Schedules (Calendar months)			
Requirements	5	5	3
Design	7	5	4
Coding	6	4	3
Integration testing	6	4	3
Total	24	18	13
Overlapped	20	15	10
Effort (person-months)			
Requirements	10	6	4
Design	15	8	6
Internal documentation	14	6	4
User documentation	29	13	11
Coding	99	30	20
Integration/test	40	16	11
Defect repairs	48	35	31
Management	25	10	7
Total	280	124	94
Monthly salary	$2,000	$3,000	$4,000
Total cost	$560,000	$372,000	$376,000
Cost per line	$18.60	$37.20	$37.60
Lines per month	107	81	106

statements in 1984. In terms of the artificial unit of equivalent Assembler, monthly output would be 321 lines per programmer in 1984 compared to the 107 lines actually shown for 1960—a 300% increase.

In sum, economic productivity must be divorced from lines of code in order to be understood. When economic productivity is uncoupled from lines of code, new and very powerful analyses may be performed that demonstrate the power of the modern and emerging programming technologies.

SUMMARY OF SOFTWARE MEASUREMENT TRENDS

As of 1985, software engineering is slowly emerging from the dark fog of lines-of-code measurements to explore new methods and new concepts of measurement. The inability of lines-of-code measures to be used for fourth- and fifth-generation languages is triggering one of the more significant waves of discovery of the century, with the recognition that all forms of communication and all symbol systems must be evaluated. This may eventually trigger a new science provisionally termed conceptual symbology, or the study of all symbols used to communicate abstract and complex ideas; this should forge a new bond between linguistic science, perceptual psychology, and the sciences which require rich symbol systems to convey their concepts.

At the pragmatic, day-to-day level, new software measures are starting to appear that come to grips with functions, with structural complexity, and with data complexity. Although these methods were developed independently by different researchers, new synergistic hybrid measurements are starting to be explored, with significant potential values.

Among the encouraging signs of measurement maturity for software are the relatively strong correlations between complexity metrics and defect rates and the apparent but not yet fully validated correlations between function points and program sizes.

The lack of satisfactory economic measures for software has started to trigger an increasing awareness that economics itself is not a complete science and that certain classes of products, such as software systems, have not been fully covered by economic theories or by economic models.

Although a full and satisfactory set of software metrics does not exist in 1985, it is safe to say that both the magnitude and the direction of metrical research is leading to the prospect of a mature science of software measurement by the end of the decade.

REFERENCES

1. Kuhn, T.S.; *The Structure of Scientific Revolutions*; University of Chicago; Chicago, IL; 1970.
2. Goldstine, H.H.; *The Computer from Pascal to Von Neumann*; Princeton University; Princeton, NJ; 1980.
3. Elshoff, J.L.; "Some Analysis of Commercial PL/I Programs"; *IEEE Transactions on Software Engineering*, June 1976; pp. 113-120.
4. Jones, Capers; *Programming Productivity—Issues for the Eighties*; IEEE Press; Silver Spring, MD; Cat. No. EHO 186-7; 1981; pp. 221-224.
5. Jones, Capers; "A Survey of Programming Design and Specification Techniques"; *Proceedings of the IEEE Conference on Specifications of Reliable Software*; Cat. No. 79 CH1401-9C; 1979; pp. 91-103.
6. Ross, Douglas T.; "Structured Analysis (SA): A Language for Communicating Ideas"; *IEEE Transactions on Software Engineering*, Vol SE-3, No. 1, January 1977.
7. Nassi, I. and Shneiderman, B.; "Flowchart Techniques for Structured Programming"; *SIGPLAN Notices*; ACM; 1973.
8. Orr, K.T.; *Structured Systems Development*; Yourdon; New York; 1977.

9. Vidondo, F., Lopez, I., and Girod, J.J.; "Galileo System Design Method"; *Electrical Communication—ITT Technical Journal*, Vol. 55, No. 4, 1980; pp. 364-371.
10. Curtis, B.; *Human Factors in Software Development*; IEEE Press; Silver Spring, MD; Cat. No. EHO 185-9; 1981.
11. Shneiderman, B. et al; "Experimental Investigation into the Utility of Detailed Flowcharts in Programming"; *Communications of the ACM*, Vol. 20, No. 6, June 1977; pp. 373-381.
12. Sheppard, S.D., Kruesi, E., and Curtis, B.; "The Effects of Symbology and Spatial Arrangement on Comprehension of Software Specifications"; *Proceedings of the Fifth International Conference on Software Engineering*; IEEE Press; Silver Spring, MD; Cat. No. 81CH1627-9; pp. 207-214. (Also in *Human Factors in Software Development*; See reference 10.)
13. Skemp, R.R.; "Understanding the Symbolism of Mathematics"; *Special Issue of Visible Language*, Vol. 26, No. 3, Summer 1982;
14. Fitzsimmons, A. and Love, T.; "A Review and Evaluation of Software Science"; *Computing Surveys*, Vol. 10, No. 1, March 1978; pp. 3-18.
15. Christensen, K., Fitsos, G.P., and Smith, C.P.; "A Perspective on Software Science"; *IBM Systems Journal*, Vol. 20, No. 4, 1981; pp. 372-383.
16. Zipf, G.; *The Psycho-Biology of Language: An Introduction to Dynamic Philology*; M.I.T.; Cambridge, MA; 1965.
17. Fitsos, G.P.; "Elements of Software Science"; *IBM Technical Report*; TR 02.900; IBM Santa Teresa; 1982.
18. Larkin, J. et al; "Expert and Novice Performance in Solving Physics Problems"; *Science*, Vol. 208, June 1980; pp. 1335-1342.
19. Curtis, B., Sheppard, S.B., and Milliman, P.; "Third Time Charm—Stronger Prediction of Programmer Performance by Software Complexity Metrics"; *Proceedings of the Fourth International Conference on Software Engineering*; IEEE Press; Silver Spring, MD; 1979, pp. 356-360.
20. Jackson, M.A.; *Principles of Program Design*; Academic; London; 1975.
21. Warnier, J.D.; *Logical Construction of Systems*; Van Nostrand Reinhold; New York; 1981.
22. Orr, K.T.; *Structured Requirements Definition*; Ken Orr & Associates; Topeka, KS; 1981.
23. Jones, T.C.; "Program Quality and Programmer Productivity"; *IBM Technical Report*; TR 02.764; January 1977; pp. 5-45.
24. McCabe, T.J.; "A Complexity Measure"; *IEEE Transactions on Software Engineering*, Vol. SE-2, December 1976; pp. 308-320.
25. Pressman, R.; *Software Engineering—A Practitioner's Approach*; McGraw-Hill; New York; 1982.
26. Sheppard, S.D., Curtis,B., Milliman, P., and Love, T.; "Modern Coding Practices and Programmer Performance"; *Computer*, December 1979; pp. 50-59.
27. Gannon, J.; "An Experiment for the Evaluation of Language Features"; *International Journal of Man-Machine Studies*, Vol. 20, No. 8, 1977; pp. 61-73.
28. Burding, B.M., Becker, C.A., and Gould, J.D.; "Data Organization"; *Human Factors*, Vol. 19, No. 1, 1977; pp. 1-14.
29. Pietsch, P.; *Shuffle Brain—The Quest for the Hologramic Mind*; Houghton Mifflin; Boston; 1981.
30. Jones, T.C.; "Technical and Demographic Trends in the Computer Industry"; keynote address, 1983 Data Structured Systems Design Conference; Ken Orr & Associates; Topeka, KS; 1983.
31. Kendall, R.; in "Reusability in Programming—A Survey of the State of the Art"; *IEEE Transactions on Software Engineering*, Vol. SE-10, No. 5, September 1984; pp. 488-493.

32. Albrecht, A.J. and Gaffney, J.E.; "Software Function, Source Lines of Code, and Development Effort Prediction: A Software Science Validation"; *IEEE Transactions on Software Engineering*, Vol. SE-9, No. 6, November 1983; pp. 639-647.

33. Gannon, J.D.; "An Experimental Evaluation of Data Type Conventions"; *Communications of the ACM*, Vol. 20, No. 8, 1977; pp. 584-595.

34. Behrens, C.A.; "Measuring the Productivity of Computer Systems Development Activities With Function Points"; *IEEE Transactions on Software Engineering*, Vol. SE-9, No. 6, November 1983; pp. 648-651.

35. Symons, C.; *Extended Function Points with Entity Type Complexity Rules*; Nolan, Norton and Company; London; 1984.

36. Halstead, M.H.; *Elements of Software Science*; Elsevier North-Holland; New York; 1977.

37. Albrecht, A.J.; "Measuring Application Development Productivity"; Proceedings of the Joint IBM/SHARE/GUIDE Application Development Symposium; October 1979; pp. 83-92.

THREE
DISSECTING PROGRAMMING PRODUCTIVITY

Programming has been a major occupation for more than 30 years; the factors which affect programming productivity and quality are finally starting to become known, although not all of them are fully quantified in terms of their measured impacts.

In this chapter, the 20 major factors for which quantified data exist are analyzed in a series of case studies. In addition, in Chapter 4, another 25 factors which lack full quantification, but which are known to be significant, are discussed in terms of their probable effects.

In order to create the case studies and demonstrate the impact of each factor in isolation, an interactive software life-cycle model was developed that allowed each factor to be changed independently of all others. In this book, the model is called the software productivity, quality, and reliability model, or SPQR. A short description of the SPQR method of operation and the inputs which drive the model are shown in Appendix A.

The 20 factors whose quantified impacts on software projects have been determined from historical data are the following:

1. The programming languages used
2. Program size
3. The experience of programmers and design personnel
4. The novelty of the requirements
5. The complexity of the program and its data
6. The use of structured programming methods

 7. Program class or the distribution method
 8. Program type or the application area
 9. Tools and environmental conditions
10. Enhancing existing programs and systems
11. Maintaining existing programs and systems
12. Reusing existing modules and standard designs
13. Program generators
14. Fourth-generation languages
15. Geographic separation of development locations
16. Defect potentials and removal methods
17. Documentation
18. Prototyping before main development begins
19. Project teams and organization structures
20. Morale and compensation of staff

In addition to the 20 major variables for which reasonable historical data exists, there are 25 other significant factors for which there is insufficient information to provide a true quantitative assessment. These somewhat ambiguous factors are discussed in Chapter 4. However, since these variables are known to be significant, even if their full impact cannot currently be evaluated, it is of interest to identify them here:

 1. Schedule and resource constraints
 2. Unpaid overtime
 3. Staff size
 4. Total enterprise size
 5. Attrition during development
 6. Hiring and relocation during development
 7. Business systems and/or strategic planning
 8. User participation in requirements and design
 9. End-user development
10. Information centers
11. Development centers
12. Staff training and education
13. Standards and formal development methods
14. Canceled projects and software disasters
15. Project redirections and restarts
16. Project transfers from city to city
17. Response time and computer facilities
18. Physical facilities and office space
19. Acquiring and modifying purchased software
20. Internal politics and power struggles
21. Legal and statutory constraints
22. U.S. export license requirements

23. Enterprise policies and practices
24. Measuring productivity and quality
25. Productivity and quality improvement steps

Collectively, the 20 quantified variables discussed in Chapter 3 and the 25 intangible variables discussed in Chapter 4 appear to account for more than 90% of the real variations in productivity that occur in industry.

This chapter's purpose is to dissect and quantify each individual factor on the complete life-cycle of a programming system, from the first tentative discussion of a new program through its development and for 5 years of customer usage. (Although many programs are used for much longer than 5 years, that period is sufficient to capture the bulk of the maintenance effort in terms of defect removal, although not necessarily for enhancements, which can continue indefinitely.)

METHODS USED IN PRODUCTIVITY ANALYSIS

Within this chapter, all of the productivity case studies are normalized to include the same basic sets of activities.

Included software development activities

Management and planning
Systems analysis and design
Programming new code
Analysis of existing code for enhancements (when this occurs)
Acquisition of reusable code (when available)
Internal documentation creation
    Cost estimates and budgets
    Development plans
    Initial and final external specifications
    Detailed module specifications
    Inspection and test plans
    Fault reports and fault responses
External documentation creation
    Installation guide
    Screen and menu creation
    User's guide
    Maintenance manual
Document production and distribution
Design and code inspections (unless specifically excluded)
Integration of code and library control

Unit, function, and system testing
Defect repairs by development personnel
Normal project meetings

Included maintenance activities

Management and planning
On-site delivery support (unless specifically excluded)
Central maintenance of reported defects
On-site field maintenance support (unless specifically excluded)

It is interesting that although the set of activities included for the case studies appears to be reasonably complete when compared to the life-cycle descriptions in the current software engineering literature, in reality these activities only account for somewhere between 60% and 80% of the probable effort that will go into a programming system.

The remaining 20% to 40% of effort varies depending upon the specific nature of the project being developed, with activities such as bidding and contract negotiations or export license applications sometimes being totally absent and sometimes being quite expensive and time-consuming.

The reason for excluding some activities is that too much variance occurs in real-life situations for a general pattern to be derived, or because quantitative data is missing or unreliable. These ambiguous and variable factors are discussed in Chapter 4. The major software activities that are excluded from this chapter's quantitative results are:

Excluded software development activities

Bidding and contract negotiations
Export license applications
Customer or user involvement in the project
Analysis and selection of tools and support packages
Tool customizing and systems programming support
Development and control of reusable code libraries
Formal quality assurance
Formal project auditing
Hiring and staffing expenses and effort
Subcontract negotiations and contract programming
On-the-job or classroom education of project personnel
Development of customer classes and textbooks
Development of maintenance classes and textbooks
Translation of textual materials into foreign languages
Travel expenses during development

Business phase reviews
Project managers above the first line
Project transfers during development
Restarts and major direction changes during development

Excluded overhead activities

Accounting
Advertising
Attornies and legal staff
Marketing
Patents and patent staff
Personnel
Pricing
Purchasing
Security

Excluded maintenance activities

Training of maintenance personnel
Training of customers
Customer maintenance activities
24-hour hot lines for maintenance information
Permanent on-site maintenance personnel at customer locations

Nonstandard Work Breakdown Structures

Because very few enterprises track software costs and activities in sufficient detail to isolate the high-cost aspects of software development and maintenance, this chapter uses a nonstandard work breakdown that emphasizes the two most expensive parts of commercial and military software development: defect removal and paperwork. For maintenance, this chapter uses a three-part work breakdown as shown below:

- The person-months of effort shown for requirements and design deal only with the meetings, verbal discussions, and mental effort of developing the design. The mechanical tasks associated with writing down the design, reproducing copies, and distributing the design for review are covered under "Internal documentation."
- The person-months of effort shown for testing deal only with writing the test cases, putting them in a test library, integrating the code, and running the test cases. All of the effort to fix the bugs which the test cases uncovered is shown in a separate category called "defect repairs."

- The general topic of maintenance is divided into three subcategories: (1) Delivery, or installing the program on the customers' computers; (2) Central maintenance, or fixing all defects reported from customers at central repair sites; and (3) Field maintenance, or sending systems engineers onto the customers' premises to aid in fault isolation, recovery, and repair installation. Subcategories 1 and 3 seldom occur, but when they do, they are expensive activities.

Source Code Line-Counting Conventions

For the program examples within this chapter, the line-counting conventions used are:

- Lines are terminated by delimiters.
- Verbs or operational statements are included.
- Data definitions are included.
- For Assembler language, macro expansions are included.
- For COBOL, included code is counted.
- The code delivered to the user is the basis for the count.
- Comments are excluded.
- Job control language is excluded.
- Temporary code developed to aid testing is excluded.

In each of the case studies in this chapter, the major variables that affect the project will be discussed in a standard manner, using the following conventions:

Project and personnel variables. This portion will discuss the class of software in terms of whether the project is internal or external; the type of software, ranging from personal programs through real-time and military systems; the skills of the personnel; and the kinds of usage expected.

Environmental variables. This portion will discuss the workstation and computer time availability and the requirements, design, and documentation methods used for the project, as well as the kinds of defect removal methods used.

Data and code-structure variables. This portion will discuss the code structure or lack thereof; the data complexity, and, from time to time, the impact of special factors, such as reusable code.

THE IMPACT OF PROGRAMMING LANGUAGES

Of all the variables that affect programming productivity, the choice of language is the most controversial and the most ambiguous. Due to the mistaken use of lines of code per unit of time as a historical productivity metric, most of the literature on the impact of languages is totally unreliable and indeed conceals the true impact of languages. Only in a few cases, such as the work of Albrecht and Gaffney (1), Behrens (2), and Jones (3) have the mathematical paradoxes concerning languages been overcome.

High-level languages have both an explicit and a subtle influence on programming productivity. The explicit influence may be stated in the following terms:

- The higher the level of the language, the smaller the amount of code that must be written to complete a given function. This reduces the direct effort of coding, and also lowers the probability of making coding errors.
- The syntactical and semantic structures of high-level languages often improve the clarity and usefulness of a given language for a given application. Thus LISP is the most convenient language for artificial intelligence programs, while APL is the most convenient language for matrix manipulation.

The subtle influences of programming languages on productivity have not been fully described in the programming literature, but they are significant:

- Interpretive languages such as APL, BASIC, and FORTH tend to reduce the design effort and the paperwork needed to develop a program, since the interpretive languages allow immediate proto-typing of many functions.
- The new fourth-generation languages, such as data base query languages, application generators, and the like, come very close to eliminating the design phase of program development efforts. The design proceeds by simply doing the program, or at least a prototype of the program.
- Third-generation languages reduce the maintenance effort of a programming system, since maintenance personnel can usually make more sense out of the listings than they can with Assembler language.
- Fourth-generation languages are currently ambiguous in terms of their impact on maintenance, and some fourth-generation languages may actually be harder than earlier languages to maintain since the lack of procedural logic makes the programs difficult to grasp.

Table 3-1 shows the same programming system developed in four different languages: a basic Assembler language, COBOL, APL, and a spreadsheet such as VisiCalc or Lotus. The examples are based on an

Table 3-1 Comparison of the same program in four languages using the lines-of-code metric

	Assembler	COBOL	APL	Spreadsheet
Size (lines)	20,000	6,500	1,600	400
Schedules (calendar months)				
Requirements	1	1	1	0.5
Design	3	2	1	0.3
Coding	3	2	1	0.2
Testing	3	2	1	0.2
Total	10	7	4	1.2
Overlapped	6	4	3	1.0
Development effort				
(Person-months)				
Requirements	2	2	1	0.2
Design	6	3	1	0.2
Internal				
documentation	1	1	0.5	0.3
External				
documentation	4	2	1	0.2
Coding	26	8	2	0.3
Testing	9	3	1	0.2
Defect repairs	10	5	2	0.8
Management	7	3	1	0.2
Total	65	27	9.5	2.2
5-year maintenance effort				
Delivery	0	0	0	0
Central maintenance	2	2	2	2
Field maintenance	0	0	0	0
Total	2	2	2	2
Project total	67	29	11.5	4.2
Staff size	$5,000	$ 5,000	$5,000	$5,000
Cost per month	$335,000	$145,000	$57,500	$21,000
Total cost	$335,000	$145,000	$57,500	$21,000
Cost per line	$16.75	$22.31	$35.94	$52.50
Lines per month	308	241	168	181

interactive planning program that estimates the number of programmers within various kinds of corporations, the backlogs of applications, attrition rates and personnel replacement costs, the growth of code libraries and the number of programmers on board over a 10-year period, and the total dollar expenditures for programming on an annual basis.

The examples and case studies within this book are all drawn from actual projects, but they have been normalized and generalized by means of the SPQR tool described in Appendix A, to ensure that variables such as line-counting methods and the activities included are the same and only the variable under discussion actually changes.

The initial assumptions for the examples shown in Table 3-1 are shown below.

Project and personnel variables. The program is developed as an internal project and is not aimed at being marketed commercially. The program is interactive and is intended to allow nonprogramming managers to model various assumptions about the growth of programming within a large multinational enterprise. This specific application is novel and had not been previously developed within the enterprise. The analysis and design is done by professional software personnel who are very familiar with the enterprise being modeled and with mathematical modeling itself. Indeed, the systems analysts will use the program themselves when it is finished, and so the requirements are very well understood.

The programming itself in the Assembler and COBOL versions is done by experienced programmers. For the APL and spreadsheet versions, the coding is done by the systems analysts themselves rather than by a programmer.

The project is done at a single development location, and the finished program will be used only at that location, so there is no travel at all. Both the computer resources and the support tools are adequate for the task. Maintenance of the program is informal and assumes that the users and the maintainers work in the same location and communicate easily. However, one aspect of maintenance is that the nonprogramming users are given some instruction in running the program. Additionally, the systems analysts occasionally perform "guest" runs for senior management who are interested in the results but not interested in doing their own terminal sessions. Since from 10 to 50 different people can run the programs, informal dialogs and conversations occur quite frequently.

Environmental variables. In all four cases, the analysts and programmers have their own terminals and essentially unrestricted access to machine time. There are no constraints on performance or the memory usage of the finished program.

The design consists of external functional specifications in English text augmented by sample output formats. Chronologically the APL version was done first and became the basis for the design of the other versions.

Since the systems analysts are also users of the program, the external documentation is informal and is prepared by the analysts themselves. Since the program is internal and not intended for commercial marketing, the documentation is informally reproduced from an ordinary daisy wheel printer and is not typeset or bound into book form.

The defect removal methods include a formal design inspection and testing against known data. For the APL and spreadsheet versions, but not for the Assembler language or COBOL versions, prototypes were used to work out the formats and user interface features before development was completed. The program was a stand-alone program that did not interface with any other programs except the host operating system, so there was no integration.

The project was staffed by personnel already on board and sufficiently versed in the subject area that no training was required or supplied.

Data and code-structure variables. The programs were all interactive, and all starting conditions were input by users. Each terminal session was self-contained, and the runs were not saved in a data base or stored. For the Assembler language and COBOL versions, structured coding techniques were used. For the APL and spreadsheet versions, structuring was not attempted, because of the nature of the languages themselves. Although the data had relatively complex interactions, there were only some 30 initial conditions to be analyzed, so the overall data complexity was not great. Output could either be displayed on a screen, printed in a predetermined format, or stored for later use and revision.

The sizes of the four versions were:

Assembler	20,000 source statements
COBOL	6,500 source statements
APL	1,600 source statements
Spreadsheet	400 source statements

From an analysis of Table 3-1, it is readily apparent why lines of code per unit of time is so hazardous as a productivity metric. While real-life economic productivity was improving by over an order of magnitude (total effort went from 67 months to 4.2 months), the net code-production rate declined from 308 to 181 lines per month, and cost per line increased from $16.75 to $52.50. Note that actual coding effort declined from 26 months to 0.3 months, for a 75-to-1 reduction, but this improvement was not even noted in terms of cost per source line. Total costs were reduced from $335,000 to only $21,000.

By contrast, note how the productivity results differ when the function-point method is used in place of lines of code, as shown in Table 3-2:

Table 3-2 Comparison of the same program in four languages using the function point metric

	Assembler	COBOL	APL	Spreadsheet
Function points	62	62	62	62
Cost per function point	$5403	$2338	$927	$338
Function points per month	0.95	2.4	6.5	9.5

Clearly, the function-point method is a much better indicator of comparative productivity for multilanguage environments than the lines-of-source-code metric.

Conclusions on the Impact of Language

Once freed from the unfortunate masking effect of lines of code per unit of time, the impact of language level turns out to be very significant indeed: an order-of-magnitude reduction in effort and an almost equal reduction in development schedules. Very high level languages such as APL, and the new nonprocedural languages such as spreadsheets, are modifying the traditional concept of a programming development cycle, and they are greatly reducing both the requirements and design tasks and changing the way those tasks are carried out. Unfortunately, these changes are totally masked by the errors of trying to measure productivity in terms of lines of code per unit of time and hence are largely unknown. One of the advantages of the function-point methodology discussed in Chapter 2 is its ability to capture productivity across languages, which lines of code can never do.

THE IMPACT OF PROGRAM SIZE

The programming and software engineering literature is almost uniform in agreeing that large programming systems tend to be more expensive to produce and to have longer schedules than do smaller programs. There are wide variations, but the general trend is relatively clear: Big is expensive and slow when it comes to software. This phenomenon was clearly analyzed by Brooks (4) in "The Mythical Man-Month", and was subsequently explored by other researchers, including the author (5) and Boehm (6).

However, within the total envelope of time and effort, what are the effects of size on individual tasks and work activities? Here the picture is not so clear-cut. One of the major reasons why size alone is difficult to analyze is that almost never does size change by itself. Usually, as programs grow larger, the data that they process becomes more complicated, the interfaces between the individual components and modules require more attention, and the need for communication between all of the team members working on the project goes up rapidly. Also, activities such as integration, which may not occur at all on small programs, begin to assume significant proportions as size climbs above a few thousand source statements.

It is possible to envision very large collections of code, such as a macro library, a repository of reusable modules, or a set of utility programs, where the total size has relatively little impact on overall productivity, because the individual modules are totally unconnected from one another and merely reside in the same repository.

In the ordinary world of commercial and systems programming, size exerts a considerable influence in a number of areas. Following are the major items that tend to grow at more than a linear rate as size increases, assuming that other factors such as the source language, the tools, and the experience levels of personnel stay relatively constant:

Planning activities
Management activities
Communication needs
Requirements development
System functional design
Interfaces between components and modules
Complexity of control flow and data flow through the system
Integration
Defect potentials (interface and complexity-related problems)
Defect removal (all forms from desk checking to delivery)
Data volumes
Internal documentation
External documentation

However, there are other activities which stay more or less constant regardless of size:

Module design
Coding
Unit testing

Since the three activities that stay relatively constant are the traditional mainline tasks of programming, it may be concluded that as systems grow larger, actual coding becomes a smaller percentage of the total effort. Indeed, for very large systems such as telecommunications systems and operating systems it often happens that fewer than 50% of the personnel engaged in the project do any coding at all, and those who do perform coding find that much of their time is spent on noncoding tasks such as resolving interface issues with surrounding modules and components.

As a generalization, all programming activities can be placed into one of three classes:

1. Project related tasks, or the work of identifying the requirements for the system, documenting the basic assumptions, coordinating group activities, handling financial and business matters, and documenting the usage and maintenance instructions.
2. Code-related tasks, or the traditional work of low-level design, coding, and unit testing.
3. Defect-related tasks, or the group activities associated with design reviews, code inspections, and testing. From time to time, performing correctness proofs will be part of this set.

Table 3-3 The impact of size increases on COBOL program productivity measured with lines of source code

	Case 1: Home finance	Case 2: Accounts payable	Case 3: General ledger
Size in line	1,000	10,000	100,000
Schedules (calendar months)			
Requirements	0.5	3	6
Design	2.0	4	10
Coding	1.5	4	6
Testing	1.5	3	8
Total	5.5	14	30
Overlapped	4.0	9	20
Development effort (person-months)			
Requirements	0.5	4	50
Planning and business	0.2	3	60
Design	0.5	6	70
Internal documentation	0.3	1	75
External documentation	0.5	3	125
Coding	1.5	18	180
Testing	0.5	9	115
Defect repairs	1.0	18	300
Management	0.5	7	110
Total	5.5	69	1,085
5-year maintenance effort			
Delivery	0.2	5	100
Central maintenance	2.3	10	380
Field maintenance	0	0	0
Total	2.5	13	480
Project total	8.0	82	1,565
Staff size	1	9	54
Cost per month	$ 5,000	$ 5,000	$ 5,000
Total cost	$40,000	$410,000	$7,825,000
Cost per line	$ 40.00	$ 41.00	$ 78.25
Lines per month	182	145	92

As programming systems grow from very small to very large, the first and third groups of activities tend to grow much more rapidly than does the second. This means that serious attempts to improve productivity at the large-system level must also include techniques that facilitate project management and that minimize the expenses of eliminating defects, either by enhancing defect prevention or by raising defect removal efficiency or both.

Table 3-3 shows the impact of size increase on programs of the same general type. Since there are almost no real-life examples of programs where size is the only variable that changes, Table 3-3 shows three programs in the same field of endeavor and written in the same language, COBOL. Case 1 represents a 1000-source-statement home finance program; Case 2 represents a 10,000-source-statement accounts payable program; and Case 3 represents a 100,000-source-statement integrated general ledger system.

Project and personnel variables. All three programs are developed internally for use within the enterprise and are not intended for external sale or lease. The programs are all interactive and are aimed at utilization by nonprogrammers. The accounting principles upon which the programs are based are very well understood by the users and the analysts alike. However, for the two larger-sized examples, the users are somewhat uncertain about what they really want the systems to do.

The programs are done within a single development location, and the finished systems will be used at that location, so there is no travel at all. Both the computer resources and the support tools are adequate for the tasks. Maintenance of the programs is formal, and when completed, they enter the official inventory of application packages owned by the enterprise.

Environmental variables. In all three cases the analysts and programmers have their own terminals and essentially unrestricted access to machine time. There are no constraints on performance or memory usage of the finished program.

Since a majority of the users are nonprogrammers and have little experience with computers, particular care is taken to make the HELP screens, menus, and user's guides clear and easy to understand, although, as with internal systems, the user's guides are merely printed from a daisy wheel printer and are not typeset or bound into book form.

Data and code-structure variables. This is the area where size as an independent variable is almost impossible to analyze. Although structured coding was used in all three programs, the data complexity of Case 3, the large integrated general ledger system, is subjectively viewed by the analysts and users alike as much greater than that of either of the two smaller examples. This causes interface problems among the components and modules of the large system, which affect the design, the programming, and the integration of the system.

The sizes of the three cases, all of which are assumed to be done in the same COBOL version and to operate on the same computer, are:

Personal finance	1,000 source statements
Accounts payable	10,000 source statements
Integrated general ledger	100,000 source statements

Note that the data in Table 3-3 is synthesized from a number of projects. From Table 3-3, several significant observations may be derived:

1. In terms of overall impact, coding dropped from being the major activity for the small home finance program to only the third-ranked activity for the large general ledger system.
2. The effort needed to produce the internal and external system documentation for the 100,000-source-statement example was significantly greater than the coding effort.
3. The effort needed to test the software and repair the defects in it emerged as the major sources of effort and expense in the 100,000-source-statement example.

Ranking the three most expensive development activities for each example is illuminating:

	Case 1: Home finance	Case2: Accounts payable	Case 3: General ledger
Size in statements	1000	10,000	100,000
Most expensive	Coding	Coding and defect repairs (tie)	Defect repairs
Second most expensive	Defect repairs	Testing	Documentation
Third most expensive	Documentation	Management	Coding

It is plain that making improvements in productivity requires a multifaceted strategy that attacks the largest cost elements. For small programs, where coding is the largest cost element, techniques such as improved languages and code-handling tools are likely to be quite effective. However, for large systems, where both defect removal costs and documentation costs are more expensive than coding, a different strategy is indicated; a synergistic set of complementary methods that include document production facilities, design and code inspections, and higher-level programming languages is an appropriate strategy.

Although the three examples were all COBOL source language programs, and hence not subject to the catastrophic paradoxes which lines-of-source-code metrics introduce into multilanguage environments, it is of interest to note the function point method analyses of productivity for small through large systems, as shown in Table 3-4.

Productivity decreases as size goes up not because coding itself takes significantly more effort, but rather because so many peripheral activities such as documentation, integration, planning, and defect removal begin to take increasingly large amounts of effort and time.

Table 3-4 The impact of size increases on COBOL program productivity, measured with function points

	Home finance	Accounts payable	General ledger
Function points	9.5	95	950
Development cost per function point	$2894	$3631	$5710
Function points per month	1.7	1.4	0.9

THE IMPACT OF EXPERIENCE

The topic of experience is very difficult to separate from the topic of skill and in many ways the two can be treated as synonymous. The programming literature is uniform in agreeing that experience is one of the most significant variables in the industry, with controlled experiments such as those of Chrysler (7) indicating that experience was a pivotal factor. Boehm (8) also cites experience and individual human variation as the largest single factor in productivity. The early observation of productivity variations of more than 20 to 1 as a result of individual experiences, by Sackman and others (9), has been replicated by other researchers, including Curtis (10).

Although there is general agreement that experience is a major variable, there is currently no real consensus on whether experience develops chronologically, develops through breadth of assignments rather than time, or is an intangible factor that varies with uncontrollable human responses. Also, the emerging situation of programmers who learn to program as very young children of perhaps 5 or 6 years of age, and hence have some 15 years of programming behind them when they first enter the job market, is too new a phenomenon to have yet been studied. Those of us who are currently in the programming profession and are older than 40 learned to program as adults, since there were no computer science curricula at most universities during the 1950s and early1960s. Those who are between 21 and 40 probably learned programming in college, but the next generation is programming right now in grade schools and high schools.

The impact of this trend is likely to eliminate or greatly reduce the shortage of programmers by as early as 1990 and to give employers an enormous pool of talent that may be unprecedented in either the sciences or business. There is a very strong possibility that programming will take a place beside reading, writing, and mathematics as a new basic skill.

Subcategories of Experience

The word "experience" can cover two different topics, both of which are important. First, experience in the problem area that is to be programmed is significant. If the program is an accounting package, for example, it is very useful for the programmers to know something about basic accounting.

Second, experience in the tools and languages used to develop the program is also significant. A programmer using a new language for the first time is likely to make mistakes, but that will pass with time.

Table 3-5 gives four examples of the impact of experience on programming. Case 1 assumes a programmer who is very experienced in both the problem area and the tools and languages used. Case 2 assumes a programmer who knows the problem area, but is using a new language, compiler, and tool set for the first time. Case 3 assumes familiarity with the languages and tools, but the programmer has not previously dealt with an application of this type. Case 4 shows a hapless programmer attempting an application of a type not previously encountered and using a new language and tools for the first time as well.

Project and personnel variables. Since the impact of experience is often most dramatic at the individual level rather than at the level of teams or departments, the program is of a size small enough to be handled by a single individual. Let us assume that the program is a subelement of an order-entry system, written in COBOL, and that it is intended to validate that incoming orders from sales personnel have the correct part numbers and quantity measures, that the customer numbers are either valid or identified as new, and that certain other information is correct. Assume that the program takes 1000 COBOL source statements to complete.

All four projects are done at a single development location, and the finished program is not aimed at being marketed commercially. The program is interactive and is intended to allow sales personnel to input order information from remote locations. The sales personnel are presumed to have no computer experience, and help and prompting information will be supplied interactively, along with a printed user's guide that covers basic operations.

Environmental variables. The programmer is also the analyst in the four examples. The requirements are constant throughout and relatively stable. The design consists of English-text functional specifications, a pseudocode module specification, and sample screen layouts which are jointly developed by the programmer and several sales personnel.

The programmer has a terminal and essentially unrestricted access to machine time. There are no constraints on memory usage and while there

Table 3-5 The impact of experience on programming productivity

	Case 1	Case 2	Case 3	Case 4
Size in lines (COBOL)	1,000	1,000	1,000	1,000
Programmer experience with:				
Application	High	High	Low	Low
Language	High	Low	High	Low
Structure	High	Low	High	Low
Schedules (calendar months)				
Requirements	0.6	0.6	0.6	2.6
Design	1.2	1.8	1.8	2.5
Coding	1.0	1.6	1.2	2.3
Testing	0.6	1.4	1.0	2.0
Total	3.4	5.4	5.6	9.4
Overlapped	2.0	4.0	4.0	7.0
Development effort (person-months)				
Requirements	0.6	0.6	0.9	1.0
Design	0.6	0.6	0.6	1.1
Internal documentation	0.1	0.1	0.1	0.1
External documentation	0.3	0.3	0.3	0.3
Coding	1.0	1.8	1.5	2.5
Testing	0.4	0.5	0.6	1.0
Defect repairs	0.6	0.7	1.4	3.0
Management	0.4	0.4	0.6	1.0
Total	4.0	5.0	6.0	10.0
5-year maintenance effort				
Delivery	0	0	0	0
Central maintenance	1.8	2.0	2.5	4.0
Field maintenance	0	0	0	0
Total	1.8	2.0	2.5	4.0
Project total	5.8	7.0	8.5	14.0
Staff size	2	2	2	2
Cost per month	$5,000	$5,000	$5,000	$5,000
Total cost	$29,000	$35,000	$42,500	$70,000
Cost per line	$29.00	$35.00	$42.50	$70.00
Lines per month	250	200	167	111

are performance constraints, there are no technical difficulties in achieving them.

The defect removal methods consist of design reviews, including user participation, coupled with both unit testing and a 1-week trial run with live data.

Data and code-structure variables. Incoming data is input by sales personnel and transmitted over telephone lines. The purpose of the program is to validate that data against a set of known criteria and then pass on correct and reformatted inputs to another program. (The program is not being done in a database environment.) Outputs are messages to the sales personnel that all input is correct, or diagnostic messages and requests for reentry if the input is not correct. Other outputs include validated and reformatted order entry to another program. Data complexity is not great, although when incoming mistakes are made, diagnosing the cause sufficiently to give reasonably helpful messages requires some programming ingenuity.

All of the four examples are in COBOL, and all assume structured programming. However, the two examples where the programmer is assumed to be a novice in COBOL (having been an Assembler language programmer previously) also assume that structured programming is also new to the programmer. To summarize the four examples:

Case 1 assumes a programmer who is experienced both in the application area and in COBOL and structured programming.

Case 2 assumes a programmer who is experienced in the application area but not in COBOL or structured programming.

Case 3 assumes a programmer who is experienced in COBOL and structured programming but not in the application area.

Case 4 assumes a programmer who is not experienced in either the application area or in COBOL and structured programming.

As can be seen from Table 3-5, deficiencies in the programmer's experience in either the application area or the language and methods to be used for development tend to stretch out schedules and increase the effort needed for development. If there is a lack of experience in both the application area and the language and methods used, the cumulative impact is even more severe.

Table 3-5 represents variations assuming reasonably competent programming in the best case and simple inexperience, not catastrophic incompetence, in the worst case. If comparisons were drawn between some of the great programming talents of the world and some of the greenest amateurs, the difference between the best- and worst-case situations would be even more extreme. There is no reason to doubt that true experts can outperform amateurs by perhaps 20 to 1. Indeed, there are many programs for which the amateurs could not finish the job at all.

THE IMPACT OF THE NOVELTY OF THE PROGRAM REQUIREMENTS

At first it might seem that the impact of novelty is indistinguishable from the impact of experience, and indeed there are certain similarities between the two.

However, the profound impact novelty has had on the industry deserves serious study, and it is often a very different phenomenon from the impact of experience or the lack of it.

From the time of programming's birth in the 1940s through about 1960, almost every application was a brand-new one that had never been computerized. It is safe to say that between 1944 and 1964, perhaps 75% of all programs written were entirely new applications in areas that had never before been automated. From 1964 through 1974, perhaps 40% of the programs being written were in application areas that had never been automated before, but an increasing amount of effort started going into conversions and rewrites of existing systems. From 1974 through today, it appears that fewer than 25% of the programs written are for new applications, and enormous energy is now being devoted to conversions, maintenance of existing systems, and functional enhancements.

For the first 20 years after the "big bang" which computers introduced into science and business, everything was new and comparatively unexplored. The universe of programming was quite a different place from what it is today, and even more different from what may occur in the future. By 1990, it is likely that fewer than 10% of the programs started will be for applications that have never been programmed before, while 90% will be for applications, such as payroll programs, that may have been programmed many thousands of times.

With many repetitions, even crude trial-and-error techniques can gradually find ways of avoiding disasters and selecting the methods that work reasonably well. Therefore, programs that are conversions, rewrites, or at least patterned after well-known earlier programs have a much higher chance of easy implementation than those which jump off in the dark into areas which have never before been automated.

Another significant aspect of novel applications is the uncertainty of the users themselves in deciding what they want, or in describing the significant aspects of the tasks that are to be automated.

Programming is turning out to be a major catalyst in its relationships with older sciences, and for many disciplines, such as psychology and linguistics, the first attempts at writing programs that would automate some of the paradigms then current revealed flaws in the older disciplines. For example, much of conventional grammar and many linguistic hypotheses turned out to be fallacious. Similarly, many psychological concepts, such as that of how human memories are stored, were found to be based on inaccurate descriptions.

In simpler activities, such as order-entry and payroll programs, it was noted time and again that even expert practitioners, such as order-entry clerks of many years' experience, could not always explain what they did in terms that lent themselves to a computer's replicating the human tasks involved.

Table 3-6   Novel versus familiar application areas

	Case 1: Reprogrammed application	Case 2: Novel application
Size in Lines (BASIC)	1,500	1,500
Schedules (Calendar months)		
Requirements	0.5	3.0
Design	0.5	2.0
Coding	1.5	2.0
Testing	1.5	2.0
Total	4.0	9.0
Overlapped	4.0	9.0
Development Effort (person months)		
Requirements	0.2	1.0
Design	0.5	1.0
Internal documentation	0.2	0.2
External documentation	0.5	0.5
Coding	1.5	3.0
Testing	1.0	1.0
Defect repairs	0.5	3.0
Management	1.1	2.0
Total	5.5	11.7
5-year maintenance effort		
Delivery	0	0
Central maintenance	2.0	9.0
Field maintenance	0	0
Total	2.0	9.0
Project total	7.5	20.7
Staff size	1	1
Cost per month	$ 5,000	$ 5,000
Total cost	$37,500	$103,500
Cost per line	$ 25.00	$69.00
Lines per month	273	128

The net of the situation is that applications that are novel and have not previously been subject to computerization have much more uncertainty and much higher failure rates than do programs that are covering known ground.

Table 3-6 shows only two examples: Case 1 is a simple reprogramming of an existing application, and case 2 is a new kind of program that has never been done before. Assume that both programs are written in BASIC. Case 1 is an inventory management program that calculates the economic order quantity for standard pharmaceuticals in a large retail pharmacy. Case 2 is a program that scans a central pharmaceutical database each time a prescription is filled, checking to be sure that the patient is not already taking medicine that would react dangerously with the current prescription.

Project and personnel variables. Assume that both programs are internal applications which the pharmacy does not intend to market commercially. The programs are interactive and are intended to be used by both pharmacists and pharmaceutical assistants, who are not expected to be highly skilled in the use of computers.

In Case 1 an older program written in COBOL for a past-generation computer is simply being rewritten for the pharmacy's new microcomputer. In Case 2, the pharmacy is pioneering a new approach to prescription safety.

Assume that the same programmer is doing both jobs and that the programmer is quite proficient in BASIC and generally familiar with medical and pharmaceutical terminology and practice.

The project is done at a single development location, and the finished programs will be used only at that location, so there is no travel at all. Both the computer resources and the support tools are adequate for the task. Maintenance for the programs is informal and assumes that the users and the programmers work at the same location and communicate easily.

Environmental variables. In both cases, the programmer/analyst who is doing the job has access to the store's microcomputer without restrictions. There are no constraints on performance or memory usage of the finished programs.

The analysis for Case 1, the reprogramming job, consists of reviewing the listings for the former program, plus informal discussions about whether any new features are desired when the program is converted.

The analysis for Case 2, the novel program, consists of discussions with the pharmacists about what drugs are likely to interact and about how they currently check for dangerous prescription mixes.

Since the programs are internal and not marketed, user documentation is informal and produced by the programmer/analyst personally. Some HELP functions are included in the programs, but they refer to the user's guide for any real complications.

The data interactions in both cases are moderately complex. The novel program, in particular, has potentially unusual Boolean combinations, due to the fact that some drugs will react in the presence of a second drug quite differently from how they react with a third or with a combination of drugs.

Data and code-structure variables. The programs are interactive and use an informal database of pharmaceutical information developed at the pharmacy. Since the programs are written in BASIC, which is difficult to structure, an essentially unmodular style was used, although the major routines were segmented and used comments to highlight the tricky areas.

Output from both programs is displayed on the screen in predetermined formats, or optionally it may be printed. The pharmaceutical database is updated in both cases.

The sizes of the two programs for the purposes of this example are the same: 1500 BASIC source statements.

When Table 3-6 is examined, the increase in time spent on requirements and design for Case 2, the novel application, implies that neither the users of the system nor the programmer really had a good idea of what was to be accomplished, and probably not of how difficult it would turn out to be.

This uncertainty in the requirements usually finds its way into the code, with redirections and partial recoding as new needs appear with distressing frequency.

Also, for the first-time and novel applications, it is not always clear how to test the program, since the kinds of real-life situations that might stress the program are comparatively unknown. This shows up in much higher maintenance than ordinary for a program of this size and nature.

Novel applications are exciting to do and often the most challenging kinds of jobs that programming offers, but the uncertainty on the part of users, designers, and programmers about exactly what needs to be accomplished leads to slow development, many restarts, sluggish productivity, and high maintenance costs afterward. As Fred Brooks wisely observed in "The Mythical Man-Month," when doing new kinds of systems, plan on throwing the first program away.

THE IMPACT OF COMPLEXITY

Complexity is perhaps the programming industry's most widely cited reason for poor quality, and one of the most widely cited reasons for low productivity as well. Unfortunately, complexity is also one of the most ambiguous and least defined topics in the domain of psychology and one of the most difficult areas to study conclusively in programming. While techniques such as McCabe's structural complexity metric (11) have been applied fairly successfully to analyzing the subjective complexity of programs, the same techniques have not been successful in studying the initial requirements on which the programs are based. That opens up the question of whether the measured complexity of the final program reflects the complexity of the original problem or is merely an unfortunate byproduct of the way the designers and programmers went about their tasks.

In an informal series of interviews carried out by the author (12) with programmers of complex modules that were being recoded to reduce their defect rates (12), the commonest reasons given for the complex original code were, in order of frequency:

1. Ambiguous and unstable requirements
2. Lack of time to do the module carefully
3. Lack of familiarity with the application area
4. Combinatorial complexity of data and functional interactions
5. Lack of training in, and understanding of, structured coding

The conclusion of the study was that much of the day-to-day complexity observed in programs either was external to the code and due to uncertain requirements or was accidental and might have been avoided under different circumstances.

Once the external and accidental reasons have been separated out of the complexity equation, the causes that remain have to do with "combinatorial complexity," or the number of variations and permutations of data connections and functional linkages that must be considered.

Functional Complexity and Data Complexity

For the purposes of this chapter, complexity will be analyzed in two aspects:

1. The control flow of a program and the linkages between its modules, or "functional complexity."
2. The interactions among the data elements which the program is processing, or "data complexity." Data complexity will be considered as the number of Boolean relations among the data elements that must be handled by the program.

High functional complexity is more or less synonymous with unstructured programming and is covered in significant detail in the books of Myers (13); Stevens (14); Constantine and Yourdan (15); and Linger, Mills, and Witt (16).

Data complexity is less well defined in the software engineering literature than functional complexity, but it is covered in a very practical and useful way in the works of Warnier (17, 18), Orr (19, 20), and Hansen (21), and in the related but somewhat different approach of Michael Jackson (22).

Four complexity examples are given in Table 3-7. In Case 1, both the functional and data complexity are low. In Case 2, functional complexity

Table 3-7 The impact of complexity on programming productivity

	Case 1	Case 2	Case 3	Case 4
Size in lines (COBOL)	5,000	5,000	5,000	5,000
Functional complexity	Low	High	Low	High
Data complexity	Low	Low	High	High
Schedules (calendar months)				
Requirements	1.5	1.5	2.4	2.5
Design	2.0	2.0	3.0	3.0
Coding	2.0	2.0	2.6	3.0
Testing	1.5	2.0	2.0	5.5
Total	7.0	7.5	10.0	14.0
Overlapped	4	5	6	10
Development effort (person-months)				
Requirements	1.0	1.0	2.0	2.5
Design	2.0	2.0	2.6	3.0
Internal documentation	0.5	0.5	0.5	0.5
External documentation	1.0	1.0	1.0	1.0
Coding	7.0	8.0	7.0	8.0
Testing	2.5	3.0	5.0	6.0
Defect repairs	4.0	5.0	16.9	30.0
Management	2.0	2.5	5.0	7.0
Total	20.0	23.0	40.0	58.0
5-year maintenance effort				
Delivery	0	0	0	0
Central maintenance	4	4	13	17
Field maintenance	0	0	0	0
Total	4	4	13	17
Project total	24	27	53	75
Staff size	5	5	7	6
Cost per month	$ 5,000	$ 5,000	$ 5,000	$ 5,000
Total cost	$120,000	$135,000	$265,000	$375,000
Cost per line	$ 24.00	$ 27.00	$ 53.50	$ 75.00
Lines per month	250	217	125	86

is high (the code is unstructured) but data complexity is low. In Case 3, the code is well structured, so functional complexity is low, but the data complexity is high. In Case 4, both the functional complexity and the data complexity are high. Assume that all of the examples are business applications and are written in COBOL and that all of them are 5000 source code statements in size.

In Case 1, where both functional and data complexity are low, assume a program to calculate the break-even points of acquiring one of two machine tools in a small factory that makes wall brackets for hanging plants. One tool costs $50,000 and will increase production by 50%, while the second tool costs $250,000 but will increase production by 100%. Capacity of the current equipment has been exceeded, and demand is rising at 15% per year. There are other variables, but this gives the gist of the problem. Assume that the program will be written in COBOL, and that company management wants to keep the program for future use and instructed the programming manager to be sure that structured coding was used and that the program would operate reliably for a long time.

In Case 2, assume that a competitive factory that also makes plant hangers is studying the same problem of whether to buy either the $50,000 or the $250,000 machine tool. However, in this case company management told the programming staff that they were in a hurry for the results and that the job should be done as quickly as possible, without taking too much time for considering future use of the program. The result is a program identical to the first example in functions, but not in structure: it has low function complexity but high data complexity.

In Case 3, with high data complexity but low functional complexity, assume that a manufacturing company has 5 factory locations making 3 different products, 15 warehouses which stock the products, and 100 delivery vans which supply wholesalers in 25 towns within a state. The manufacturer wants to optimize the delivery costs and storage costs of its products, and a linear program using the simplex method is written.

In Case 4, with both high data complexity and high functional complexity, assume that a consumer electronics company is thinking of bringing out a new stereo receiver or a new tape deck or both. They are interested in what would happen if from one to five of their chief competitors brought out similar models either simultaneously or within a year of product introduction. They want to know what the results might be if the new products were either very low in price compared to the competition but less reliable, or somewhat higher in price but very reliable. This is a multivariate problem with significant Boolean interactions. Assume also that company management is in a hurry and told the programming staff not to worry much about future usage of the program, so unstructured COBOL coding is used.

Project and personnel variables. The programs being developed are all internal, and are not aimed at being marketed commercially. The programs are interactive and are aimed at allowing nonprogrammers to use them to model various assumptions. The programs are in the general class of mathematical models, and the specific applications may be complicated but they are not novel. The analysis and design are done by personnel who are very familiar with modeling, with programming, with COBOL, and with the enterprises for which the programs are being written.

The projects are all done at a single development location and there is no travel at all. Both the computer resources and the support tools are adequate for the tasks. Maintenance of the programs is informal and assumes that users and maintainers work in the same location and communicate easily.

Environmental variables. In all four cases, the analysts and programmers have their own terminals and essentially unrestricted access to machine time. There are no constraints on performance or the memory usage of the finished programs.

The design consisted of external specifications done in English text augmented by sample output formats. The internal design was done using the Yourdon (23) version of the structured design method, actually developed by Constantine, Myers, and Stevens, in Cases 1 and 3 (the two cases with low functional complexity). For Cases 2 and 4 (the two cases with high functional complexity), the internal design was done "on the fly" as the coding proceeded.

The external user documentation for the programs is informal and produced by the analysts themselves. Since the programs are internal and not aimed at being marketed, the documentation is merely printer output from an ordinary daisy wheel or line printer, and it is not typeset or bound into book form.

The defect removal methods in all four cases assume an informal design review and informal testing carried out by the programmers themselves.

The projects were staffed by personnel already on board, so there were no hiring expenses, and the personnel were sufficiently versed in the applications that no training was required or given.

Data and code-structure variables. All four examples are in COBOL and are assumed to be 5000 source lines in size. In Case 1, both the functional and the data complexity are low. In Case 2, the functional complexity is high because of unstructured programming, but the data complexity remains low. In Case 3, the code is well structured, but the data complexity is high. In Case 4, the code is unstructured and the data complexity is high: a worst-case situation.

In examining Table 3-7, it is apparent that data complexity carries a much more significant penalty than functional complexity, although both are significant factors.

The really major productivity impacts are concentrated in the areas of defect removal and maintenance, with the high maintenance effort being simply because the programs did not work very well when first turned over to the users.

The impact of defect removal is so extreme that it may be questioned; but in several cases examined by the author, programs appeared superficially to be more or less on track until testing began, when it was revealed that systems did not work and could not be made to work without major repairs and even redesign. In the most extreme case, a project on an 18-month contract for delivery started system testing at the 17th month and was found to be unworkable as a system, although some of the components had been successfully tested alone. The testing and repairs continued for 36 consecutive months before the developers and the customer called a halt to discuss canceling the project. Since at this point the customer realized that if the contract were canceled, no other vendor could do the job without perhaps starting another long development cycle, the project was eventually completed in a total time of about 5 years from the start of the contract to final delivery.

Very few enterprises track defect removal carefully, and hence few are aware that the sum of all forms of defect removal (i.e. desk checking, reviews, inspections, documentation reviews, quality assurance reviews, and testing) comprise the largest identifiable cost element of many software systems.

The final point on complexity is that much of the complexity in commercial programming appears either to be external to the code, and caused by ambiguous and uncertain requirements, or to be accidental rather than necessary, and sometimes due to haste, to inexperience, and to other factors that might be eliminated. Perhaps the commonest reason leading to unnecessary complexity is haste, where the programming team is directed to do things fast rather than directed to do things well. Weinberg's classic study (24) of teams asked to perform projects fast, compared to teams asked to perform projects well, brings home the point that much software complexity is due to the directives given to the team.

Such directions are often self-defeating; haste early in the development cycle in the design and structure of the system may cause enormous delays or may even cause the project to be canceled if those problems show up at a time in the cycle when repairs are expensive and difficult.

THE IMPACT OF THE STRUCTURED PROGRAMMING METHODS

In both adverbial and adjectival forms, the word "structured" has now been joined to almost every action and object in the programming industry. In approximate chronological sequence, following are some of the activities in which the word "structured" has recently appeared:

Structured Analysis
Structured Requirements
Structured Design
Structured Code

Structured Documentation
Structured Data
Structured Development
Structured Walkthroughs
Structured Integration
Structured Testing
Structured Maintenance

The word "structured" is now so widely used that it has lost a rigorous definition. and has become a kind of stock phrase.

The first use of "structured" was in the context of code, where it meant achieving a rational level of modularity by eliminating jumps in control flow by means of restricting modules to a single input and output sequence. Professor Edsger Dijkstra's open letter to the ACM in November of 1968 (25) on the harmfulness of GOTO statements is the most visible landmark in the origin of the structured methods, although the logical foundations of structured code had been worked out by Bohm and Jacopini (26) and Mills (27) a few years earlier.

From this beginning, the term "structured" was applied to other deliverables and tasks; its general concept means to use a predefined plan and predefined inputs and outputs and carry out the activities in a rational and predetermined manner. In other words, programming development should somewhat resemble a stage play where actors are following a written script, as opposed to the improvisational methods where things are made up as the project goes along.

At this level, planning and following a known scenario, the structured methods are generally beneficial. However, in many cases a term, such as "structured design," has so many different meanings that there is no formal definition. For example, between the United States and Europe, no fewer than six different techniques are described under the name "structured design."

In this chapter, three different aspects of the structured methods will be considered:

1. Structured requirements, or studying the needs of the program's users in a methodical way. The technique of Kenneth Orr (19) is used in the case study presented in Table 3-8. This method is based on the general approach of Jean Dominique Warnier (17); it asserts that requirements analysis should start with the data rather than with the functions to be provided and that the data analysis should start with the output rather than with the input. Thereafter the analysis moves methodically from the output toward the input, and it derives the functions of the program from the number of data transformations

Table 3-8 The productivity impact of structured methodologies

	Case 1	Case 2	Case 3	Case 4	Case 5
Requirements	U*	S**	U	U	S
Design	U	U	S	U	S
Code	U	U	U	S	S
Size in lines	10,000	10,000	10,000	10,000	10,000
Language	COBOL	COBOL	COBOL	Pascal	Pascal
Schedules (calendar months)					
Requirements	2.5	1.5	2.5	2.5	1.5
Design	3.5	3.5	2.5	3.5	2.5
Coding	3.0	3.0	3.0	2.5	2.5
Testing	3.0	2.5	2.5	2.0	2.0
Total	12.0	10.5	10.5	10.5	8.5
Overlapped	9.0	8.0	8.0	8.0	6.0
Development effort (person-months)					
Requirements	4	3	4	4	3
Design	6	6	4	6	4
Internal documentation	1	1	1	1	1
External documentation	3	3	3	3	3
Coding	16	16	16	13	13
Testing	8	7	7	7	6
Defect repair	17	17	17	14	10
Management	7	6	6	6	5
Total	62	59	58	54	45
5-year maintenance effort					
Delivery	0	0	0	0	0
Central maintenance	30	12	13	26	7
Field maintenance	0	0	0	0	0
Total	30	12	13	26	7
Project total	92	71	71	80	52
Staff size	7	7	7	7	7
Cost per month	$ 5,000	$ 5,000	$ 5,000	$ 5,000	$ 5,000
Total cost	$460,000	$355,000	$355,000	$400,000	$260,000
Cost per line	$ 46	$ 35	$ 35	$ 40	$ 26
Lines per month	161	169	169	185	222

*U = Unstructured
**S = Structured

needed to feed the output. This method has been unusually successful in developing large commercial application programs.

2. Structured design, or decomposing the general program into sets of discrete functional modules. The technique of Myers (13), Stevens (14), and Constantine (15) is used. In this technique, considerable care is taken to analyze and minimize the communication and control flow between modules and to maximize the internal cohesiveness of individual modules.

3. Structured coding, or the actual development of programs in a way that minimizes the complexity of the resulting code. In this chapter, the techniques of Nicklaus Wirth as embodied in the Pascal language (28) is used. Pascal is the first language specifically developed to make structured programming a convenient and normal approach, by providing the now-common IF-THEN-ELSE and DO-WHILE structures to supplement the hazardous GOTO statements.

One of the problems facing researchers of the structured programming methods is the fact that it is not clear how the various structured concepts fit together. For example, the Warnier-Orr structured-requirements-and-design approach overlaps some of the domain of the Constantine-Myers-Stevens methodology, and both of these overlap structured coding.

To a certain degree, the problem is analogous to that of a physician who is treating a patient suffering from tuberculosis, ulcers, and heart disease at the same time. The most effective therapy for one of the conditions is likely to either interfere with one or both of the other therapies or even make the other illnesses worse.

In the case of the three structured methods discussed in this chapter, it is possible to use hybrid methods, starting with the Warnier-Orr method until the requirements and data structures of the program have been satisfactorily analyzed, and then following that up with the Constantine-Myers-Stevens structured design approach for ensuring that module communication and cohesion will be satisfactory. Then the program can be actually coded in a structured way using Wirth's concepts as embodied in Pascal.

Five examples for the same application are shown in Table 3-8. This is a bill-of-materials processor for a medium-sized manufacturing company that makes room air conditioners. All of the examples are assumed to be 10,000 source statements in size, with the first three being done in COBOL and the last two in Pascal. For the purposes of this chapter, COBOL and Pascal are treated as languages of approximately the same level, or roughly 3 times the level of a basic Assembler language.

Case 1 shows the application as it might have been if it had been written circa 1965: 10,000 lines of unstructured COBOL developed from an ad hoc requirements analysis and designed on the fly.

Case 2 shows the impact of structuring the requirements using the Warnier-Orr method, but we will make the assumption that only the systems analysts in direct contact with the users were trained in this method, and the programmers continued as always with unstructured COBOL designed on the fly.

Case 3 shows the system where the requirements were informally studied without benefit of any structured analysis, but the programmers and designers were impressed by the Constantine-Myers-Stevens approach and tried to embody the ideas in the decomposition of the program.

Case 4 shows the problem under the assumption that the requirements had been casually developed in an ad hoc manner, and so had the design. However, the assignment to do the coding was passed on to programmers who were software engineering graduates well versed in Pascal, and so the code itself is very well structured.

Case 5 shows the problem as it might be tackled in 1984, where a rigorous requirements study using the Warnier-Orr method is followed by a careful decomposition using the Constantine-Myers-Stevens principles, and finally the job is programmed in a structured manner using Pascal.

A certain amount of suspension of disbelief is required to follow all of these permutations of methodological change, but in real life the author has observed all of these combinations and many that are even less probable.

Project and personnel variables. Assume that all five examples are internal applications that are not intended to be marketed commercially. The programs are interactive and are intended to allow production engineering to automate the bill-of-materials processing application.

Assume that the personnel involved are very experienced in the current handling techniques for bills of materials and are also data processing professionals of many years' experience. The application area is not a novel one, and many other systems are available for comparison and study.

The projects are all done at single locations, and there is no travel cost at all. Both the computer resources and the support tools are adequate for the tasks. Maintenance for the programs is informal and assumes that the users and the programmers work at the same location and communicate easily.

Environmental variables. In all cases, the analysts and programmers who are doing the job have access to computers essentially without restrictions. There are no constraints on performance or memory usage of the finished programs.

The analysis for the project consists of discussions with the production engineering personnel, in two different ways: ad hoc unstructured conversations for Cases 1, 3, and 4; and formal structured analysis using the Warnier-Orr method for Cases 2 and 5.

Since the programs are internal and not marketed, user documentation is informal and is produced by the programmers and analysts themselves. Some HELP functions are included in the programs, but they refer to the user's guide for any real complications.

In all cases, defect removal consisted of fairly well defined structured walkthroughs (although that fact is not part of this example) and normal testing from unit through system test.

Data and code-structure variables. The data interactions in all cases are moderately complex, as is typical with bill-of-materials applications.

Output from the programs consists of printed bills of materials and routing instructions, statistical information reports, and inventory management information. The interactive portion of the program allows production engineering personnel to query the number and kinds of bills of materials during various historical periods and for the current work in progress.

The five examples are all 10,000 source statements in size; three of them are written in COBOL and two in Pascal.

The five examples have these attributes:

	Requirements	Design	Code
Case 1	Unstructured	Unstructured	Unstructured
Case 2	Structured	Unstructured	Unstructured
Case 3	Unstructured	Structured	Unstructured
Case 4	Unstructured	Unstructured	Structured
Case 5	Structured	Structured	Structured

It may be seen from Table 3-8 that the structured methods have a generally beneficial effect that can achieve quite respectable improvements in development schedules and development productivity and very significant improvements in maintenance effort after delivery. Although Table 3-8 was synthesized using the SPQR model discussed in Appendix A, all of the effects of the structured methods are derived from real-life experiences with actual systems.

There is a synergism at work from simultaneously structuring the requirements, the design, and the code; this is much more than using the structured methods for only one of these key activities.

Case 4, in which structured coding was used but the requirements and design were unstructured, deserves special comment. This case had the second-highest productivity during development, but the second most expensive maintenance. How did this unlikely combination come about?

The literature on programming is relatively unanimous that most of the troublesome defects after delivery have their origin either in the requirements or the design of the program. Endres (29), Jones (30), Basili (31), and many others have discussed this topic at length. What has not been discussed is the fact that in the absence of structured requirements and structured design, it is very difficult to write test cases for these defects. Usually it happens that no test cases that would catch the problems are even created, because the problems are due to omissions and factors left out of the design. What resulted in Case 4 was fairly quick testing and fairly low defect repair expenses during the development cycle, but very high maintenance and enhancement costs. The reason is that the bugs that cause the high maintenance costs are not picked up by testing, since there usually are no test cases that cover omissions brought on by incomplete specifications and partial design. When the requirements and design problems that are not found by testing do show up, it is during the maintenance and enhancement phase, when it is inconvenient and expensive to make design corrections.

The structured methods, by themselves, have not solved all of the problems of development of programming systems, nor are they able to turn amateurs into topflight professionals. But their records of improvement are solid when rigorously applied, and they do much to lower the risks of massive overruns and perhaps outright project failures that historically were associated with the unstructured programming methods.

THE IMPACT OF PROGRAMMING CLASSES

The topic of programming classes is almost never dealt with in the programming and software engineering literature. This is surprising, because the impact of this variable is one of the most significant of any in the industry.

The program class defines the reason for which the program is being developed. There are 11 programming classes that currently have a significant impact:

1. Personal programs developed for private use
2. Internal programs developed for use within an enterprise
3. Internal programs developed for reuse or commonality
4. Internal programs whose services are rented externally
5. External programs to be put in the public domain
6. External programs leased to customers but not sold
7. External programs bundled with hardware that is sold
8. External programs unbundled and marketed commercially
9. External programs developed under private contract
10. External programs developed under government contract
11. External programs developed under military contract

One of the main reasons for the significance of these classes is that as the program class goes from 1 through 11, the amount of documentation goes up at a very significant rate. That is, programs with identical functions but in different classes will tend to have notably different amounts of both internal and user documentation, with the general thrust being more and more documentation as the class goes up. Whether or not the documentation is really needed is currently an unanswered question, but the existence of massive quantities of documentation in classes 5 through 11 is readily apparent to both developers and users.

Following are discussions of the major attributes of the 11 programming classes.

Class 1: Personal programs. Personal programs, usually written at home for private use, are somewhat outside the scope of this book. However, these programs reflect the habits of their developers, which often means fairly sparse documentation. There are of course no management costs at all and no overhead expenses for quality assurance, program librarians, computer operators, and the like. The significance of this class is that it is the way most programmers learn the business, and it exerts a strong influence over what they think about when planning and estimating.

Class 2: Internal programs not marketed externally. For many years, this has been the commonest form of application programming in the world. Most of the tools and books on programming tacitly assume that the programs are being done for internal use within an enterprise; hence they do not usually discuss factors such as marketing, field maintenance, customer hot lines, and some of the aspects which must be considered for leased or marketed programs.

Another significant aspect of internal programming concerns documentation. Usually, internal programs are documented informally and the documentation is merely output from a line printer or daisy wheel, then stapled together and distributed informally. The graphics, if any, are often done by hand and interpolated into the text. The costs of such documentation are primarily those of writing, and comparatively little expense or effort goes to editing, proofreading, generating professional art and illustrations, using a composer or photocomposer, binding, warehousing, distribution, and marketing.

Maintenance is another significant aspect of Class 2 internal programming. Most articles and books on maintenance tacitly assume single-site internal maintenance, and so they omit discussions of the enormous costs of sending field maintenance people to remote customer locations. Similarly, the very high costs of installing large commercial systems at the customer computer centers is not covered. Now that the marketed-software business is growing, many small companies are finding that the maintenance costs are far above anything they ever anticipated, because the available sources of data on maintenance costs totally ignore the two most expensive aspects of maintenance: delivery support and field service.

Class 3: Internal programs intended for reuse or commonality. The third class of software is usually found inside large corporations and government agencies. It comprises software systems that are used at multiple locations or offices. Common systems are halfway between true internal systems and commercial software in terms of development rigor, documentation, and maintenance efforts. It often happens that common systems are very slow during requirements and design, since so many needs must be dealt with simultaneously. Also, if the code runs at many different computers in different locations, then maintenance can be hectic and expensive compared to that of ordinary single-site systems and programs.

Class 4: Internal programs marketed as services. Class 4 programs are those where the source and object code is not directly leased or marketed, but customers can access the programs and use their functions from remote sites by means of timesharing networks or dial-in facilities. The usual reason for this kind of approach is to keep trade secrets well protected.

Compared to internal programs, Class 4 programs usually have higher documentation costs. To make a good impression, the user guides are almost always professionally written and edited and are produced with professional art and composition.

Class 5: External programs to be put in the public domain. Class 5, or public-domain software, has emerged as a minor subindustry within the microcomputer world, and some government-sponsored software is in the public domain also. This is a very mixed class, with programs ranging from state-of-the-art artificial intelligence applications through crudely written games. However, since the costs range from nothing to some minimal fee for disks or tape, the field is not a very interesting one from a cost estimating viewpoint.

Class 6: External programs leased to users. Class 6 programs are the common way that the mainframe computer manufacturers such as IBM have unbundled their large operating systems and major application packages. The code may be utilized on the customers' computers, but legal ownership is not transferred; any attempt at unauthorized use or copying of the source code is certain to lead to remonstrances, and if the violations are flagrant, to litigation.

Since the programs in Class 6 are often large, outright purchase could easily amount to more than $100,000 per program, and many large data centers will have dozens of such programs in daily use. Leasing provides near-term cash flow advantages for the customers and long-term advantages for the vendors.

Class 6 programs are usually supported by formal documentation that is professionally produced and composed, and hence fairly expensive.

Maintenance for Class 6 programs often includes field service and may include a 24-hour hot line facility so that users can get questions and problems addressed at any time of day or night. Since they are not purchased outright, Class 6 programs are often installed on the customers' computers by vendor personnel, which adds significantly to the cost of maintenance.

Class 7: External programs bundled with hardware. The costs of Class 7 programs are the most ambiguous and difficult to explore. Many corporations that make high-technology products for which the operational software is bundled or included in the purchase or lease price of the hardware do not even have separate accounting codes for software personnel or other kinds of engineers, so the software development costs are sometimes lost from view.

Similarly, software maintenance costs may be indistinguishable from the hardware maintenance costs of Class 7 products unless careful accounting practices are used.

Indeed, the problems with keeping track of the software aspects of Class 7 products are so great that they have probably thrown off the U.S. Department of Labor statistics which deal with numbers of programmers in the United States, since many corporations do not actually know how many software professionals work for them.

Class 7 products are also ambiguous in isolating documentation costs, because of the same tendency to use accounting structures that blur hardware and software activities indistinguishably into one set of accounting codes.

Class 8: External programs unbundled and marketed to users. Class 8 programming is one of the most amazing industrial phenomena of the 20th century. Class 8 programs are the ordinary commercial programs that can be purchased over the counter in computer stores, bought by mail from advertisements in journals, acquired from information utilities directly into home computers, and also bought from pirates and unscrupulous sources.

With Class 8 programs, a limited form of ownership is transferred to the purchaser. The agreement usually includes the right to run the program on one or more computers, and sometimes the right to make backup copies for private use. The right to make secondary copies for unauthorized resale, however, is not transferred, just as purchasing a book does not give the buyer the right to make copies for resale. One new and fairly expensive aspect of developing Class 8 software is that of protecting the packages from unauthorized copying, by means of a host of techniques ranging from faith in human nature through elaborate crypto-graphic techniques.

The distinguishing aspects of Class 8 programs from a programming productivity point of view are these: Documentation is a mixed bag, ranging from barely legible mimeographed sheets containing insufficient information to even boot the program through elaborately printed and even elegant manuals. Many Class 8 programs also feature interactive on-line menus and HELP information, including the new iconographic pictorial screens and pull-down menus. It is interesting that as of 1984, microcomputer-based software in Class 8 is sometimes technically superior to the large institutional systems in Class 2 in terms of ease of use.

Although the topic is not yet fully explored in the programming literature, menu-driven on-line documentation that is primarily text, mixed with graphics, should cost about 50% more than ordinary type-script to prepare initially, but since there are no printing, binding, or distribution costs, the net costs for the on-line documentation are often somewhat less than for conventional documentation produced in bound and printed form.

Class 8 programs may or may not have delivery support and field service. One thing Class 8 maintenance often has, which sets it apart, is the concept of only maintaining the code of authorized purchasers, to discourage piracy. This implies a fairly extensive database of customer information and some query facilities available to the maintenance administrative staff: expense items that to date have not been covered at all in the maintenance literature.

Another aspect of Class 8 programming, which may grow to be increasingly significant, is the need to communicate changes and updates very rapidly to very large numbers of customers. For example, a leading spreadsheet product has now sold more than 250,000 licenses, and to mail a letter to all purchasers would cost $50,000 in stamps alone, to say nothing of the cost of handling the materials to be mailed, presorting the envelopes, and the like.

An interesting new solution to this problem is to establish a special interest group or a service on one of the information utilities, such as CompuServe or The Source. This can even allow users to acquire updates directly into their microcomputers, as well as informing them about what is occurring with the product.

Class 9: External programs under commercial contract. Commercial contract programming runs the gamut from individual job shoppers who might work for a week or less on a program of a few hundred lines to massive projects that may take more than five years and involve hundreds of programmers. For example, the large insurance and banking application systems developed by Electronic Data Systems under contract are major undertakings which rank among the largest and most sophisticated systems yet developed.

In Class 9 programming, one significant productivity factor is the expertise of the users who are controlling the contract. The Walston and Felix study (32) from IBM's Federal Systems Division identified user involvement as a key issue. Experienced users, who have administered programming contracts before and know how such things go, can affect productivity beneficially. Inexperienced users, who are uncertain of what they want and don't realize how difficult changes are after certain points in programming development, can affect productivity in a negative way.

Another aspect of Class 9 programming, also true in Classes 10 and 11, is the nature of the contract itself. Contracts come in many varieties, and Brandon and Segelstein's Data Processing Contracts (33) is a very thorough discussion of all of them, especially those dealing with hardware. Remer's Legal Care for Your Software (34) is more specific, in dealing with software alone, and it includes sample contracts in an appendix. Finally, Pooley's work on Trade Secrets (35) covers aspects of programming that are becoming increasingly important; for example, who owns intellectual property such as software?

The reason we discuss legal issues in a book on productivity is that software developers finding themselves faced with penalty payments for nonperformance of a contractual obligation, or corporations who discover that the ownership of one of their programs is being challenged in court by the programmer who did the work, will discover that conventional definitions of productivity have very little meaning if the costs of penalties or litigation are significant.

Class 10: External program under government contract. This form of programming is comparatively common among academic and commercial institutions working under government grants or under contract with federal, regional, and local governments.

While the programming itself may range from relatively ordinary to very exotic, there is one distinguishing feature that usually affects productivity: documentation. Not every government agency, especially outside the United States, requires large amounts of documentation, but the trend is relatively clear that government contract projects are accompanied by quantities of documentation that often exceed the documentation requirements for similar programs done for private enterprise.

Another aspect of government contracts, which is even more notable in programs done under military contract, is a frequent lack of maintenance on the part of the program developers, because the contracting agency assumes all maintenance responsibilities after delivery. This is true especially in high-security or defense applications, but it may also simply be a result of policy.

Class 11: External program under military contract. Military contract programming ranges from ordinary applications programming such as payrolls and Post Exchange inventory management through highly intricate command and control packages to exotic real-time software for weapons and navigational purposes.

As with civilian government contracts, one of the distinguishing attributes of military contract programming is documentation. However, in the United States at least, the documentation is controlled in considerable detail by military specifications, or "MilSpecs" as they are called. Military specifications on software documentation are so precise, so exacting, and so necessary in order to complete the contracts that a whole generation of specialists has grown up who earn their livings by documenting systems in accordance with MilSpecs.

On the plus side, MilSpecs are certainly thorough, and not much of value is left out. On the minus side, they are rigid and change more slowly than technology is changing, so that often programs documented in MilSpec fashion could be handled somewhat better in the commercial domain.

Maintenance in military contract programming is often not part of the contract, since the contracting agency will assume software maintenance after delivery.

A future aspect of military contract programming of enormous importance—indeed, one of the most important changes in the history of programming—is the new U.S. Department of Defense requirements centering around the Ada programming language (36) and the supporting environment (37) under which Ada programs will be written.

The U.S. Department of Defense (DOD) is the largest single user of computers and programs in the world, and one of the most active organizations in programming research in the world as well. The new DOD-sponsored Ada programming language is large and powerful, and it will grow to be supported by a full-scale repertory of tools covering the entire life cycle from preliminary planning through the last days of maintenance. However, as of 1984 the proposed Ada environment has some notable gaps, of which one is extreme: For military contract software, documentation is usually the largest cost element, and the proposed Ada environment has few plans or recommendations for addressing this problem.

The Ada language is so new that as this book is written, almost no pragmatic results have been obtained covering the productivity of Ada for large programming projects; no such projects have yet been completed. The Ada environment is still in the early planning stage and is some years from full operational capabilities. Nonetheless, the significance of Ada and the new support environment merit an attempt to assess their productivity.

Table 3-9 The impact of programming class on software productivity

	Case 1	Case 2	Case 3	Case 4
Program Class	Class 2	Class 6	Class 11	Class 11
Size in lines	100,000	100,000	100,000	100,000
Language	PL/I	PL/I	Ada	Ada
Schedules (calendar months)				
Requirements	4.5	4.5	4.5	4.5
Design	11.0	13.0	14.0	12.0
Coding	8.0	8.0	8.0	8.0
Testing	6.0	6.0	6.0	6.0
Total	29.5	31.5	32.5	28.5
Overlapped	19.0	20.0	21.0	17.0
Development effort (person-months)				
Requirements	48	60	70	63
Design	74	88	99	81
Internal documentation	15	376	778	259
External documentation	32	407	519	173
Coding	165	165	165	145
Testing	93	106	116	98
Defect repairs	400	406	406	408
Management	100	193	258	147
Total	927	1,801	2,411	1,347
Staff size	49	90	114	80
Cost per month	$ 5,000	$ 5,000	$ 5,000	$ 5,000
Total cost	$4,635,000	$9,005,000	$12,055,000	$6,870,000
Cost per line	$ 46.35	$ 90.05	$ 120.55	$ 68.70
Lines per month	107	55	41	72
Internal pages	1,196	5,019	10,380	10,380
External pages	2,542	5,438	6,920	6,920
Total pages	3,748	10,747	17,380	17,380

Four examples in Table 3-9 show the impact of programming class on productivity. All of the examples are 100,000 source lines in size and represent a fairly complex system that monitors aircraft status either for a large commercial airline or for an Air Force command. The system records planes in and out of service; kinds of repairs being made; rate of new plane acquisitions; and rates of aircraft retirements, sales, mothballing, or losses. For safety purposes, the system also keeps statistics of aircraft accidents and crashes by time, kinds of plane, and circumstances of the event.

The civilian (PL/I) and military (Ada) versions of the systems are essentially identical, except that the military version has higher levels of security authorizations for making queries and includes some additional data types, such as planes damaged or lost in combat.

Of the four examples given for the case study in Table 3-9, Cases 1 and 2 are written in PL/I, and Cases 3 and 4 are assumed to be written in Ada. Note that in real life, no systems of this magnitude have yet been written in Ada, and the results are synthesized by means of the SPQR estimating model discussed in Appendix A.

Case 3 shows Ada as it might appear early in its lifetime, say 1985, before the full supporting environment is complete. Case 4 shows the potential impact of the full Ada environment, as it might occur in 1990.

The four examples are:

Class 2: Internal program not for outside marketing
Class 6: External program leased to users
Class 11: External program under military contract in 1985
Class 11: External program under military contract in 1990

Project and personnel variables. The system is highly interactive and is intended to allow authorized users to make queries about a variety of aircraft status conditions. The users are presumed to know nothing in particular about programming.

The development personnel are very familiar with the application area and are also data processing professionals of many years' experience. The experience with Ada is of necessity only a few years in Case 3, but in Case 4 it is quite extensive.

The project is done at a single location, so no travel costs at all are involved. Both the computer resources and the support tools, especially in Case 4, are adequate for the task.

Documentation is in both on-line and hard-copy form, for backup purposes and for contractual reasons.

Maintenance for the program is not shown, since in every case the customers take over maintenance responsibility after completion of the project. In place of maintenance, Table 3-9 shows the estimated total quantity of documentation pages produced for both internal documents (i.e. specifications, plans, etc.) and external documents (i.e. user's guides, maintenance manuals produced to aid the customers, etc.).

Environmental variables. In all cases, the analysts and programmers doing the job have access to computers essentially without restrictions. There are no constraints on performance or memory usage of the finished programs.

The analysis of the project consists of in-depth studies of aircraft maintenance data from existing sources, interviews with maintenance personnel on their needs and plans, and interviews with senior executives to ascertain what they hope the sytem to achieve.

The specifications are formally documented and subjected to rigorous design reviews. A small-scale model of the system is constructed to prove the concepts (costs of model building is excluded from the four examples, however).

Other defect removal operations include correctness proofs of key algorithms, code inspections, and a full series of testing that includes unit test, function test, subsystem test, system test, and customer acceptance test.

Data and code-structure variables. Both the data and its interactions are very complex, as is typical with such applications. Rigorous code-structuring conventions are assumed in all examples. The segmentation of the system into components and modules is assumed to start with the techniques of Warnier-Orr diagrams, followed by the decomposition methods of Constantine-Myers-Stevens.

Several conclusions may be drawn from Table 3-9, of which the most obvious is that any attempt to improve large-scale programming productivity that does not address documentation costs is doomed to failure. For Class 11 programs, it is quite possible that more than half of the total development resources will be devoted to documentation and that no more than about 30% of the personnel will do any coding at all, if the system is a sizable one.

The second conclusion is that Class 11 (military contract) programming brings with it a significant amount of work that is not always performed in the commercial sector. Chief among the additional tasks are documentation to U.S. military standards. The standards themselves may be laudable and are certainly thorough, but they require powerful documentation facilities if their implementation is to be reasonably cost-effective. Given the impact of documentation costs on military programming, it is surprising that the proposed Ada environment did not initially cover this topic or even appear to note the existence of what is perhaps the major software expense element for the Department of Defense.

Whether Class 11 programs will ever be developed as rapidly as commercial software is another question, and the answer depends to a large extent on the kinds of documentation support packages that enter the Ada programming environment. The 1990 Ada example in Case 4 assumes very powerful integrated text/graphics capabilities for all documentation.

Overall, the impact of programming classes has not been covered in the software engineering literature to the extent that its importance merits. The kinds of contractual obligations that surround programming systems can have a major impact on costs and productivity, and in extreme cases they can add nonperformance penalties or litigation expenses to the overall costs of the projects.

THE IMPACT OF PROGRAMMING TYPES ON PRODUCTIVITY

In the industry at large, the phrase, "programming type" is ambiguous and has no standard definition. In the context of this book, there are 12 recognizable types of programming that can influence productivity, ranked below in order of difficulty:

1. *Nonprocedural programming*, or developing software by means of a fourth-generation language, a spreadsheet processor, a program generator, a query program, or the like.
2. *Batch applications programming*, or developing programs for eventual use by nonprogrammers. These include the ordinary commercial programs that handle payrolls, accounting, order entry, and the like, usually on a periodic basis such as daily, weekly, or monthly.
3. *Interactive applications programming*, or developing programs that have a high degree of interaction with users and which are intended to be invoked or controlled from a terminal or office computer.
4. *Batch database applications programming*, or developing programs for a database environment such as dBase III or IBM's Information Management System (IMS), or on some other commercial or locally developed database system.
5. *Interactive database applications programming*, or developing programs that have a high degree of interaction with users via a terminal and also interrogate or update a database system.
6. *Scientific or mathematical programming*, or developing programs that tend to involve relatively complex and lengthy calculation sequences, often requiring supercomputer power, such as long-range meteorological studies.
7. *Systems or support programming*, or developing programs that are intended primarily as tools for computing professionals. These include compilers, test tools, and operating systems such as CP/M, Unix, MS-DOS, MVS, and the like.
8. *Process-control programming*, or developing systems that are intended to monitor and operate sensors and mechanisms that deal with continuously moving materials, such as the flow of oil through a refinery.
9. *Communications or telecommunications programming*, or developing software that is intended to facilitate the linkage of distributed users, terminals, telephones, or computers.
10. *Embedded programming*, or developing software that is used within an operational device such as a radar set, but whose action is more or less concealed from the human operators of the device.
11. Real-time programming, or developing software that is aimed at

reacting immediately to events that occur at high speed, such as the target tracking of a military aircraft warning system.
12. *Graphics and image processing*, or developing software that digitizes and manipulates visual information.
13. *Artificial intelligence programming*, or developing software that is intended to replicate some aspect of human decision-making or cognitive processes, such as the new medical diagnostic expert systems.

Not only are the 12 categories loosely defined, but hybrid forms are also common, such as "real-time embedded programming" or "real-time process-control programming." Further, several new potential types may emerge over the next few years, with robotics programming, audio/music programming, and game programming being the major candidates for becoming full-fledged specialties.

Ever since programming became a recognized occupation, there has been a general hypothesis that the difficulty of programming is greater for some types than for others and that the skills required for the more difficult types of programming are harder to achieve. This hypothesis is intuitively plausible, but there is not a great deal of hard data that either confirms it or challenges it. However, the practical implications of the hypothesis are evident in the pay scales of programmers, which seem roughly proportional to the type of programming being performed (38).

Variations in type of programming are a difficult challenge to productivity researchers, because nowhere are the problems of using lines of code as a productivity indicator more troublesome. For example, in the domains of embedded and real-time programming, a significant amount of effort is devoted to removing excess and redundant code in order to achieve the required memory and performance targets. Since this reduction in code is a major consumer of human resources, and yet the end result is to make programs smaller, it is obvious that rather low productivity will result if lines of code per unit of time is the indicator selected, or unless some kind of credit is given for the deleted code.

Because the reliable data that covers programming-type differences is sparse, only two examples are given in Table 3-10 to show the productivity variations: a Type 2 (batch applications) program and a Type 11 (real-time) program. The batch application program is assumed to be a payroll program for a small company, and the real-time program is assumed to be an aircraft radar controller. Both programs in the examples are assumed to be written in the C programming language, to simplify the variations of the projects; the examples are synthesized from several actual projects.

Project and personnel variables. The programs being developed are both intended for a single user and are developed under standard commercial

Table 3-10 The impact of programming type on productivity

	Type 2 (Batch application)	Type 11 (Real-time program)
Size in lines (C language)	5,000	5,000
Schedule (calendar months)		
Requirements	0.9	1.6
Design	2.6	3.4
Coding	1.6	2.6
Testing	1.3	2.3
Total	6.4	9.9
Overlapped	3.8	5.9
Development effort (person-months)		
Requirements	1.4	2.4
Design	2.0	3.3
Internal documentation	1.6	1.6
External documentation	2.5	2.5
Coding	5.4	8.5
Testing	3.7	4.5
Defect repairs	5.0	6.5
Management	2.5	4.0
Total	24.1	33.3
5-year maintenance effort		
Delivery	0.3	0.3
Central maintenance	2.5	2.5
Field maintenance	0	0
Total	2.8	2.8
Project total	26.9	36.1
Staff size	6	6
Cost per month	$ 5,000	$ 5,000
Total cost	$134,500	$180,500
Cost per line	$ 26.90	$ 36.10
Lines per month	207	150

contracts. The programmers in both examples are equally skilled in their application areas, have the same number of years or experience, and have equal familiarity with the languages and design tools available to them. Both the batch application payroll program and the real-time radar controller are written in C and are 5000 source instructions in size. However, assume that the radar controller was initially developed at 6000 source lines and was then examined and condensed to achieve the 5000-source-line final delivery target.

Environmental variables. In both cases, the programmers had their own terminals and essentially unrestricted access to machine time. The design consisted of external specifications in response to the customer requirements, done in English text augmented by pseudocode. The internal design was done using the Constantine-Myers-Stevens structured design approach.

The external user documentation for both projects was informally produced by the programmers and analysts, since only a single customer was involved.

The defect removal methods in both cases assume relatively formal design and code inspections by trained personnel, and full testing was performed beforehand.

The projects were staffed by personnel already on board, and there was no hiring expense. Since the personnel were experienced in the application areas, there was no training or education expense for either project.

Data and code-structure variables. Both examples are in C and are assumed to be 5000 source lines in size. In both the payroll and the radar controller programs, the data complexity is considered subjectively to be medium. In the payroll program, the code is well structured; in the radar controller program, the initial highly structured program was modified for performance reasons, and the result is less structured than normal.

In looking at Table 3-10, it may be seen that the overall impact of programming type is fairly significant: The extra time and effort needed to compress code and speed up throughput in the real-time example triggers an increase in both schedule time and development effort and therefore must inevitably drive productivity down.

Since all project personnel are aware of the need for tight code and memory constraints in the real-time example, this fact tends to affect every aspect of the project. The requirements exploration must be carried out in some detail to be sure that the requirements are not redundant or superfluous; the design must be very carefully thought out in terms of memory utilization and performance; the coding must be done once to achieve an operational level and then substantially redone to achieve the compression and performance targets. These constraints and the tight code may introduce bugs and operational problems, which in turn affect the testing schedules and resources. In other words, real-time systems require evaluating more variables and responding to more challenges than a standard batch programming system, and these extra factors tend to reduce productivity.

THE IMPACT OF TOOLS AND ENVIRONMENTAL CONDITIONS

Much of the productivity literature and almost all of the commercial advertising relative to programming productivity assume that better tools and a better programming environment will yield major productivity gains. Advertising claims of a 90% reduction in programming time or increase in productivity of 1000% are not uncommon. When explored closely, most of these assertions tend to disappear because ambiguous data was used or because the claim was based on only a small portion of total development, such as coding measured for a few hours and then turned into an annual rate.

As an example of measurement difficulties, some of the program-generator advertisements that speak of order-of-magnitude productivity improvements do not mention or deal with user requirements, design, customer documentation, integration, or maintenance. Even if coding productivity is improved by an order of magnitude, the overall impact on a project may be much smaller if coding represents only 15% to 30% of the total effort.

Another problem in exploring the productivity impact of tools and environments is the lack of any kind of normative standard for exactly which tools comprise a "good" or "excellent" environment and which tools, if missing, would cause the environment to be considered "poor." Both Reifer and Trattner (39) and Wasserman (40) give interesting views of what a good program environment might be like circa the early 1980s, but it is possible to envision a new kind of environment quantitatively and qualitatively far beyond anything currently available. By the 1990s, it should be possible to have a full life-cycle support environment for commercial and government programming that will integrate well over a hundred different tools and applications and will include new generations of expert systems for areas such as planning and estimating.

The following pages list the kinds of tools that may be available in the next generation of programming environments.

Planning and estimating support tools

• Knowledge-based estimating program that predicts software quality, reliability, resources, costs, and schedules, with an accuracy of plus or minus 5%

• Reverse estimating tool that predicts the optimum set of tools, design methods, programming languages, and defect removal steps to achieve any constraints or targets for delivery schedules, quality, costs, and resources

• Expert planning tool that will predict the optimum work breakdown structure for up to 1000 interrelated software activities, including the appropriate kinds of support personnel and subcontract personnel, as well as the major milestones and PERT (Program Evaluation and Review Technique) or Gantt charts to any desired level of detail

• Skeleton formats and interactive tools for constructing all planning documents required by standard commercial contracts, by government contracts, and by military specifications, as well as those required by foreign countries

• On-line access to all standards that will affect the project, including ANSI, ISO, CCITT, U.S. Department of Defense, and other standard-setting organizations

Contract- and bid-support tools

• On-line standard commercial contract forms and proposal outlines, plus both civilian and military request-for-proposal outlines, references, and issuing office

• On-line standard contracts for joint ventures, research agreements, and subcontract agreements for working on multicompany projects

• On-line access to major regulations and guidelines covering overseas contracts, technology export licenses, and other aspects of international business

Financial- and budget-support tools

• On-line support for annual business plans and unit budgets, including skeleton forms and facilities that are the equivalent of VisiCalc templates

• On-line support for project and departmental accounting, using the approved accounting practices established by academic institutions, commercial enterprises, and both civilian and military government organizations

• On-line support for capital expenditure requests and for purchase-order processing

• On-line support for travel authorization; travel expense accounting; airline, hotel, and rental car reservations

• On-line support of personnel requisitions and job openings and of subcontract and consulting agreements

Calendar and schedule management tools

• Standard calendar and schedule management facilities for meetings, with communication facilities for polling other participants to avoid conflicts. Calendar can be linked to project-planning facilities to highlight milestones and checkpoints as they come due.

• On-line access to public calendars of meetings, trade shows, and conferences sponsored by major organizations such as the IEEE, CCITT, ACM, SHARE, and GUIDE.

• On-line telephone directories with automatic dialing by name or number.

• On-line access to public telephone directories in all cities in the United States and for many overseas locations.

Requirements tools

• Expert-system requirements analyzer for common application types in major industries such as banking, insurance, and telecommunications, and for civilian and military government application areas.
• High-speed modeling and prototyping of system outputs, inputs, and major functions, using generators, standard module packages, or interpretive languages

Design and specification tools

• On-line skeletons to meet standard commercial specifications and to meet both civilian government and military specification requirements
• On-line access to library of reusable design, reusable modules, and other standard elements
• On-line expert data design and analysis tools, optimized for common application types in major industries and for both civilian and military government applications
• Fully integrated text/graphics/simulation capabilities for design construction

Documentation tools

• Skeleton outlines of all standard document types both for commercial program products and for civilian government and military contract projects
• On-line pilot facility for preparing interactive menus, icons, and user documentation
• Fully integrated text/graphics support with multiple type fonts, scientific and mathematical symbols, all European language symbols, and standard graphic symbols for engineering and software schematics
• Interactive 100,000-word spelling checkers for all major languages, including scientific and mathematical terms
• Interactive grammar and style analyzers, coupled to major style guides such as the U.S. Government Printing Office Style Guide

Communications tools

• Full communications facilities for data, voice (including voice storage and forwarding), graphics, and images such as facsimile transmission and video
• Full teleconferencing and videoconferencing support from the workstation itself, without requiring a special teleconference room

• On-line facilities for merging documents by different authors and from different sources (i.e. spreadsheets, illustrations, text) into cohesive packages

• Full program- and data-transfer capabilities, remote test capabilities, and remote maintenance capabilities.

Reference and education tools

• On-line interactive reference to major technical libraries for textual, graphic, and video materials, with full interactive search capabilities by title, subject, author, and chronology

• On-line access to technical courses and seminars at both public and private educational facilities

• Interactive pilot facilities for creating custom on-line course materials, including linked facilities for video-disk selection and creation

• On-line access to catalogs of major university and technical schools, catalogs of commercial technical symposia and courses, and curriculum analyses for major technical fields

Data dictionary and database tools

• Expert system for planning databases and data dictionaries for major enterprise classes, such as banking, insurance, telecommunications, and both civilian and military government organizations

• Extended database concepts that allow voice, graphics, and image databases as well as conventional alphanumeric data

• Extended database facilities to access historical data and past values of current records, to allow a new class of time-dependent applications to be created

Configuration control and change control tools

• Extended database facility to keep all historical information and all past values of current records, to allow reconstruction of system to approximately any given minute. Requires high-volume optical or perpendicular magnetic storage, plus a new type of chronological access method.

• Configuration control tools that provide a superset of all current government and military requirements.

Programming and code generation tools

• Full support of all major programming languages (i.e. Ada, ALGOL, APL, Assemblers, BASIC, C, CHILL, COBOL, FORTH, FORTRAN, JOVIAL, LISP, LOGO, MODULA-2, Pascal, PROLOG, SMALLTALK, etc.)

• Full support of and access to libraries of reusable modules and utility programs, in all major languages and under all major operating systems

• Full support of and access to program generators and fourth-generation languages (i.e. database query languages, etc.)

• Full support of access to a variety of editors, syntax checkers, cross-reference tools, sorts, and miscellaneous programming tools

Defect removal and quality assurance tools

• Full interactive support of design and code inspections, without requiring physical travel by the participants (i.e. shared screens, teleconferencing, and an interactive fault-reporting and response facility)

• Fully interactive modeling and prototyping facilities, using reusable code, generators, or interpretive languages

• Life-cycle defect tracking and analysis system, from requirements through maintenance period, with all defects recorded, categorized, analyzed, and repaired interactively

• Remote facilities for fault identification and isolation and for code replacement, via telecommunications lines, satellite, or single sideband radio

Maintenance tools

• Support for 24-hour hot-line trouble calls and for fully warrantied software repairs.

• Remote fault identification and symptom monitoring, with the ability to query the defect database to see if other users have experienced the same problem, and if so, whether or not a fix is available

• For high-volume programs with thousands of customers, fully interactive communication via 24-hour information utilities that can download patches and refresh releases to authorized customers

• For systems installed in remote or inconvenient locations (i.e. satellite, underwater, or untended mountain or jungle locations), the ability to modify software via radio or microwave

The tools and environments just described go significantly beyond what is commercially available today, but not beyond the limits of actual technologies.

Table 3-11 illustrates the impact of tools and environmental factors on productivity. Three cases are shown: a best case that is typical of a leading-edge tool set in a major software research organization; an average case that is typical of commercial programming environments in corporations and government; and a worst case that illustrates the impact of insufficient capital and inadequate tool sets on productivity.

It is interesting to discuss the broad difference in the costs of the tools among the three cases. In the best-case example, the total cost per

Table 3-11 The impact of tools and environment on software productivity

	Best environment	Average environment	Worst environment
Size in lines (C language)	100,000	100,000	100,0000
Schedules (calendar months)			
Requirements	3.5	3.5	3.5
Design	7.5	9.0	9.5
Coding	4.5	4.5	4.5
Testing	4.0	5.0	5.0
Total	19.5	22.0	22.5
Overlapped	11.5	13.0	13.5
Development effort (person-months)			
Requirements	42	42	42.5
Design	53	63	67.0
Internal documentation	122	366	610.0
External documentation	113	338	564.5
Coding	158	188	233.0
Testing	85	95	103.0
Defect repairs	132	128	124.0
Management	85	147	209.0
Total	790	1,367	1,953.0
5-year maintenance effort			
Delivery	0	0	0
Central maintenance	19	61	113
Field maintenance	0	0	0
Total	19	61	113
Project total	809.0	1,428.0	2,066.0
Staff size	68	105	144
Cost per month	$5,000	$5,000	$5,000
Total cost	$4,045,000	$7,140,000	$10,330,000
Cost per line	$40.45	$71.40	$103.30
Lines per month	126	73	51

programmer/analyst for the tools in question would be in the vicinity of $50,000 in 1985; for the average case, the costs would be in the vicinity of $6,000 per programmer/analyst; while for the worst case, the cost would be in the vicinity of $2,500 per programmer/analyst.

In a 1981 IEEE workshop on productivity issues (41), one of the two major issues that surfaced was the lack of any definitive information on the optimum capital spending for tools and support to achieve maximum productivity. (The second issue was the need for extended facilities to support reusable software.)

Project and personnel variables. In all three cases, assume that the programming system to be developed is a new compiler for the Ada language that will consist of 100,000 source code statements. The compiler itself will be written in the C language, by programmers who are very familiar with compiler development and reasonably familiar with the new Ada language definition. Assume that the compilers will be sold to 100 customers (for the maintenance calculations) and that the delivery to the first customer must take place in less than 14 months, so personnel will be added if needed.

Best-case environment

• Integrated text/graphics support for requirements, design, and documentation.
• Good technical libary and information access
• Automated configuration control and project libraries
• One terminal per programmer/analyst in his or her office, with extra terminals available upon request for home use
• Full repertory of cross-reference tools, debugging tools, and formal test library tools
• Adequate office space per programmer/analyst, with ample storage for listings and reference materials
• Numerous small conference rooms for reviews and inspections
• Automated defect reporting and tracking system

Average environment

• Some word processing support but no automated graphics.
• Small and sparse technical library.
• Some automation of configuration control, but only for the source code. Documentation is controlled manually.
• One terminal per three programmer/analysts, with the terminals being in terminal rooms. No home terminals.
• Some debugging tools, but test library is manual.
• Shared offices for three or four programmer/analysts. Barely adequate storage for listings and references.
• One or two small conference rooms available for reviews
• Manual defect recording system.

Worst-case environment

• Only typewriters for documentation; no graphics at all.
• No technical library or reference sources.
• No automation of configuration control, for either the source code or the documentation.
• One terminal per four or more programmers, with frequent downtime of the terminals and computer system.
• Minimal debugging tools, but test library is under manual procedures and not under central control.

• No offices for technical personnel, but only desks in a common working room. No storage for listings and references.

• No small conference rooms available for reviews.

• No defect recording system at all.

Data and code-structure variables. In all three cases, assume that the code is reasonably well structured and the data complexity is typical of compilers: high, but well understood.

In considering the impact of environmental variables on productivity as shown in Table 3-11, it can be stated that lack of an adequate tool set coupled with a poor physical environment exacts a penalty of more than 100% in the human resources needed to carry out a significant programming project. If the delivery schedules are not constrained, there can also be an impact on development time.

Probably the greatest single harmful element in both average and worst-case environments is lack of adequate documentation support. As discussed in subsequent sections, the documentation for a large programming system is often the largest or second-largest element of cost, yet few software-producing enterprises are aware of this and have taken steps to minimize documentation effort.

The internal documentation for a large programming project can total more than fifty English words for every line of source code when the contents of requirements documents, design documents, planning documents, and business documents are added together.

The external documentation, supplied to customers, can sometimes exceed more than 100 English words for every line of source code in the sum of the installation guides, user's guides, text on menus and HELP screens, maintenance manuals, operator's guides, educational materials, and marketing brochures.

The effort, costs, and schedule time needed to complete the documentation is often on the critical path leading to product delivery, and yet lack of integrated text/graphics support is an almost universal condition of commercial and government programming installations. Only a few leading-edge commercial enterprises and some academic and research facilities currently provide really adequate documentation support.

THE IMPACT OF PROGRAM ENHANCEMENTS

As programming moves past the 30-year mark as a professional occupation, an unforseen and perhaps permanent change is starting to occur in much of the work that is performed throughout the industry. Many programmers and analysts find themselves working on enhancements to programming systems that have been in existence for some time, rather

Table 3-12 Estimated worldwide programming population and annual code production of all types from 1950 to A.D. 2000

Year	Number of programmers	Annual production of source code (lines)	Cumulative active code (lines)
1950	100	200,000	200,000
1960	10,000	20,000,000	5,000,000
1970	100,000	200,000,000	250,000,000
1980	2,000,000	4,000,000,000	5,000,000,000
1990	7,000,000	14,000,000,000	17,500,000,000
2000	10,000,000	20,000,000,000	25,000,000,000

than working on the creation of new systems. While this phenomenon is not difficult to explain, its impact has crept up on much of the industry, and neither commercial programming organizations nor computer science schools have fully geared up to meet the changing requirements.

Based on demographic studies by Jones (42), Table 3-12 shows the approximate numbers of professional programmers in the industry from 1950, with predictions to the year 2000.

Even though the retirement rate of active systems was found by Kendall to be very high (43), the total worldwide inventory of active code is quite large and is growing much larger each year. This code is of course not frozen, and it changes fairly often as requirements change and the external world evolves.

One of the challenges of the computer and programming industry is that of dealing with this growing inventory of existing systems. Indeed, a new subindustry has started to appear in the tools and services for restructuring and restoring aging systems.

The work involved in modifying an existing system usually carries with it added costs and schedule time, relative to developing new programs, for the following reasons:

1. The existing program must be explored and fairly well understood, and quite often the original documentation is not adequate; also undocumented patches and changes may have been added.
2. For even small changes, it may be necessary to recompile much of the original program, and it will certainly be necessary to regression-test the system to ensure that the modification has not degraded prior functions.
3. If the original code is unstructured, or written in a language such as assembler with insufficient comments to understand the logic, the task of safely updating the code is intrinsically difficult. It may be necessary to use one of the new restructuring products or services.

Table 3-13 Worldwide totals of programmers working on new programs and enhancements from 1950 to A.D. 2000

Year	Programmers on new programs	Programmers on enhancements	Worldwide total
1950	90	10	100
1960	8,500	1,500	10,000
1970	65,000	35,000	100,000
1980	1,200,000	800,000	2,000,000
1990	3,000,000	4,000,000	7,000,000
2000	4,000,000	6,000,000	10,000,000

Table 3-13 shows the approximate percentages of industry programmers working on brand-new programs and on enhancements to existing programs from 1950 through the year 2000, taken from the previously mentioned demographic study by Jones.

Enhancements versus Maintenance

Enhancements in the commercial programming world are often formal development efforts that resemble new projects in terms of the rigor of reviews and inspections, formal cost estimating, contractual negotiations, and the like. Defect repairs, on the other hand, are often done as rapidly as possible and with only the minimum rigor needed to ensure that the repair does not introduce fresh problems; fresh defects often do get introduced anyway, as noted by Jones (44). Moreover, defect repairs are often covered by a product warranty, so the expenses are borne by the system developer rather than by the customers explicitly.

Table 3-14 shows the major distinctions between maintenance in the sense of enhancing an existing project and maintenance in the sense of defect repairs.

The business and technical differences between enhancements and defect repairs are so significant that it is very unfortunate that the two concepts have become blurred together.

Table 3-14 Summary of differences between maintenance types

	Enhancing an existing program	Defect repairs on an existing program
Funding source	Customers	Often internal
Requirements	Customers' needs	Developer's needs
Workers involved	Development team	Maintenance team
Design	Often formal	Little or none
Documentation	Often formal	Little or none
Coding style	Often structured	Often unstructured
Defect removal	Often formal	Little or none

Table 3-15 Five-year enhancement and maintenance effort for a 50,000-source-statement COBOL application program (person-months)

| | Years | | | | | | |
	0	1	2	3	4	5	Total
Initial development	345	—	—	—	—	—	345
Maintenance (defect repairs)	—	50	30	15	5	—	100
Enhancements (new functions)	—	30	50	40	75	50	245
Total effort	345	80	80	55	80	50	690

Another significant difference between enhancements to a program and maintenance, or defect repairs, is the chronological weights of the two activities. Given reasonably thorough prerelease reviews, inspections, and tests, it is likely that the bulk of the defect repairs of a program will be accomplished within 3 years after delivery to customers. Enhancements, on the other hand, may continue at a high level throughout the life of the product and may even grow in magnitude after 7 to 10 years of field experience.

Table 3-15 shows the approximate efforts devoted to defect repairs and to enhancements against a typical 50,000-source-statement COBOL application program of a common type, such as an accounting program for handling accounts payable and accounts receivable. Assume the program is developed internally for a single enterprise and is not marketed commercially.

Although Table 3-15 is simplified to illustrate a point, note that the 5-year total amount of effort devoted to the sum of both defect repairs and enhancements equaled the initial development effort. However, if the three activities are analyzed separately, as good accounting practice would call for, the initial development equaled 50% of the lifetime total; defect repairs equaled less than 15% of the lifetime total; and enhancements equaled about 36% of the lifetime total, but showed no sign of reduction and would have eventually become the major cost element if the lifetime stretched out another 3 or 4 years.

Cost Elements of Enhancements

Estimating the time, effort, and costs is both logically and mathematically more difficult for enhancement work than for new development, because the additional factors of the status and structure of the base system must be included in the equations.

Moreover, enhancement work also presents major difficulties in measuring productivity, because of the ambiguity in whether or not to include the base code in the productivity figures. One school of thought, with which the author tends to agree, asserts that the productivity of the delivered product is the most important factor, and therefore any code in the delivered system should be used in the productivity measures, regardless of whether it was freshly coded or old code from previous versions. The opposing school asserts that including the base code in the productivity measures dilutes the value of measuring and prevents any understanding of the technical productivity of development; i.e. the actual design and coding of the new work.

The method used in this book in the SPQR estimating tool for evaluating the productivity of enhancements is based on the following rationale: If the base code on which the enhancement is built becomes a permanent part of the new product and is no longer used or supported in its original form, then it is included in the productivity measures of the new version or program. On the other hand, if the base code is merely "borrowed" from an existing system or library and will retain an independent existence regardless of its utilization in the new version, then it is excluded from the productivity measures.

For example, if a new program is constructed in which 2000 new source statements are added to an existing program of 3000 source statements, and the old program is discarded and no longer supported, then the productivity measures of the new project would be against all 5000 source lines. For example, in a new version of a word processing program that offered new features and replaced a former version, the base code would be counted.

However, if a new utility program of 2000 source statements was created to provide additional capabilities for a 3000-source-statement application program that would continue to be used on its own, then the productivity measures would be based on only the new 2000-line development effort. For example, for a separately priced and marketed spelling checker that augmented an existing word processing program, only the new code for the spelling checker, and not the original program, would be counted.

The underlying rule of this method is that anything becoming permanently a part of the new version is counted, and anything not permanently becoming a part is excluded.

Enhancement work can be divided into three major modes on the basis of the nature of the relationships of the new code to the old:

1. The new code will be added as discrete modules,
2. The new code will be added partly as discrete modules, and partly as changes or modifications to the existing base code, or
3. The new code will be added entirely as changes or modifications to the existing base code.

As a general rule, cases 2 and 3 are usually more difficult to perform than case 1 because of the need to explore the inner workings of the base system in considerable detail.

Another aspect of enhancement that differs from new development, but which is one of the most significant determinants of both the costs and schedules of doing the enhancement, is the status of the base code. In this book and in the SPQR estimating tool, five main plateaus are significant:

1. The base code is stable—few if any bugs remain in it, and the annual number of defect reports against the base code is usually less than 0.5 per 1000 source code statements.
2. The base code is stabilizing—it is still generating fault reports from customers using the program, but the annual volume of defects is less than 3.0 per 1000 source code statements.
3. The base code is unstable—sufficient bugs are being reported to cause relatively frequent changes that can interfere with the work of adding new functions. Rates of 3.0 to 6.0 defects per 1000 source lines per year often indicate unstable base code.
4. The base code is error-prone—it often fails dramatically when customers use it, and the annual quantity of defect reports is in the range of 6.0 to 10.0 per 1000 source code statements.
5. The base code is hazardous—it barely works at all, and the annual number of incoming defect reports is greater than 10.0 per 1000 source code statements.

Any attempts to add new functions to error-prone or hazardous base systems will meet major problems and usually experience notable cost and schedule overruns.

Table 3-16 shows the combinations of these factors. Four cases are illustrated:

Case 1: A new 10,000-source-statement COBOL program, to provide the basis for comparison

Case 2: Adding 10,000 lines of new code as discrete modules to a stable base system of 30,000 COBOL source statements, to show how the need to understand and test the base affects productivity relative to new code

Case 3: Adding 10,000 lines of new code partly as new modules and partly as changes and modifications to the original code of a stable 30,000-source-statement program in COBOL, to show the difficulty of scattered changes

Case 4: Adding 10,000 lines of new code partly as new modules and partly as changes and modifications to an error-prone base system of 30,000

Table 3-16 The productivity impact of making enhancements to existing programs (COBOL)

	Case 1	Case 2	Case 3	Case 4
New size in lines	10,000	10,000	10,000	10,000
Base size in lines	0	30,000	30,000	30,000
Schedules (calendar months)				
Requirements	2.2	2.7	2.8	2.9
Design	3.3	3.7	4.3	4.5
Coding	3.0	3.8	4.4	5.2
Testing	3.5	4.8	5.5	6.4
Total	12.0	15.0	17.0	19.0
Overlapped	8.0	9.5	11.0	12.0
Development effort (person-months)				
Requirements	3.5	4.0	4.5	4.5
Design	5.0	5.5	6.4	6.5
Internal documentation	0.5	0.5	0.5	0.5
External documentation	2.0	2.0	2.0	2.0
Coding	16.0	22.0	25.0	29.0
Testing	9.0	13.0	15.0	15.0
Defect repairs	18.0	17.3	26.9	30.0
Management	6.5	7.5	9.5	10.5
Total	60.5	71.8	89.8	98.0
5-year maintenance effort total)				
Delivery	6.0	6.0	8.0	9.0
Central maintenance	15.0	15.0	19.0	21.0
Field maintenance	0	0	0	0
Total	21.0	21.0	27.0	30.0
Project total	81.5	92.8	116.8	128.0
Staff size	8	8	8	8
Cost per month	$ 5,000	$ 5,000	$ 5,000	$ 5,000
Total cost	$407,500	$455,000	$585,000	$640,000
Cost per line	$ 40.75	$ 45.50	$ 58.50	$ 64.00
Lines per month	165	143	111	102

COBOL source statements, to show how hard it is to work with unstable and poorly structured base code

Project and personnel variables. The programs being developed are internal and are not intended for outside commercial marketing. The programs are all general application programs, in the area of accounting systems. The analysis and design is done by personnel familiar with the application areas and reasonably familiar with the base system which is to be enhanced.

The projects are all done at a single development location, and there is no travel at all. Both the computer resources and the support tools are adequate to the tasks.

Environmental variables. In all four cases, the analysts and programmers have their own terminals and essentially unrestricted access to machine time. There are no constraints on performance or memory usage of the finished program.

The design consists of external specifications done in English text, augmented by sample output formats. In Cases 1 and 2, the code is well structured using the principles of Constantine-Myers-Stevens. In Cases 3 and 4, the base programs are assumed to be older and relatively unstructured. In Case 4, the code is assumed to be error-prone.

The defect removal methods in all four cases assume informal design reviews and testing carried out by the programmers and analysts themselves.

The projects were staffed by personnel already on board, and there were no hiring expenses. The personnel were well versed in the application areas, so no education was needed.

Data and code-structure variables. All four examples are in COBOL. Case 1 is for 10,000 source code statements of well-structured new code with average data complexity. Case 2 is for a 10,000-source-statement COBOL addition to an existing 30,000-source-statement base system; both the base and the new code are well structured and of average data complexity. Case 3 is for a 10,000-source-code-statement COBOL addition to a fairly complex and unstructured 30,000-source-code-statement COBOL base system; data complexity is average. Case 4 is for a 10,000-source-code-statement COBOL addition to an unstructured and error-prone 30,000-source-code-statement COBOL base; the data complexity again is average.

In considering Table 3-16, the points of significance are these:

1. Enhancing an existing system tends to be more time-consuming and somewhat more costly than developing an equivalent amount of new code, because of the overhead associated with learning the base system, integrating the new code with it, and ensuring that no regressions have been introduced.
2. The defect status and the structure of the base system exert considerable influences on the effort and schedules for adding new functions, as does fragmentation of new code.
3. Enhancing an error-prone or hazardous, poorly structured base system is one of the most unpredictable and difficult challenges faced by both development and estimating personnel, as well as by estimating tools.

The trend toward modifying or enhancing existing systems is likely to be permanent. The emerging subindustry which specializes in restructuring and restoring aging software is likely be a high-growth activity throughout the 1980s and 1990s. The tools, methods, education, and literature on this subject are generally inadequate in 1985, and correcting these deficiencies is an urgent priority for academic, commercial, and government enterprises.

THE IMPACT OF PROGRAM MAINTENANCE

Because of the ambiguous definition of the term "maintenance" that includes both enhancements and defect repairs, and because of the shortage of controlled studies that distinguish between the two, the topic of maintenance is both confusing and underreported in the software engineering literature.

Here we restrict the word "maintenance" to mean only defect repairs on a program or system after it is delivered to customers. The other aspect of maintenance, or adding new functions and enhancements, is discussed above.

Maintenance in the sense of defect repairs has three major cost elements, of which the two largest are so severely underreported in the literature that most books and articles on maintenance surprisingly make no reference to them at all. The three cost elements are:

Delivery support. If a program is delivered to its customers and installed by systems engineers who are employed by the developer or vendor, the costs of this support are directly proportional to the number of customers and the number of defects still present in the software. While a majority of programs have no delivery support at all, those that do find this a very expensive undertaking. Indeed, this is one of the reasons why major software enterprises such as IBM, Digital Equipment Corporation, Control Data Corporation, Honeywell, and Burroughs charge so much for their software packages. For a large system with more than 1000 customers and less-than-average quality, cost of delivery support can be higher by order of magnitude than the total of all development expenses for the system. This cost element is almost never discussed in print or included in the functions of software cost-estimating tools, except for proprietary ones by the software houses themselves.

Central maintenance. Central maintenance is the traditional task of responding to defect reports that come in from customers, developing and testing the repairs, and distributing the repairs back out to the customer base. This is the only form of maintenance that is usually discussed in the maintenance literature, since this is the most common maintenance activity. However, it is not usually the most expensive, and its costs can range from less than 1% of development expenses for a high-quality program used only by a single customer to perhaps 40% of development expenses for a low-quality program with many customers.

Field service. Field service refers to sending vendor systems engineers onto the customer's premises in order to assist in defect analysis and removal and patch installation and otherwise keep systems healthy and operational. While many programs and many vendors have no field service at all, for those that do this is either the most expensive or the second most expensive single activity of maintenance, depending upon delivery support. For large low-quality programming systems with more than 1000 customers and a field life of 7 to 10 years, field service costs will often exceed the total development costs for the program by 300% to 500%.

High-Volume Program Maintenance

The rapid emergence of the microcomputer industry has spread computer usage to millions of individuals, and there are now software packages that exceed 250,000 licensed users on a global basis. A new maintenance problem, to date not covered in the literature, is that of providing adequate service and defect repairs to high-volume programs. This is likely to become a major topic in the future, and already in 1985 a single action such as sending a letter to registered customers of a program with 250,000 licenses would cost $50,000 just for first-class postage stamps. This is why many software companies are starting to use the information utilities for maintenance purposes and to download patches from central computers and databases rather than depending upon more traditional methods.

The Cost Elements of Software Maintenance

There are six primary and six secondary factors that are significant in determining total software maintenance costs. The primary factors are:

1. The number of latent defects in the program
2. The number of customers of the program
3. The number of maintenance personnel assigned to the program
4. The tools and support for maintenance
5. The structure and maintainability of the program
6. The vendor's contractual obligations governing maintenance

The secondary factors are:

1. Multiple defect reports for the same problem
2. Unrecreatable defect reports (reports that can not be duplicated)
3. Invalid defect reports, because of customer errors or other reasons
4. Training available for maintenance personnel
5. Maintenance documentation available for the program
6. The presence or absence of customer systems programmers

The number of permutations among the 12 variables is large, but the two chief variables, which together account for perhaps 50% of the total maintenance cost ranges, are the number of defects in the program when it was delivered and the number of customers who use the program.

Four examples are given in Table 3-17 to illustrate the impacts of these variables. All of the examples are based on a 50,000-source-

Table 3-17 The impact of defect levels and numbers of users on total software maintenance effort

	Case 1	Case 2	Case 3	Case 4
New size in lines (COBOL)	50,000	50,000	50,000	50,000
Number of customers	1	1	10,000	10,000
Number of defects	250	1,000	250	1,000
Development effort (person-months)				
Requirements	26.0	27.0	26.0	27.0
Design	35.0	39.5	35.0	39.5
Internal documentation	97.5	97.5	97.5	97.5
External documentation	105.0	105.0	105.0	105.0
Coding	88.0	103.0	88.0	103.0
Testing	55.5	78.0	55.5	78.0
Defect repairs	111.0	198.0	111.0	198.0
Management	62.0	77.0	62.0	77.0
Total	580.0	725.0	580.0	725.0
5-year maintenance effort				
Delivery	0	0	3,982	4,146
Central maintenance	70	365	87	383
Field maintenance	0	0	2,233	2,775
Total	70	365	6,302	7,304
Project total	650	1,090	6,882	8,029
Cost per month	$ 5,000	$ 5,000	$ 5,000	$ 5,000
Development cost	$2,900,000	$3,625,000	$ 2,900,000	$ 3,625,000
Maintenance cost	$ 350,000	$1,825,000	$31,510,000	$36,520,000
Total cost	$3,250,000	$5,450,000	$34,410,000	$40,145,000
Cost per line	$ 65.00	$ 109.00	$ 608.20	$ 802.90
Maintenance percentage of total cost	10.8%	33.5%	91.6%	90.9%

statement COBOL application program, such as an accounting package. Case 1 assumes a high-quality program with only a single user. Case 2 assumes a low-quality program with only a single user. Case 3 assumes that the high-quality version of the program has been sold to 10,000 customers worldwide. Case 4 assumes that the low-quality version of the program has been sold to 10,000 customers worldwide.

In Cases 1 and 2, which represent the typical situation of internal software developed and used inside a company, the delivery support and field service costs are essentially nothing, since the developers install the product themselves.

In Cases 3 and 4, the assumption is that the program will be installed on the customer computers by vendor personnel and that any subsequent trouble reports will have on-site visits by vendor personnel to aid the customers in handling the problems. This is typical of the major commercial software packages marketed by computer companies and large software houses; i.e. database systems such as IMS or ADABAS, manufacturing support packages, integrated accounting systems, and the like.

From analysis of Table 3-17, several conclusions may be drawn. First, the traditional task of central maintenance is not the major element of overall maintenance expenses, although it can become significant. Even for a relatively high defect rate, the central maintenance costs did not exceed one-third of the total costs for development and 5 years of maintenance.

However, as the number of customers increases, the costs of delivery support and field service go up dramatically: For the cases with 10,000 customers, about 90% of the total lifetime expenses were devoted to various on-site support activities. Note also that for programs that were essentially identical except for the number of customers, a difference in maintenance costs of more than an order of magnitude was brought on by the large number of customers.

In the entire set of software activities, the ranges of costs are greater for maintenance than for any other cost-bearing element, while the number of quantitative studies on the nature of those costs and the reasons for them is lower than in any other domain. The recent books on maintenance by Martin and McClure (45) and Parikh and Zvegintzov (46), coupled with the beginnings of an IEEE special interest group on maintenance and a Naval Postgraduate School conference on maintenance, may be signals that this long-neglected topic might soon emerge as a true professional subject and target of controlled research.

The large expenses for delivery support and field service are a significant reason for the high market costs of major application and system software packages. Entrepreneurs and start-up enterprises need to be aware that attempts to provide delivery support and field service are very expensive undertakings, and the larger the market success of the product, the greater these costs become.

Not illustrated, but very significant, is the cost of maintaining an entire inventory of programs and applications. Large enterprises such as ITT and IBM may have in excess of 30,000 separate programs in their overall corporate inventories, which can approach 100,000,000 source code statements. The Department of Defense and the combined portfolios of the U.S. military may have over 100,000 programs and a total size of 250,000,000 source code statements. Maintenance against such an inventory is very expensive, even if individual maintenance costs are quite low for each separate program or application.

THE IMPACT OF REUSABLE MODULES AND FUNCTIONS

The economic incentive for reusing software is the same as that for the use of standardized parts in automotive and aircraft design: standard parts are cheaper, more reliable, and usually easier to fix or replace when something goes wrong.

Most programmers and software designers have spontaneously reused logic, modules, and design elements since the industry began. Macro libraries were an early attempt at reusability in assembler language programming, while an international organization, SHARE, was created to facilitate reusability of code and logic among the scientific customers of IBM computers.

However, the ad hoc and spontaneous reuse of a few basic algorithms is a long way from achieving the economic leverage that might be possible if 50% to 80% of every major application and system program could be constructed from "off-the-shelf" components.

As noted in a previous study by T.C. Jones (47), the topic of reusability includes five major subtopics that must be evaluated:

1. Reusable data, or techniques for standardizing the flow of information from module to module and application to application.
2. Reusable architecture, or planning the inclusion of reused parts as a basic step in program and system design from requirements onward.
3. Reusable designs, or encapsulating the optimum skeletal structures of major generic application programs, such as word processing packages and accounting packages.
4. Reusable programs, or creating commercial software that is useful on a wide variety of computers and, in addition, has adopted a standard data interchange so that any given program can transmit information to other programs, as the need arises. Standard invocation and control sequences will also be a necessity for reusable programs.

5. Reusable modules, or standard functional elements that can be linked together to create new programs and systems. Here too is a need for a standard data interchange and for standard invocation and control sequences.

In addition to these five primary topics, the subject of reusability has a variety of secondary considerations, of which the more signifcant are:

• Library and catalog support for a repertory of standard reusable modules and functions

• Library and catalog support for the user and maintenance documentation accompanying standard modules or functions, so that such information need not be recreated each time a standard function is included in a program

• Nomination and certification of candidate standard reusable modules, to ensure that they meet very high criteria of quality and reliability

• Construction of a new class of specification and design methods which include the ability to specify standard elements of systems, as well as the new and unique functions that will require hand coding, i.e. design methods that have explicit verbs based on standard functions

• Language, tool, and environmental support for reusable code and standard functions, to encourage widespread adoption of such methods within enterprises

• Selective migration of standard functions that are used with high frequency from software to VLSI or microcode, to augment their performance

• Architectures and computers capable of handling very high levels of parallelism and concurrency, since standard functions are intrinsically capable of parallel execution if the machines on which they execute can support parallelism

• Augmentation of conventional programming techniques with a new generation of application and system generators, which operate by selecting and coupling standard modules that meet application needs

• Internal financial and accounting changes within the enterprises that adopt standard functions and reusable code, so that the initial creator of a standard module has a way of receiving some form of compensation, while the users of the standard functions make some form of payment

In 1985, reusability is an emerging technology, but not yet a mature or well-formed one. However, it is significant that all of the enterprises reporting productivity rates in excess of 20,000 delivered source code statements per programmer-year make use of reusable designs and reusable code in order to achieve those high levels.

Because a fundamental design attribute of the new Ada language is support for separate compilation of modules and the inclusion of preexisting functions in new Ada programs, the topic of reusability will become one of the major technical subjects of the late 1980s. Other languages also specifically supporting standard modules and reusable code include MODILA-2, FORTH, OBJECTIVE-C, and SMALLTALK/80, while more informal techniques for reusing code exist for most other languages.

Financial Considerations of Reusable Software

Reusable software and standard designs present both interesting technical challenges and very interesting business challenges. Some of the major problems facing reusable code and standard functions in commercial enterprises are financial: how to pay for the overhead costs of running a shared reusable code library that many projects can utilize; how to compensate the developers of standard functions so that they have some incentive to create reusable modules in the first place; and how to change internal cost apportionment methods so that reusable code can be purchased by projects, and yet still be economical to use.

When reusable code is first considered by commercial programming organizations, even such major ones as IBM, it is usually slow to succeed, for the following reasons:

1. Given the current environment in most enterprises, there is absolutely no incentive for developers to create candidate standard functions. Since the costs tend to be slightly higher and the schedules somewhat longer for standard functions, and since secondary users benefit rather than the developer, no one is willing to take the extra time and cost to develop a reusable module in an ordinary commercial programming environment.
2. Since reusable code is by definition shared by many projects, the central library and catalog function for the reusable code needs special funds and staffing. Few enterprises have been willing to bear the startup costs.
3. Since a defective or error-prone reusable module that found its way into many applications would be as large a disaster as a defective chip in a circuit board, any enterprise considering reusable functions needs a very thorough certification and quality assurance review of the candidate functions before accepting them into the standard library. This is one of the major reasons why reusable code costs more than ordinary code and why it takes longer to develop.
4. Since both the usage information and the maintenance documentation must accompany reusable code in order for the concept to really work, it is also necessary to develop new and very modular forms of documentation.
5. To pay for the startup and overhead costs of entering the domain of

reusable code, it is usually necessary to change an enterprise's internal policies and sell reusable code to the projects which plan to reuse it.

Collectively, the financial issues of entering the domain of reusable code are perhaps more challenging than the technical issues. The startup costs for a large enterprise such as an insurance company or a bank to establish a reusable code library and begin to stock it will often approach $1,000,000, while the time period for the initial establishment of the library may exceed a year. Even if the enterprise is willing to bear the expense, it is not always easy to begin without careful handling of the financial issues.

Productivity Impact of Standard Functions and Reusable Code

There would be little value in bearing the startup costs of a reusable code program unless there were significant payoffs. The payoffs are impressive: reductions of application development cycles for large projects from 36 months to perhaps 8 months, cost reductions in excess of 50% per project, and the elimination of application backlogs and the stabilization of the application programming population within the enterprises.

Four examples are given in Table 3-18 to show the increasing benefits of reusability as the amount of reusable code increases. Case 1 is for a 10,000-source-statement COBOL business application program developed in the traditional manner, with no use of reusable code from requirements through implementation but with utilization of structured design and coding techniques. Case 2 shows the same project, but with 25% of the code and documentation taken from a library of standard COBOL routines; this is the approximate quantity of reusable code for the first year or so of typical use. Case 3 shows the same project, but with 50% of the code drawn from a library, and with the program being based on a standard program skeleton that gives the optimal structure for the application; this was the approximate situation of leading-edge enterprises that had ongoing reusable code libraries in 1983. Case 4 is intended to illustrate application programming in the late 1980s. Here 75% of the code is assumed to come from a standard-function library; the program's skeleton is also predefined; and the development environment supports high-speed modeling and prototyping of the finished program, so users can work out all their requirements by means of actually using the prototypes.

Table 3-18 The impact of reusable code and standard disigns on software productivity

	Case 1 No Reuse	Case 2 25% Reuse	Case 3 50% Reuse	Case 4 75% Reuse
New code in lines (COBOL)	10,000	7,500	5,000	2,500
Reused code in lines	0	2,500	5,000	7,500
Total	10,000	10,000	10,000	10,000
Schedules (calendar months)				
Requirements	2.2	1.8	1.7	0.8
Design	3.3	2.5	2.3	1.5
Coding	3.0	2.3	2.0	1.4
Testing	3.5	2.4	2.0	1.6
Total	12.0	9.0	8.0	5.3
Overlapped	8.0	6.0	5.0	3.0
Development effort (person-months)				
Requirements	3.5	2.5	1.6	0.6
Design	5.0	3.5	2.3	1.0
Internal documentation	0.5	0.5	0.5	0.5
External documentation	2.0	1.5	1.0	0.7
Coding	16.0	10.0	6.5	3.0
Testing	9.0	5.5	5.6	2.0
Defect repairs	18.0	10.5	6.8	3.0
Management	6.5	4.0	2.7	1.2
Total	60.5	38.0	27.0	12.0
5-year maintenance effort				
Delivery	6.0	3.0	2.0	0.5
Central maintenance	15.0	4.0	3.0	2.5
Field maintenance	0	0	0	0
Total	21.0	7.0	5.0	3.0
Project total	81.5	45.0	32.0	15.0
Staff size	8	6	5	4
Cost per month	$ 5,000	$ 5,000	$ 5,000	$ 5,000
Total cost	$407,500	$225,000	$160,000	$75,000
Cost per line	$ 40.75	$ 22.50	$ 16.00	$ 7.50
Lines per month	165	263	370	833

Project and personnel variables. The programs being developed are internal and not intended for outside commercial marketing. The programs are all general application programs, indeed the same application program, in the area of market forecasting. The analysis and design in all four examples is done by personnel who are familiar with the application area.

The programs are done at a single development location, so there is no travel. Both the computer resources and the support tools are adequate for the tasks.

Environmental variables. In all four cases, the analysts and programmers have their own terminals and essentially unrestricted access to machine time. There are no significant constraints on performance or memory usage of the finished program.

In Case 1, the design consists of external specifications done in English text, augmented by sample output formats. The code is structured using the technique of Constantine-Myers-Stevens. In Cases 2 and 3, the design is drawn from a library of program skeletons. In Case 4, the design is drawn from a library of program skeletons, and in addition, the users are able to experiment with a working prototype to finalize their requirements.

Data and code structure variables. All four examples are in COBOL. The code is well structured in all examples, and the data complexity is only moderate.

In analyzing Table 3-18, it should be noted that the first three cases, although artificially constructed from SPQR, are based on real systems. Case 4 is an extrapolation, but the basic technologies of reusable code are such that gains of that magnitude are likely to be achievable in leading-edge enterprises by the late 1980s.

Of all the variables discussed in this book, reusable code and standard designs have perhaps the largest single impact on productivity. Because of the need to certify the reusable components and modules to very high levels of quality, they have a similar impact on quality as well. Although reusable software is not a mature technology in 1985, the economic advantages it offers are such that many major enterprises are exploring ways of incorporating the concept into their repertory of programming tools. J.H. Frame, vice president of programming, and Dr. Ted Biggerstaff of the ITT Corporation hosted the first international conference on reusability in October 1983 (48), and selected papers from that conference were republished by the IEEE (49); this indicates the emerging importance of reusability.

However, achieving a practical level of reusability has both technical and financial challenges that must be faced, and the financial challenges may be more difficult to overcome than the technical ones.

THE IMPACT OF PROGRAM AND APPLICATION GENERATORS

As of the end of 1985, no fewer than 50 commercially available application and program generators are being advertised. There are no agreed definitions of "program generator" and "application generator." In this book, a program generator is defined as a tool which produces an executable stand-alone program in a target language such as COBOL from a nonprocedural source language or from menu screens. An application generator is defined as a tool which produces an executable application from a nonprocedural source language or from menu screens, but the application thus created uses services and features from the application generator and can only execute with the generator as a host. That is, program generators yield source code that can be executed at will; application generators yield running code but are permanently tied to the generator itself.

Program and application generation are logically related to reusable code, and indeed program generators usually have a repertory of standard functional elements as their base, coupled to a menu-driven or nonprocedural front-end language that allows the generator to select the specific functions that will be linked together to form the completed program.

Program generators originated in the 1960s in the field of compiler generation, which was one of the first subdisciplines of computer science that was well enough understood to make generation possible. However, the commercially marketed generators in the 1980s are largely aimed at business application programs, especially those in database environments, and are usually set up to handle menu creation; output report and output screen formatting; queries; and various selections, joins, and mathematical operations on data.

While it is not always necessary to be a professional programmer to use a program generator, it is still necessary to understand the application area in considerable depth and to know at least the rudiments of file organizations, database structures, Boolean logic, and system design.

Experience to date indicates that while generation can be relatively effective in speeding up development, generated programs may have three handicaps compared to conventional development: (1) They often require much more computer time and may not execute as rapidly; (2) they may take more memory; and (3) they may be difficult to maintain, due to the lack of procedural logic. Thus large high-volume applications may not be good candidates for generation, while low-volume or short-lived applications may be suitable.

In exploring a full program life cycle, the commercially available program and application generators in 1985 usually are most effective in the internal design and coding phases and have comparatively little impact elsewhere. Also, to date commercial program and application generators are used by professional programmers or by very sophisticated end users. Indeed, a subdiscipline of professional programming is emerging in those programmers who are expert in one or another of the new generators and are able to write sizable programs using them.

Following is a list of the effects of program and application generation on typical life cycle phases circa 1984.

Life-cycle phase	Impact of program generation
Requirements	Minimal
Function design	Minimal
Logic design	Significant
Coding	Significant
Internal documentation	Varies
External user documentation	Minimal
Test case preparation	Minimal
Defect repairs	Varies
Integration	Minimal
Maintenance	Varies

Table 3-19 shows one example of program generation, which is compared to conventional coding using COBOL for the same application. The COBOL example is the same 10,000-source-code-statement program utilized in Table 3-18.

Project and personnel variables. The programs being developed are internal, not intended for outside marketing. The programs are both general application programs, in the area of market forecasting. Both Case 1, the COBOL version, and Case 2, the generated version, are intended to contain the same functions: i.e., interactive utilization by end users of a database with market information, and the ability to change various assumptions and predict the results. In both examples, the projects are handled by professional analysts and programmers who are in direct contact with the potential end users.

The programs are done at a single development location, so there is no travel. Both the computer resources and the support tools are adequate to the tasks.

Environmental variables. In both cases, the analysts and programmers have their own terminals and essentially unrestricted access to machine time. There are no significant constraints on performance or memory usage of the finished program.

In both examples, the specifications consist of external requirements and function design done in English text, augmented by sample output formats.

Data and code-structure variables. Case 1, the COBOL example, is well structured, and the data complexity is only moderate. Case 2, the generated example, uses the same data structure, so its complexity is the same as that of Case 1. The coding structure of Case 2 is derived from the output of the program generator; it uses a nonprocedural source language to create an intermediate COBOL version, which is then compiled and executed automatically. The number of source statements in the nonpro-

Table 3-19 The impact of program generation on productivity measured with lines of source code

	Case 1: Conventional COBOL Program	Case 2: Generated Program
Size in source lines	10,000	2,000
Size in secondary lines	10,000	14,000
Schedules (calendar months)		
Requirements	2.2	2.2
Design	3.3	2.7
Coding	3.0	1.8
Testing	3.5	2.3
Total	12.0	9.0
Overlapped	8.0	6.0
Development effort (person-months)		
Requirements	3.5	3.5
Design	5.0	2.5
Internal documentation	0.5	0.5
External documentation	2.0	2.0
Coding	16.0	3.0
Testing	9.0	2.5
Defect repairs	18.0	9.0
Management	6.5	2.5
Total	60.5	25.5
5-year maintenance effort		
Delivery	6.0	2.0
Central maintenance	15.0	6.0
Field maintenance	0	0
Total	21.0	8.0
Project total	81.5	33.5
Staff size	8	4
Cost per month	$ 5,000	$ 5,000
Total cost	$407,500	$167,500
Cost per line	$ 40.70	$ 83.75
Lines per month	165	78

cedural source language that drives the COBOL generator is approximately 2000, so that the program generator can be viewed as essentially a language that is 5 times higher in level than ordinary COBOL. However, the amount of generated COBOL source code is somewhat higher than the amount of code in Case 1: Assume that 14,000 COBOL source statements are generated.

As can be seen from Table 3-19, program generation can be an effective way of reducing development schedules and costs. Not shown in the table, however, are the production and execution costs or the response time for the resulting system. Generation is not alway appropri-

Table 3-20. The impact of program generation on productivity measured with function points

	Case 1 Conventional program	Case 2 Generated program
Function points	95	95
Development cost per function point	$3184	$1342
Function points per month	1.6	3.7

ate for systems with high volumes of data or where extremely quick response times are needed.

Maintenance may also be troublesome with generated programs and applications, although not with the example used in Table 3-19, where the generator merely produced COBOL source code.

In analyzing Table 3-19, note the impact of the mathematical paradox dealing with economic productivity versus apparent productivity based on lines of code. Although the lifetime costs of program generation versus conventional development dropped from $407,500 to $167,500, for a 59% economic productivity improvement, the apparent productivity in terms of both cost per source line and lines per programmer-month moved in a negative direction and concealed the economic gains.

The efficiency and effectiveness of program and application generation is essentially unmeasurable with lines-of-code metrics (especially for application generators, where the resulting application depends upon built-in functions in the host generator and does not produce true source code). Table 3-20 gives the productivity rate expressed in the function-point method.

Program generation is not in 1985 a mature technology, but it is becoming a hotbed of research and new products, and the technology has sufficient economic potential to make it worth exploration. However, it is not clear how easily such generated programs can be linked together to form large systems. Also, note that program generation has no impact on requirements or on external user documentation and has comparatively little impact on external design. The impact of code generation on maintenance is currently ambiguous.

THE IMPACT OF FOURTH-GENERATION LANGUAGES

As of 1985, no single phrase in the software world is as ambiguous and lacking in true meaning as the phrase "fourth-generation language." In scanning the commercial advertisements in the data processing journals, we note that the phrase is currently being applied to products that range from minor COBOL preprocessors through entire program development environments. James Martin (50) suggests as a practical definition that the term "fourth-generation language" be restricted to products whose results are ten times better than COBOL, with the assumption that applications can be finished with one-tenth the effort, in one-tenth the time, or both.

If Martin's concept is defined strictly to include total effort and total time—with requirements, design, documentation, integration, and testing included as well as coding—then most of the current products calling themselves fourth-generation languages do not meet this criterion, and only query languages, spreadsheet applications, and some of the more interesting special-purpose tools for graphics and decision support systems remain in the set of proper fourth-generation languages.

Following is a list of the effects of fourth-generation languages upon typical life cycle phases circa 1984:

Life-cycle phase	Impact of fourth-generation languages
Requirements	Minimal
Functional design	Minimal
Logic design	Significant
Coding	Significant
Internal documentation	Varies
External user documentation	Minimal
Test case preparation	Minimal
Defect repairs	Varies
Integration	Minimal
Maintenance	Varies

Table 3-21 shows an example of the use of a fourth-generation query language and conventional COBOL for an application being developed to interrogate a database and extract information on sales status.

Project and personnel variables. The programs being developed are internal, and not intended for outside marketing. The programs both query the same database and present the same report to the end user. Both versions are developed by an experienced programmer/analyst who knows the application area, the database contents, and the languages very well. The programs are done at a single location, so no travel is required. In both cases, the client for the application is a single user, whose requirements are clear and unambiguous. Since only a single user is involved, no formal user's guide or external documentation are created. Since the life expectancy of the application is planned for only a few months, no maintenance documentation is prepared either.

Table 3-21 The impact of a fourth-generation language on productivity measured with lines of source code

	Case 1: Conventional COBOL program	Case 2: Fourth-generation program
Size in source lines	1000	50
Schedules (calendar months)		
Requirements	0.2	0.1
Design	0.6	0.0
Coding	1.5	0.1
Testing	0.5	0.1
Total	2.8	0.3
Overlapped	2.8	0.3
Development effort (person-months)		
Requirements	0.1	0.0
Design	0.5	0.0
Internal documentation	0.1	0.0
External documentation	0.0	0.0
Coding	1.5	0.1
Testing	0.5	0.1
Defect repairs	0.2	0.1
Management	0.1	0.1
Total	3.0	0.4
5-year maintenance effort		
Delivery	0	0
Central maintenance	0	0
Field maintenance	0	0
Total	0	0
Project total	3.3	0.4
Staff size	1	1
Cost per month	$ 5,000	$5,000
Total cost	$16,500	$2,000
Cost per line	$ 16.50	40.00
Lines per month	303	125

Environmental variables. In both cases, the programmer/analyst has a terminal and essentially unrestricted access to machine time. There are no significant constraints on performance or memory usage of the finished program.

In both cases, the specifications consisted of a requirements document created jointly by the user and the programmer/analyst.

Data and code-structure variables. Case 1, the COBOL example, is well structured in the method of Constantine-Myers-Stevens and consists of 1000 source statements. Case 2 is nonprocedural and consists of a menu-driven query language, which required some 50 responses to finish the application.

From Table 3-21, it may be seen that a fourth-generation language can have a significant impact on development and economic productivity if the application is suited for such a method.

One of the unexpected byproducts of the fourth-generation methods is the dramatic reduction in design time: Often the applications require very little in the way of flowcharting or internal design, other than defining the fields and data elements which the program will access. With fourth-generation methods, the work of design can often be subsumed in merely doing the application.

It is clear that the lines-of-source-code unit of measure is not adequate for expressing productivity in the fourth-generation environment. Table 3-22 gives the function-point rates for the same two examples:

Table 3-22. The impact of a fourth-generation language on productivity measured with function points

	Case 1: Conventional COBOL Program	Case 2: Fourth-generation program
Function points	10	10
Development cost per function point	$1,650	$200
Function points per months	3	25

If James Martin's stricture that fourth-generation languages should cause an order-of-magnitude productivity gain relative to COBOL is taken seriously, then very few products can actually achieve that goal. However, the word "productivity" itself has more than one definition and can be variously interpreted to mean schedule time, costs, or yield.

In the example shown in Tables 3-21 and 3-22, the total time savings introduced by the fourth-generation language was just under 10 to 1, while the cost savings were 8 to 1. Yield, or the ability to deliver a given set of functions for specified time and cost amounts, was improved by about 9 to 1. The tasks of working with users on requirements, plus the other peripheral activities of software development, remain significant factors even with fourth-generation languages and methods.

THE IMPACT OF GEOGRAPHIC SEPARATION
OF DEVELOPMENT SITES

Because most software projects in the industry are developed at a single location, the impact of geographic separation is not very significant in terms of the number of projects that are affected. However, for those projects that are developed at different physical locations, and especially so for projects developed jointly by several companies or enterprises, and for large international development projects, the impact is quite severe.

Multilocation and international development projects stress the coordination and communication abilities of most enterprises to their limits and are a primary justification for two rather capital-intensive technologies: full networking of voice, data, programs, and images; and the use of teleconferencing or at least telephone meetings.

In 1985, both technical and international legal issues are emerging that will have a profound impact on communication, but their final results are still unpredictable. The technological issues concern the emergence of satellite communication, local-area networks, cellular mobile telephony, and radio-linked computer communication which theoretically can make multilocation coordination a great deal easier. The legal issues involve the emerging restraints and even taxation on the transfer of technical information and data across national boundaries; these restraints are moving to restrict coordination and make it both more difficult and expensive. Added to the equation is the still-unfolding aftermath of the breakup of AT&T, which is very ambiguous in 1985 in terms of its final implications.

The costs and expense elements in multisite development are so volatile and changing so rapidly that readers are cautioned that recalculation of the costs at approximately monthly intervals would be needed to stay current with the emerging trends; currency fluctuations and the tariffs for international airfare must also be included.

Three examples are given in Table 3-23. Case 1 is for the development of a large, 250,000-source-statement COBOL system for a general business area such as inventory management, where the system is developed entirely at a single location. Case 2 is for the same system developed cooperatively among six different locations, with two of the cities being in the United States and four in Europe. This is the kind of situation in which large multinational corporations frequently find themselves involved. In Case 2, it is assumed that all six locations are networked together for voice, data, and program transfer and that teleconferencing facilities are available. Case 3 assumes the same system and the same six locations but with no network communication among them and no teleconferencing; communication between the project teams consists primarily of travel to one or another of the sites for frequent meetings. Case 3 is perhaps typical of multicompany projects where subcontractors from different enterprises are working on a common system.

Project and personnel variables. In all three cases, the system is assumed to be identical in functions and technical content: a 250,000-source-statement COBOL system intended for inventory management. The

Table 3-23 The impact of multiple development sites and communication facilities on software productivity

	Case 1: One Site	Case 2: Six sites (networked)	Case 3: Six sites (not networked)
Size in lines	250,000	250,000	250,000
Schedules (calendar months)			
Requirements	5.5	6.0	7.0
Design	17.0	18.0	20.0
Coding	11.5	13.0	15.0
Testing	12.0	14.0	15.0
Total	46.0	51.0	57.0
Overlapped	30.0	36.0	42.0
Development effort (person-months)			
Requirements	130	135	150
Travel & meetings	400	550	1,200
Design	175	250	325
Internal documentation	730	800	900
External documentation	790	900	950
Coding	420	500	600
Testing	290	325	400
Defect repairs	765	850	1,000
Management	400	550	650
Total	4,100	4,860	6,175
5-year maintenance effort			
Delivery	450	450	450
Central maintenance	455	455	455
Field maintenance	875	875	875
Total	1,780	1,780	1,780
Project total	5,880	6,640	7,955
Staff size	136	136	147
Number of trips	10	50	750
Travel costs	$ 50,000	$ 250,000	$ 3,750,000
Cost per month	$ 5,000	$ 5,000	$ 5,000
Total cost	$ 29,450,000	$ 33,450,000	$ 43,525,000
Cost per line	$117.60	$133.80	$174.10
Lines per month	61	51	40

system will be delivered to a total of 100 customer locations, from whom maintenance requests will subequently be received if needed.

In all three cases, the development teams are assumed to be skilled and experienced in the area, and the user requirements are not particularly ambiguous or troublesome.

Environmental variables. In all three cases the analysts and programmers have their own terminals and essentially unrestricted access to machine time. The specifications consist of external requirements and functional design done in English text, augmented by sample output formats.

The primary technical differences between the environments consist of the way the personnel communicate and coordinate. In Case 1, all personnel are at the same development location, and hence communicate face to face at live meetings and by phone calls and memorandums. In Case 2, four of the development locations are in Europe and two are in the U.S., but they are linked together by a network and by teleconferencing facilities. In Case 3, the same four European and two U.S. cities are involved, but there are no network or teleconferencing facilities, so communication is handled by ordinary telephone lines, by mail, by limited use of facsimile transfer, and above all by actual travel of key personnel from city to city.

Design reviews are primarily local ones within each development location, but there are key phase reviews and frequent business and strategic meetings that require involvement from managers at all locations. Technical personnel travel as the need arises to solve problems and resolve interface issues.

Although all of the six locations are working on a common project and cooperate fully, certain political problems arise during periods when it appears that a milestone or major deliverable will be late, and each location tends to point a finger at one or more of the other locations as the cause of the delay.

For Case 3, at the critical stages of integration and testing the test personnel are formed into roving teams that visit each of the six locations in turn, while one location is designated the master integration site. The code which successfully passes local integration is then shipped via courier to the master integration site for final integration and testing.

Data and code-structure variables. The COBOL examples are all well structured, but the data complexity is fairly high due to the numerous interactions. Interface problems where the opposite sides of the interface are in different geographical locations provide a major technical challenge.

In analyzing Table 3-23, the intuitive notion that distributed development is expensive is borne out. Indeed, although it is not widely recognized or covered in the literature, the travel costs for multinational software projects lacking full networks and teleconferencing tend to significantly outweigh almost any other single cost factor for the project.

For large multisite programming projects within a single country, the three chief expense elements are usually defect removal, paperwork, and travel, in that order. For multisite international projects, the chief expense element is usually travel, followed by defect removal or paperwork, depending upon the nature of the project. Regardless of the order, these three activities collectively often absorb 75% of all development resources and are the major factors to be considered in attempting to improve productivity for large multisite development projects.

Moreover, poorly supported distributed development that lacks network and teleconferencing facilities is both much more expensive and much slower than either single-location or properly supported distributed development because of the difficulty of coordinating at a distance and the slowness of turning around documents circulated for review. In addition to the direct costs for travel, significant penalties of both development time and effort must be overcome as well. Relative to single-site development, the cost penalty is perhaps 45%, while the schedule penalty is a full calendar year, or about 40% in the example shown in Table 3-23.

Large corporations with distributed development, or small corporations working cooperatively as subcontractors on larger efforts, will find it advisable to do considerable thinking and planning about communication and network facilities, so that they do not find themselves agreeing to schedules and costs that will be eroded by the high impact of travel and meeting expenses needed to coordinate multi-site and international projects.

The existence of large multisite development projects is a major reason for the business-class seating sections now featured by almost all international airlines. It is not uncommon for as many as 15 employees and managers of a major international software project to find themselves on the same flight; this raises issues regarding disaster and contingency planning that go outside the scope of this book.

Distributed and multinational development projects are comparatively rare in the software industry, except among very large corporations, but when they occur they add time and cost penalties of significant magnitude, and the topic is not covered in the standard software engineering texts.

THE IMPACT OF DEFECT POTENTIALS AND DEFECT REMOVAL METHODS

The measurement of the major causes of error in programming systems is not discussed as widely in the literature as its importance merits, although the studies of Endres (29), Basili (31), and Weiss (51) are very thorough, and a report by Gaffney gives general predictions (52).

The measurement of defect removal efficiencies appears not to be discussed at all, except in the pioneering study of Fagan (53) and the reports by the author. Yet of all of the attributes of programming that are likely to affect the perceptions of end users of the program, no topics are more important.

Defects and defect removal efficiency are discussed in this book on productivity because of the expenses involved: Defect removal costs are always among the top three expense elements for software projects (paperwork and travel are the other two high-cost items). One of the most direct and effective methods for improving productivity, therefore, is to utilize better defect prevention and defect removal technologies and hence shorten project schedules and minimize defect removal costs.

Also, while most software managers view schedules as their chief source of concern, if the resulting software is intended for the commercial market, its actual market success will be more heavily affected by customer-perceived quality than by any other factor.

The Essential Mathematics of Defect Removal

Most software projects that are released to commercial customers experience at least a three-level series of defect removal steps (desk checking, unit testing, and final testing) before release. Some experience as many as 13 steps (requirements review, top-level design review, detailed design reviews, quality assurance reviews, independent validation and verification, correctness proofs, desk checking, unit testing, function testing, component testing, system testing, field testing, and customer acceptance testing). There are basic mathematical factors surrounding defect removal that should be considered.

If the total number of defects present in the system is at some finite level, such as 50 per 1000 source code statements, and the defect removal efficiency of each removal step is fairly high, such as 80%, then it is obvious that most programs will come close to running out of bugs before they are released. For example, at 50 defects per 1000 source code statements and 80% defect removal efficiency, a three-level series of defect removal operations would yield the following:

Initial quantity of defects	50 per 1000 statements
Step 1 removal efficiency	80%
Defects removed by step 1	40 per 1000 statements
Defects left after step 1	10 per 1000 statements
Step 2 removal efficiency	80%
Defects removed by step 2	8 per 1000 statements
Defects left after Step 2	2 per 1000 statements
Step 3 removal efficiency	80%
Defects removed by step 3	1.6 per 1000 statements
Defects Left after step 3	0.4 per 1000 statements
Latent defects at delivery	0.4 per 1000 statements

Most commercial software projects whose postdelivery defect rates have been quantified appear to have in the vicinity of at least 4 or 5 defects per 1000 source code statements at delivery. There are two possible explanations:

1. The defect potentials of the programs may be higher than 50 per 1000 source statements, and
2. The defect removal efficiencies may average less than 80%.

Both these conditions appear to be true. From considering the mathematics of commercial software's defect removal activities, it is obvious that a 7- to 13-level series of defect removal activities, even with efficiencies of 50%, would essentially exhaust any realistic quantity of defects before delivery to customers. From the fact that defects are not exhausted, it may be inferred that removal efficiencies may be less than 50% or that the starting quantity of defects may be in excess of 100 per 1000 source code statements.

The highest proportion of defects actually observed by the author was 274 per 1000 source code statements, when the sum of the defects found during reviews, inspections, and testing were accumulated for several modules of a commercial program. The highest proportion of defects observed after delivery of a commercial program to customers was 31 per 1000 source code statements, when the first 3 years of customer-reported defects were summed. (Both programs, incidentally, were written in Assembler language.)

The lowest defect removal efficiency observed by the author for a four-level series of defect removal steps was 44%; the removal series consisted of unit test, function test, component test, and system test. The lowest efficiency for one step was in a unit test of a single module, where the efficiency was approximately 13%. (The defects found during this series were compared to those found in the first 2 years of customer usage, and it was noted that 56% of the total discovered defects came in from the customers. The highest efficiency observed by the author for the same series of steps was 84%, incidentally, which occurred 2 years later on a subsequent release of the same product, for which significant improvements in defect removal methods had been introduced.)

While these anecdotes have no statistical relevance, the underlying mathematical situation is inescapable: Unless defect potentials are higher than 50 per 1000 source lines and defect removal efficiencies are lower than 50% per step, programs should run out of defects before delivery. This plainly is not the case.

The general formula under which defect removal efficiency is measured is:

$$\text{Efficiency} = \frac{\text{defects found}}{\text{defects found} + \text{defects not found}}$$

The part of the formula difficult to apply in real life is "defects not found." When measuring the efficiency of a given removal activity, such as unit test, there is no way to know how many defects were not found by the test. The custom which this book adopts is to keep track of all subsequent defects, found from the removal step being measured through the rest of the development cycle and then for a certain time after delivery to the customer. Usually a period of 2 years after delivery is adequate to form an approximation of defect removal efficiency.

As an example of the above general formula, say that a unit test of a module found 20 defects, subsequent testing before release found another 70, and 2 years of customer usage found 10; then the approximate efficiency of the unit test would appear to be 20%, since 80 defects out of the total of 100 were found after that activity.

It should be noted that this technique is subject to error from a variety of sources. Defects in additional functions created after the measures begin is one of the chief sources of error. Another source of error, to be discussed presently, are "bad fixes," or fresh bugs introduced as a result of repairing previous bugs. However, in spite of the error margin, which may reach 30%, the method gives a useful approximation of the day-to-day efficiencies of defect removal methods. At the very least, the method dilutes the widespread optimism that defects might be "tested out" of a program, since it usually yields efficiencies of less than 50% per step, and cumulative efficiencies are often less than 75% for all predelivery defect removal methods summed together.

A second way of assessing defect removal efficiency is to "seed" a program with a known quantity of defects prior to a removal step such as system testing. If the removal step finds, for example, 60% of the seeded defects, then it can be asserted that the efficiency of the removal operation is in the vicinity of 60%. However, few enterprises actually practice defect seeding.

Defect Potentials

Although Endres has described almost 200 kinds of software defects, a simpler six-category system is sufficient for day-to-day practical work. A defect is roughly defined as a problem which if not removed would cause the system to either produce incorrect outputs or to stop its operation. The six categories and a brief explanation of their meaning follow:

1. *Requirements defects.* This category refers to user requirements that are either mutually inconsistent, so ambiguous as to be prone to more than one interpretation, or missing even though logically necessary.

2. *Design defects*. These include requirements that are accidentally omitted from the design; overt design errors, such as inappropriate segmentation of a system into components and modules; and detailed design errors that may overlap coding errors, such as failing to validate incoming data before using it for processsing.
3. *Coding defects*. This category refers to defects that are not traceable to precursor requirements or design problems. It includes such common problems as looping too often or not often enough, branching to incorrect locations, and incorrect setting of switches or incorrect interpretation of switch settings.
4. *Documentation defects*. Documentation defects are often problems in the user's guides or menus supporting software projects: examples that don't work, missing information, ambiguous text passages, failure to put explanations in manuals at the places where the topics are logically expected, and the like.
5. *Administrative defects*. These are common with commercial software marketed to many customers. This category includes sending customers a back level or incorrect disk or tape, losing customer defect reports, or failing to respond at all.
6. *Bad fixes*. As the name implies, bad fixes are new bugs that are accidentally injected into a program as a result of trying to fix previous bugs. This category of defects is much more common than might be expected.

The rationale for having only six broad categories of defects, rather than a more granular set of categories, is that these six categories appear to be the minimum set that clearly distinguish between defect origins and thereby allow rational defect prevention strategies to be planned in response. For example, if owners of a commercial software product discover 40% of incoming customer problem reports are either for bugs in the user documentation or for being sent the wrong patch, they might very well explore the need for improved technical writing and tighter administrative controls.

The defect potentials of a program are dependent variables that cannot be predicted in isolation. They are the end results of the interactions of the novelty of the program or system to be developed, the skills of the development personnel, the design and coding methods selected, and several other factors as well. Indeed, the number of interacting variables needed to predict defect potentials is so large that only computer-aided methods are convenient for analysis.

What is a surprise to most researchers who have access to fairly complete counts of defects is the unexpectedly large numbers that often occur. Table 3-24 gives a few examples based on projects observed by the author.

Table 3-24 Observed defect quantities and origins for representative programming systems

	Case 1	Case 2	Case 3	Case 4	Case 5
Size	1K	20K	200K	250K	350K
Language	BASIC	COBOL	COBOL	Assembler	Assembler
Type	Application	Application	Application	System	Real-time
Defect origins	Number of defects by category				
Requirements	4	220	1,800	1,750	4,900
Design	6	280	2,600	5,500	8,050
Coding	30	360	2,400	7,500	9,800
Documentation	10	160	1,400	2,750	4,200
Administration	0	20	110	550	1,300
Bad fixes	12	130	1,600	3,300	4,850
Totals	62	1,170	9,910	21,350	33,100
Defects per 1000 lines	62	58.5	49.5	85.4	94.6

For small programs, such as shown by Case 1, coding errors appear to be the chief source of trouble. As programs grow larger, and as they become full-scale systems, the relative impact of coding errors tends to diminish as errors attributable to requirements and design become more severe.

The Common Forms of Defect Removal Methods

There are more than 40 varieties of defect removal methods in use for software projects, their accompanying documentation, and other deliverables:

Removing defects in requirements and design

1. Personal editing
2. Reader/author cycles of others' work
3. Management reviews
4. Informal group design reviews
5. Group structured walkthroughs
6. Quality assurance reviews
7. Formal group inspections
8. Independent verification and validation
9. Design simulation or modeling
10. Formal proofs of correctness

Removing coding defects

1. Personal desk checking
2. Code reading by a peer

3. Code reading by a manager
4. Code reading by a chief programmer
5. Informal code reviews
6. Group structured walkthroughs
7. Formal code inspections
8. Quality assurance review
9. Modeling or prototyping code
10. Unit testing of individual modules
11. Function testing of related modules
12. Integration testing of all modules
13. Quality assurance testing of all modules
14. Simulation testing
15. Stress and performance testing
16. Regression testing
17. Field testing
18. Customer acceptance testing

Removing defects in user documentation and training material

1. Personal review by author
2. Reader/author cycles of others' work
3. Review by manager
4. Professional editing
5. Quality assurance review
6. Automated dictionary and grammar checkers
7. Customer reviews
8. Usage of documentation with system prototypes
9. Prototyping educational materials
10. Trial usage of documentation and educational materials
11. Independent verification and validation
12. Professional proofreading

Removing defects in supporting and peripheral material

1. Personal reviews by authors
2. Audits of project status
3. Phase reviews
4. Quality assurance review of plans
5. Formal document inspections of plans
6. Independent verification and validation

As of 1985, there are no thorough or exhaustive studies that cover the costs, efficiencies, and general applicability of these various defect removal methods. From observational data by the author on internal IBM programs and from the pioneering studies of Fagan on defect removal methods, it is possible to state the approximate ranges of efficiency for a subset of the most common defect removal methods and to discuss the approximate costs for those methods as well.

It is unfortunate that so important a topic has so few controlled studies to back up the claims and assertions that are common in the literature. For example, correctness proofs are now becoming widely recommended, but no hard evidence has yet been published to demonstrate that the operational reliability of programs that used correctness proofs is any better than the reliability of those that did not.

Following are short discussions of the commoner types of defect removal methods, for which some quantitative information is available.

Removing defects in requirements and design. Although many industry studies have concluded that requirements and design problems are the chief source of error in all programming systems (other than very small ones), there is a shortage of reliable information on the quantitative successes or failures of various aspects of defect removal in rectifying this situation. The previously mentioned studies of Fagan and a series of interviews with software practitioners and managers provide the source of the methods listed for removing requirements defects.

Of the common methods for removing requirements and design errors, the weight of available evidence indicates that formal group inspections and design simulation or modeling where users are able to work with running examples of the program's functions have the highest overall efficiencies, and alone may remove in excess of 65% of the requirements and design problems. Personal editing of one's own work has not been reported on in the literature, but experiments by the author on his own program designs indicate a low efficiency of 30% or less. Quality assurance reviews, if properly staffed, seem to be moderately successful, but their efficiency is only speculative. The most controversial of the methods for removing design defects is the correctness proof; there are many references to this topic in the literature but essentially none that demonstrate that the operational reliability of programs proved correct is any higher than that of programs that use only conventional defect removal methods.

In terms of balancing schedules, costs, and resources against quality, the most successful approach may be a combination of (1) formal design inspections for the critical functions of a system, (2) prototyping or modeling its major outputs so users can see the results, and (3) informal reviews and standard testing.

Testing alone, with no precursor reviews, models, or prototypes, is invariably inefficient and is usually expensive as well. One of the classic causes of late delivery schedules is that of shortcutting reviews or prototyping in order to start testing early, and then finding that the program doesn't work and can't be made to work without extensive redesign.

Removing coding defects. Although testing is the most widely used method for finding coding errors, the measured efficiencies of all forms of testing are distressingly low and usually less than 50% for common test steps, such as unit test, function test, component test, and system test. The cumulative efficiency of the whole series may total less than 75%. Not only is testing alone inefficient in terms of defect removal, but the costs are quite high.

Testing costs are seldom discussed clearly in the software engineering literature, because the common usage of cost per defect as a productivity indicator tends to distort the costs and lead to major misunderstandings.

Testing costs, like any other kind of defect removal, have three separate elements of expense that need to be evaluated:

1. Preparation costs, or writing the test cases, putting them in a test library, and preparing the test scripts or scenarios. This cost element is not dependent upon the number of defects and will stay relatively flat even for programs that approach or achieve zero-defect status.
2. Execution costs, or running the test series and writing fault reports for any errors that are discovered. This cost element is roughly proportional to the number of defects in the program, but even for zero-defect code the test library must still be exercised at least once, so the costs never drop to zero even if defect levels do.
3. Defect repair costs, or fixing the bugs that have been identified by the test process. Defect repair costs are directly proportional to the number of defects in a program, and this cost element alone can drop to zero if the code achieves zero-defect status. Since most test cycles tend to uncover 3 to 20 defects per 1000 source lines, in day-to-day testing this is the largest cost element, but the one with the greatest amount of uncertainty and fluctuation.

The way the three major variables interact is so complex and so prone to dramatic fluctuation that only computerized predictive methods allow reasonably accurate and convenient estimation of testing and other defect removal costs.

Another problem with testing is the fact that both test plans and test cases themselves often contain defects, and indeed an informal study by the author in 1975 at IBM indicated that the error density in the test materials for a program exceeded the error density in the program itself. Fagan points out the need to inspect the test materials themselves.

So far as can be determined from the literature to date, formal code inspections and modeling or prototyping the final code (using some kind of interpretive language such as APL or BASIC, or at least using a fourth-generation query language if it is an MIS project) provide the highest efficiencies in code defect removal, at more or less moderate costs. Only those two methods appear to consistently rise above 60% in overall defect removal efficiency.

Field testing with live data in customer environments is also efficient, but it comes so late in the development cycle that any major design or requirements errors noted will be found too late for convenient repair.

Long-term production running with the full set of customers is the only method that approaches 100% in defect removal efficiency, although at substantial cost and often great embarrassment for developers and aggravation for users of the programs.

The sales of millions of microcomputers to both enterprises and private owners is bringing with it new problems and new cost elements relative to defect repairs. A program with a large number of users, such as the 250,000 or so licensed customers of major spreadsheet programs introduces enormous overhead costs in defect repairs. A recall or replacement of a high-usage program because of severe errors could drive small companies out of business. For such reasons, software and hardware companies are exploring alternative methods for receiving fault reports and distributing repairs, such as the use of the information utilities or a central site for downloading repairs directly into users' computers.

Removing defects in user documentation and training. A short and informal study by the author of approximately 150 software and hardware reviews in *InfoWorld*, *BYTE*, *Personal Computing*, and *Creative Computing* revealed that over 75% of the reviewers commented that the documentation was difficult to understand and poorly written, while almost half found errors of fact that were sufficient to slow down the evaluation of the program.

The publications profession has long had a variety of effective methods for eliminating technical and stylistic errors in professional materials, which include referees, professional technical editors, professional proofreaders, pilot studies, style guides, and skeleton outlines. However, such methods tend to be time-consuming and also expensive, and the fact appears to be that most software user information is written in a hurry and rushed out without adequate controls.

One of the most effective methods for minimizing documentation problems, which couples both defect prevention and defect removal aspects, is the use of patterns or archetypes for document construction. In other words, find the documents that have been the biggest sellers or the most popular with users, and copy their style and structure. Some years ago, IBM carried out an analysis of the comments forms and letters from readers about IBM manuals and then selected the most popular reference manuals and tutorials to be used as patterns for future manuals. These manuals were used as training aids for new writers, and the results appeared reasonably successful, judging by the comments on the subsequent manuals produced using these patterns.

One of the major complaints noted in the study of software and hardware reviews carried out by the author was the failure of examples to actually work. Few things are more frustrating to a user seeking to learn a new program than to copy an example keystroke for keystroke, only to have it fail. The cardinal rule of defect removal against documentation is that all examples should be tried out and should work exactly as stated.

The emergence of Apple Computer's new Macintosh, of the Xerox Star, and of the Graphics Environment Manager product of Digital Research is introducing a new form of user documentation termed "iconographic," which means roughly that pictures or icons, rather than conventional text, are used to represent basic functions and objects. This form of documentation is likely to bring new and special requirements for defect removal, but the topic is new enough so that controlled studies have not yet been published.

In terms of training users in new products, conventional instruction using live instructors, texts, and case studies has a long history of being effective in removing defects. However, the conventional instruction methods are expensive. The emerging optical storage technology should soon be introducing computer-controlled, linked video, audio, textual, and graphic instructional material as the new standard methodology. This field is still too new for the most effective defect removal methods to be clear, although some methods such as pilot studies and prerelease validation, will be carried on in different forms.

Removing defects in supporting and peripheral material. Not only are the specifications, code, and user documentation sources of error in programming projects, but so are the business and planning documents, such as cost estimates, forecasts, development plans, schedules, and even job accounting for hours and dollars expended. Several projects have notably overrun their budgets because of serious errors in support materials. For example, a programming manager once neglected to include the cost of writing user documentation in the cost estimate for a new project, which escaped notice until after the bid had been accepted.

Since development cost estimates, development schedules, and market forecasts appear to be in error more often than not, a major field of endeavor which is not adequately covered in either the technical or business literature surrounding software is determining the efficiency and cost-effectiveness of the methods for eliminating defects in supporting plans.

Many descriptions of programming life cycles assume that reviews between key phases, such as between requirements and design or between design and coding, will be effective in providing early warnings and heading off trouble. This seems not to be the case. Indeed, the author has seen no evidence in real life, or citations in the literature, that indicate that projects are actually canceled or redirected as a result of normal phase reviews. Usually it is an audit or some extraordinary management or customer action that triggers the redirection.

One of the most widespread and apparently effective methods used for evaluating the supporting plans of commercial software projects is the customer review, while a second is the use of outside consultants, although no quantitative information has been published on either topic.

The IBM Corporation has had unusual success in defect removal in supporting plans and documents by requiring that the Quality Assurance Department sign off on the accuracy and adequacy of the plans before a product can be announced to the external world or delivered to customers. While there are ways of appealing and overriding what IBM calls "nonconcurrences" by quality assurance, those ways are usually seldom resorted to. The origin of this effective but uncommon approach and the unusual power that the Quality Assurance Department possesses in IBM, stem from some of the antitrust allegations that asserted IBM would announce products which they could not deliver. IBM determined that anything announced would be deliverable and gave quality assurance strong powers to ensure that all claims were valid.

Although only a subset of the industry's defect removal activities have been measured for the efficiency, the topic is significant enough to report what findings there are, even if the information is drawn from uncontrolled observations. Table 3-25 gives the approximate ranges of efficiencies observed for 10 common defect removal methods.

There are several thought-provoking aspects to Table 3-25. One of them is that the modal efficiencies do not rise above 65% per removal step (except for the comparatively rare use of prototypes), and even the highest efficiencies do not rise above 80% per step. This means if a project is striving toward high reliability and a cumulative defect removal efficiency for a whole series in the 95% range or higher, it is necessary to string together a well-planned series of reviews, inspections, and tests, with each step aimed at the class of defect where the step's efficiency is greatest.

Although the supporting evidence is not conclusive in 1985, it can be stated that less than a five-level series at average efficiencies will not yield a cumulative efficiency high enough to be really effective for commercial software. For example, a three-level series of unit testing, function testing, and system testing will often return cumulative efficiencies of less than 60% for the entire series, which is inadequate for commercially marketed programs.

Table 3-25 Observed ranges of defect removal efficiency for programming defect removal methods

Removal step	Lowest efficiency	Modal efficiency	Highest efficiency
Personal checking of design or documents	15%	35%	70%
Informal group design reviews	30%	40%	60%
Formal design inspections	35%	55%	75%
Formal code inspections	30%	60%	70%
Modeling or prototyping	35%	65%	80%
Personal desk checking of code	20%	40%	60%
Unit testing (single modules)	10%	25%	50%
Function testing (related modules)	20%	35%	55%
Integration testing (complete system)	25%	45%	60%
Field testing (live data)	35%	50%	65%
Cumulative efficiency of complete series	93%	99%	99%

In searching for a balance between defect removal efficiency, schedules, and costs, the weight of evidence indicates that a series which skips or omits design reviews and design inspections will suffer from high tail-end costs, when the undiscovered bugs start showing up during integration and testing.

The most effective combination today appears to be (1) formal design inspections of the critical sections of a system, (2) modeling or prototyping using a high-speed method such as an interpreted language, and (3) normal testing. The extra time and effort at the front for the inspections and prototyping will be compensated for by very short test cycles, with low defect repair and minimal overtime costs.

Removing Defects in Error-Prone Modules
In the late 1960s, IBM's Endicott laboratory carried out a frequency analysis of the field-reported defects against IBM's OS/360 operating system and discovered a surprising skew. The defect reports appeared not to be smoothly or randomly distributed through the code, but instead tended to clump in a fairly small number of modules with very high error

rates. Studies of other systems, both within IBM and by other companies, revealed that error-prone modules occurred in virtually all large systems and were responsible for a high percentage of overall defect repairs and overall maintenance costs.

Error-prone modules, as they came to be called, were soon revealed to be the most expensive entities in programming. These modules sometimes contained more than 50 defects per 1000 lines of source code after delivery to customers and in some cases were almost responsible for withdrawing the products from usage.

Fixing the defects in the error-prone modules often costs more than the development expenses by an order of magnitude for products with many customers and with delivery support and field maintenance. Moreover, a point was usually reached where the error-prone modules had been patched so often that they tended to become difficult to maintain any further. IBM, for example, embarked on a fairly effective program of redesigning and recoding the error-prone modules in IMS over a 3-year period, which ultimately led to an overall reduction of about 45% in maintenance costs and reduction of an order of magnitude in field-reported defect reports.

Although some 30 different factors have been identified as causative agents for error-prone modules, there are three major ones that account for more than 90% of all cases yet observed:

1 *Individual human errors.* It often happens that programmers are not properly trained in a particular application area or even in structured programming methods, and they often get assigned to projects that exceed their current abilities.
2 *Lack of design or specifications.* Almost a third of the error-prone modules studied by the author had never been formally tested after unit test. Some were not intrinsically bad modules, but the lack of any test coverage simply allowed all latent defects to exit to the outside world. In tracing back to find out why this occurred, what was an initially surprising observation occurred: Most of the untested error-prone modules had no written designs or specifications, and the testing groups were not aware of their existence. This situation often occurred when requirements and design changes were introduced fairly late in the development cycle. The introduction of early design inspections, code inspections, and a requirement to make new inspections after every major functional or code addition essentially eliminated this source of the error-prone module.
3 *Size of the modules.* A majority of the error-prone modules in the IBM systems studied were larger than 500 source lines. Large modules tend to exceed the capacity of most human minds in terms of the internal structures and data interactions. (Modules smaller than 50 lines tend

not to have sufficient functionality and hence make frequent calls to other modules.) Modules larger than 500 lines tend to become error-prone in more or less direct correlation to their sizes.

Once the importance of error-prone modules is understood, there are two practical strategies for eliminating them: one for new projects, and one for existing projects already in use.

For new projects still undergoing development, the strategy is to query the designers and programmers about which sections of the system are the most difficult and then give those sections extra inspections and very thorough testing. No code that lacks specifications and design documentation is allowed to be added to the system.

For existing operational systems, the strategy is to scan the fault reports for peaks or spikes, and then do a formal code inspection on any module that has accumulated more than 10 defects per 1000 source statements in the last year or 18 months. If the enterprise has large systems but lacks a defect-reporting method of sufficient granularity to do this, then there is a very high probability of unsuspected error-prone modules. A fallback is to interview the system programmers doing maintenance and get their subjective opinions on the topic.

Two examples of defect removal's impact on schedules and productivity are given in Tables 3-26 and 3-27. Case 1 shows an average defect removal cycle as practiced on the internal software which enterprises

Table 3-26 Defect potentials and removal efficiencies for internal and commercial software projects

	Case 1: Internal system	Case 2: Commercial system
Size in lines (COBOL)	250,000	250,000
Defect potentials (all types)	20,350	20,350
Reviews and inspections of defect removal efficiency	60%	76%
Defects still present at integration and testing	8,140	4,884
Defect removal efficiency of testing	56%	74%
Defects still present at delivery	3,581	1,269
Mean time to failure at day of delivery (hours)	0.36	1.75
Time after delivery until product stabilizes (months)	9	5

Table 3-27 The impact of defect removal methods on project schedules and resources

	Case 1: Internal program	Case 2: Commercial program
Size in lines (COBOL)	250,000	250,000
Schedules (calendar months)		
Requirements	5.5	5.5
Design	13.5	16.5
Coding	9.5	11.0
Testing	15.5	12.0
Total	44.0	45.0
Overlapped	27.0	28.0
Development effort (person-months)		
Requirements	99	117
Design	139	161
Internal documentation	75	175
External documentation	125	325
Coding	395	395
Testing	282	275
Defect repairs	671	763
Management	255	353
Total	2,041	2,564
5-year maintenance effort		
Delivery	0	0
Central maintenance	1,408	460
Field maintenance	0	0
Total	1,408	460
Project total	3,449	3,024
Staff size	75	91
Cost per month	$5,000	$5,000
Total cost	$17,245,000	$15,120,000
Cost per line	$68.98	$60.48
Lines per month	122	97

develop for their own usage: personal desk checking, informal group design review, unit testing, function testing, and integration or system testing.

Case 2 shows the more rigorous defect removal series utilized by major software-producing corporations for marketed products: personal desk checking; formal design inspections; formal code inspections; test plan and test case inspections; user documentation inspections; and a full test cycle of unit testing, function testing, system testing, and field testing at selected customer locations with live data.

Project and personnel variables. Both projects are 250,000-source-statement COBOL applications for general business purposes, such as accounting. Case 1, the internal project, has only a single user, the enterprise which develops the program. Case 2, the marketed product, has 1000 customers that are authorized to submit defect reports in case of trouble. Although a software product of this magnitude would normally have both delivery support and field service, those two aspects of the project have been blanked out to show the essential comparisons.

Both examples are developed at a single location, so there is no travel at all. Neither example has any particular constraints on speed or memory utilization. The analysts and programmers in both examples are familiar with the application area and need no special training.

Environmental variables. In both cases, the analysts and programmers have their own terminals and essentially unrestricted access to machine time. The analysts and programmers in both examples use English text augmented by output formats for functional design, and the two systems are both fairly well structured using the method of Constantine-Myers-Stevens.

Data and code-structure variables. Both examples are fairly well structured COBOL systems. The data complexity is moderately high.

Table 3-26 gives the defect potentials and removal efficiencies, and Table 3-27 gives the resource information.

As surprising at it seems when first encountered, achieving a high level of defect removal efficiency actually tends to lower software costs and can even benefit schedules, compared to the ordinary, somewhat ineffective series of reviews and tests that most projects utilize. The reason for this is that if the troublesome requirements-and-design-based defects can be eliminated prior to integration and testing, then the usual rash of overtime and around-the-clock defect repairs that often occur are eliminated also.

In comparing the two projects shown in Tables 3-26 and 3-27, note that the net development schedule difference between them is 1 calendar month. However, the testing schedule is 3 months shorter for Case 2, the project that used full inspections prior to testing. (The 2-month net schedule increase actually is not a function of defect removal at all but is caused by the second project's need to produce commercial-grade external manuals and training materials.)

Even more significant from the point of view of overall schedule, the internal project required 9 months after its initial installation to achieve a stable trouble-free status, for a true schedule of 36 months from project startup to stable run mode. The commercial project, on the other hand, with a 5-month stabilization period after delivery, required only 33 months from project startup to stable running. While delivery dates are the factors project managers usually worry about, achieving a stable and trouble-free operational system is in many ways a more significant milestone.

The overall life-cycle costs are revealing: It is slightly cheaper to have a high defect removal efficiency than it is to have a low one. An unpublished analysis of IBM's delivered software systems, carried out by the author between 1973 and 1978, revealed the interesting conclusion that those systems with the lowest defect rates in field use were also the systems with the lowest incidences of slipped schedules and delayed deliveries, and they also had somewhat higher productivity.

The fundamental thesis that can be derived from observations on software defect rates and defect removal efficiency is both surprising and counterintuitive: Projects that aim from the beginning at achieving the shortest possible schedules regardless of quality considerations, tend to have fairly high frequencies of both schedule and cost overruns. Software projects that aim initially at achieving the highest possible levels of quality and reliability tend to have the best schedule adherence records, the highest productivity, and even the best marketplace success.

THE IMPACT OF PROGRAMMING DOCUMENTATION

While small software projects have relatively low documentation costs, the cost of documentation for large systems is very high. For commercially marketed software, contractually produced software, and both civilian government and military software, documentation costs will invariably be among the top three items in terms of effort and expense; not infrequently documentation will be the most expensive of all, with defect removal and travel costs, the other two competitors for the highest-cost place, dropping to second and third place.

For many years, the programming, software engineering, and cost-estimating literature contained very few references to documentation costs, with the result that until quite recently very few tools have been aimed at solving software documentation problems. For example, in spite of the fact that documentation to military specification standards causes paperwork costs to be the largest item in military contract software, the proposed Ada environment as of 1983 had essentially no plans for documentation support—an omission of a significant nature.

From 1968 through 1979 the author intermittently studied the documentation requirements, tools, and packages used within the IBM corporation. It had become obvious that the incoming specification sets were critical factors in both the workload and the quality of the user documentation being produced and that the whole topic of paperwork needed analysis.

The total set of documents produced by IBM in support of software products fell naturally into eight different categories:

1. Planning documents, comprising the technical and marketing strategies for emerging products
2. Control documents, or periodic reports of actual performance contrasted to expected performance, with monthly budget variance reports being typical
3. Business and financial documents, or cost estimates, forecasts, and the like
4. Technical documents, comprising the requirements, objectives, and functional and logic specifications for the software projects
5. Explanatory documents, comprising the user's guides and maintenance manuals and the educational materials aimed at teaching users and IBM personnel how the systems operate
6. Marketing documents, or sales brochures, price lists, and the like, which describe the products to customers and sales personnel.
7. Correspondence, or internal memorandums regarding a project, which circulated among the project personnel and between the various IBM divisions
8. Miscellaneous documents, comprising mostly flipcharts, viewgraphs, and meeting agendas

The number of specific documents required by the IBM Corporation in support of major software projects totaled 81 when all eight categories were summed. Following is a list of the specific documents noted circa 1979:

Large-system planning documents

Marketing plan
Comprehensive evaluation plan
Build and integration plan
Quality assurance checkpoint plan
Product distribution and support plan
Performance measurement plan
Audience requirement statement
Information implementation plan
Design review plan
Inspection plan
Information inspection plan
Information test plan

Unit test plan
Functional test plan
Component test plan
System test plan
Field test plan

Large-system control documents

Monthly budget variance reports
Monthly computer utilization reports
Quality assurance tracking reports
Quality assurance checkpoint reports
Quality assurance announcement concurrence reports
Quality assurance delivery concurrence reports
Monthly project highlight reports
Test status reports
Phase review reports
Build and integration reports
Design review reports
Inspection reports
Project postmortems

Large-system business and financial documents

Forecast assumptions
Market forecast
Cost estimates (one per product for each of six phases)
Department budgets
Capital expenditures
Travel authorization

Large-system technical documents

Programming requirements and objectives
Information requirements and objectives
Reliability and serviceability requirements and objectives
Performance requirements and objectives
Initial functional specifications
Final functional specifications
Logic specifications
System structure document
Component structure document
Design change requests
Prerelease defect reports
Postrelease defect reports

Large-system explanatory documents

Introduction
Installation guide
Principles of operation
User's guide
Programmers' guide
System programmer's guide
Operations manual
Messages and codes
Maintenance manual

Large-system marketing documents

Announcement letter
Sales manual updates
Brochures

Large-system correspondence

Standards compliance memorandum
Vital records retention memorandum
Phase review invitations
Inspection invitations
Audit invitations
Trip reports
Technical concurrence or nonconcurrence memoranda
Other correspondence

Large-system miscellaneous documents

Flipcharts
Viewgraphs
Meeting agendas
Meeting minutes

The IBM documentation set is not unusual in the world of large commercial programming systems, and the rather lengthy list of titles is intended to make plain a very important fact: Programming systems exist "on paper" for sometimes many years before they exist in real life, and the cumulative costs of creating, reading, reviewing, and updating the artificial paper system is often a much greater portion of life-cycle costs than the code itself. In fact, for some international systems where the informational materials are translated into different languages, the actual

Table 3-28 Documentation set produced for IBM's IMS/360 Version 2.3

Document categories	Number of documents	Number of pages	Number of words
Planning	14	2,654	1,327,264
Control	13	1,990	995,448
Financial	4	330	165,000
Technical	10	12,277	6,138,596
Informational	5	5,309	2,654,528
Official correspondence	6	2,322	1,161,356
Miscellaneous	2	1,324	33,101
Totals	54	26,206	12,475,293

cost of coding will not even be in the top four expense elements—paperwork, travel, defect removal, and delivery support.

Within IBM, as elsewhere, not every document is required or created for every system, and especially not for functional enhancements to existing systems. The mode or average within IBM is to produce somewhere between 50 and 60 document sets for any given product.

Table 3-28 gives the approximate count of the documentation produced for IMS/360 Version 2.3, which consisted of 165,908 lines of Assembler language source code. The data was collected by means of sampling and extrapolation, so it is not as accurate as it appears, but it is close enough to reality to demonstrate the basic point that documentation is an activity that can not be ignored or left out of software planning without peril.

Since IMS/360 Version 2.3 consisted of approximately 166K lines of source code, Table 3-28 indicates a level of 157 pages per 1000 source statements, or 75 English words for every line of source code delivered to customers.

Note that almost half of the total documentation, or pages and words, are found in the set of technical documents, comprising the requirements, functional specifications, logic specifications, and several other document types. This observation led to a more detailed analysis of system design documentation, published by the author in 1979 (54), which contained some initially surprising findings:

1. Documentation quantities were not linearly related to program size: For programs of 1000 through about 128,000 source statements, documentation grew faster than code size. Above 128,000 source statements, documentation size began to grow more slowly and even decline. Figure 3-1 contains the general curve derived from this study.
2. The completeness of programming system design began to decline

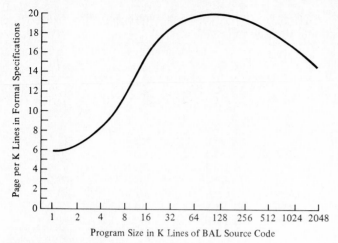

Figure 3-1 Relationship between program size and design documentation quantities in the sum of requirements, functional design, and logic design.

steadily as a function of program size, from a high of perhaps 98% of functions being described in the documentation set to a low of less than 60% for very large systems. This observation was derived by working backward from program listings and noting what functions were or were not described in the system specifications. Figure 3-2 gives the curve that was developed for specification completeness.

The overall conclusion that stems from Figures 3-1 and 3-2 is that if programming systems were developed only from the written specifica-

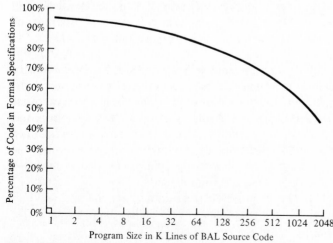

Figure 3-2 Relationship between program size and the completeness of specifications and design.

Table 3-29 Specification preparation times in hours for production of requirements, functional design, and logic design

Program size (thousands of lines)	Longhand drafts	Text entry	Graphics	Total
1	4.5	0.75	1.35	6.6
2	10.5	1.75	3.15	15.6
4	24.0	4.0	7.2	35.2
8	60.0	10.0	18.0	88.0
16	192.0	32.0	58.0	282.0
32	480.0	80.0	144.0	704.0
64	1,008.0	168.0	302.0	1,478.0
128	2,112.0	352.0	634.0	3,098.0
256	4,032.0	672.0	1,210.0	5,914.0
512	7,680.0	1,280.0	2,304.0	11,264.0
1024	14,874.0	2,304.0	4,462.0	21,840.0

tions, large-system programming would perhaps be impossible. However, in real life the project personnel are able to compensate for the lack of completeness in the specifications by meetings, telephone calls, memorandums, and similar ways of keeping one another informed of the true status.

Another conclusion, which is not intuitively obvious but which has both theoretical and practical support, is that it is not possible to fully specify the functions of a large system by using only English text, since for systems of 1,000,000 source statements and up, the complete specifications would be large enough so that they would tend to go beyond the lifetime reading capacity of development personnel.

At the time this study of design methods was done in the 1970s, interactive graphics systems were comparatively rare in support of software projects, and most U.S. systems were specified in English text augmented by hand-drawn diagrams such as flowcharts or HIPO diagrams, with some low-level informal pseudocode. Since only a minority of design personnel were touch-typists, the mode of operation was to draft the design longhand, turn it over to a text preparation group for input into a system (if indeed word processing systems were even used), and then interpolate the graphics manually. Using this mode of specification development, Table 3-29 gives the approximate number of hours of longhand drafting, text entry, and graphics preparation found within IBM circa 1977, with the data normalized to thousands of lines of Assembler.

Note that Table 3-29 covers only the essentially mechanical tasks of writing and producing the design; the mental effort, the dialogs with users, and the travel (if any) are not shown.

As time-consuming and expensive as paperwork preparation is for software projects, it is not the largest documentation expense. Reading

Table 3-30 Large-system programming specification distribution list recipients and the quantity of documentation read

Number of recipients	Percentage of material stated as read
10	100
10	50
20	25
40	10
80	5
20	<5
180	<15

the documents is considerably more expensive, because so many people have to read them. Within IBM on typical large-system projects, the primary distribution lists for technical documents average over 75 names, while the distribution lists for major products such as a new operating system sometimes have more than 200 names.

It is true that not everyone on the distribution lists actually reads everything. An informal survey by the author was based on one of the IBM distribution lists to find out how many of the recipients actually did read the materials sent to them. Table 3-30 gives the results; but note that the study was a single sample and was not controlled, although the findings are interesting.

Even though a relatively low overall percentage of material is read, reading costs still total significantly more than document production costs for medium to large commercial software projects developed in typical enterprises with internal checks and balances and sizable internal distribution lists.

However, even reading costs may not be the most expensive aspect of programming paperwork, and there is fairly clear evidence that one other item outprices it: the face-to-face meetings and discussions between development personnel to discuss what has been written and reviewed, and even more significantly, what gaps have been noted. Since perfectly clear and lucid specifications appear not to exist, nor do perfectly designed and specified systems, the largest cost item surrounding paperwork appears to be trying to compensate for documentation shortcomings by means of face-to-face meetings. However, since the meetings usually cover a broad range of topics, it is not possible to break out the exact percentage devoted to compensating for specification and documentation shortcomings.

Within IBM, programming development managers appeared to average more than 15 hours per week in meetings, for medium-sized and large projects involving multiple departments. Assuming a nominal 40-hour week, that makes live meetings a good candidate for the most expensive single activity of programming development management, with reading and document creation in second and third place. Note that since managers are only 12% to 15% of a project's staff, and technical meetings occur less frequently, the overall impact of meetings on a project's total effort is lower: perhaps 10%.

To demonstrate the impact of documentation, two examples are shown in Table 3-31. Case 1 is for a 50,000-source-statement COBOL project intended for internal use, where the documentation consists of normal internal project plans and specifications that are merely printed on a line printer and informally distributed. Case 2 is for an identical 50,000-source-statment COBOL project, which differs from the first only in that it is intended for commercial marketing, and hence both the project

Table 3-31 The impact of documentation volumes on project schedules and resources

	Case 1: Internal program	Case 2: Commercial program
Size in lines (COBOL)	50,000	50,000
Schedules (calendar months)		
Requirements	4.0	4.0
Design	8.0	9.0
Coding	5.5	5.5
Testing	6.0	6.0
Total	23.5	24.5
Overlapped	15.0	16.0
Development effort (person-months)		
Requirements	20	27
Design	35	39
Internal documentation	30	99
External documentation	78	148
Coding	108	108
Testing	58	63
Defect repairs	150	155
Management	58	76
Total	537	715
5-year maintenance effort		
Delivery	26	182
Central maintenance	100	107
Field maintenance	0	388
Total	126	677
Project total	663	1,392
Staff size	36	45
Cost per month	$5,000	$5,000
Total cost	$3,315,000	$6,960,000
Cost per line	$66.30	$139.20
Lines per month	93	70

planning documents and the external documentation are more volumi-
nous. Also, the external user's documentation is produced by professional writers, editors, and production personnel and printed in 5000-copy
lots.

Project and personnel variables. Both projects are identical 50,000-
source-statement COBOL application packages for general business
purposes, such as accounting. Case 1, the internal version will be installed
at a single site, and hence has no requirement for professionally produced
external documents. Case 2 is intended to be marketed commercially and
is supported by tutorial materials, primers, user's guides, reference
manuals, message manuals, and maintenance manuals; perhaps 20 internal documents are also produced, such as market forecasts, quality
assurance plans, defect removal plans, and marketing plans.

Both examples are developed at a single location, so there is no travel
at all. Neither example has any particular constraints on memory or
performance. The analysts and programmers in both cases are reasonably
familiar with the application area and have no need for special training.

For Case 1, the internal program, the internal documentation totaled
some 400 text pages of specifications and business documents. The
external user documentation totaled approximately 1000 pages, divided
among a primer of 50 pages, a self-study guide of 100 pages, a user's
reference manual of 250 pages, an installation guide of 150 pages, a
messages manual of 100 pages, and a systems programming and maintenance manual of 350 pages.

For Case 2, the external version, internal documentation, which
included a market forecast, a quality assurance plan, a market plan, and
several other plans in addition to the specifications, totaled over 1300
pages. The external user documentation was about 2000 pages of professionally written, edited, and printed and illustrated materials, including a
primer of 100 pages, four self-study guides of 125 pages, a user's reference
manual of 350 pages, an installation guide of 200 pages, a messages
manual of 100 pages, a systems programming guide of 350 pages, and a
maintenance manual of 400 pages. The larger number of pages in Case 2 is
partly due to the greater use of graphics and the professional typography,
and partly due to the need for both longer and more basic explanations of
system concepts.

Environmental variables. In both cases, the analysts and programmers have their own terminals and essentially unrestricted access to
machine time. The analysts and programmer use English text augmented
by output formats as the primary specification medium for functional
design. Both systems are fairly well structured, using the method of
Constantine-Myers-Stevens. Assume that the actual support for the
documentation consists of word processing equipment, but manual graphics are used in both cases.

Data and code-structure variables. Both examples are fairly well structured COBOL systems. The data complexity is moderately high.

In analyzing Table 3-31, it may be seen that commercially marketed software projects, when compared to internal projects developed for an enterprise's own use, tend both to have larger quantities of documentation and to have higher documentation expenses due to the need to use professional writers, editors, artists, and production personnel. Also, if photocomposers and typesetting equipment are used, then the capital costs are somewhat higher also.

Note also that the greater quantity of documentation exerts a subtle influence as well as an overt influence: There is more material to read; the reviews take longer; and when defects are noted in the documentation, there is more effort devoted to updating the documents whenever a technical problem changes the contents. All in all, documentation is a significant expense element of commercial programming, and the sum of all document expenses will often exceed 30% of the total development costs.

The information in Table 3-31 assumes ordinary printed documents, not interactive on-line documentation. Documenting the system interactively, especially when making heavy use of graphics and icons, typically requires special skills and may drive up the initial documentation production costs somewhat, although not enough hard data has yet been published to state the total costs authoritatively. Modification and updating of interactive documentation usually requires extensive support and languages such as SMALLTALK or OBJECTIVE-C for making the changes easily.

Although documentation has been one of the weak links of software development in the past, the emerging awareness of the cost impact which documentation exerts, coupled with the new iconographic development tools soon to be released, indicates a very favorable prognosis for improved documentation in the future.

THE IMPACT OF HIGH-SPEED PROTOTYPING

For the first 25 years of the computing era, prototyping was not a normal part of typical software system development lifecycles. The reason why this powerful technology was uncommon centers around the limitations of the available programming languages. To do a prototype with languages such as Assembler, COBOL, or FORTRAN would have required coding perhaps 50% of the system, and by then the value of having a prototype would be greatly diminished.

Prototyping as a standard technology is only becoming widespread in 1985; the surge of interest is caused by the availability of very powerful nonprocedural languages, such as those which support the many commercial database products.

These new languages allow very rapid development, often measured in hours or days, of at least the primary input and output screens and key algorithms of the systems being designed. Since hands-on experience by system users is the most effective known way of eliminating requirements ambiguities and external design problems, high-speed prototyping is turning out to be one of the most effective technologies to emerge since the computing industry began.

As a general rule, all systems that will have significant interactions with end users and which are larger than about 5000 source statements are good candidates for prototyping. If the system is a low-volume application, then the prototype can often evolve directly into the finished software. If the system is a high-volume application, the performance of the prototype in a nonprocedural language may not be sufficient, so in this case the prototypes tend to be discarded, and primary system development continues with a third-generation language to achieve the system's performance goals.

Even when the prototype is discarded, the activity of prototyping is valuable. If the time and resources devoted to prototyping total to perhaps 5% or 10% of the amounts planned for development, it is not uncommon for the system to finish slightly early and within its budget, even after the costs and schedules of the prototype have been absorbed. The reason for this phenomenon is that prototyping is so effective in minimizing mid-development requirements and scope changes.

A recent controlled study described by Boehm, Gray, and Seewaldt (55) indicated the surprising finding that prototyped software projects averaged 45% less development effort than did conventionally specified software. While the study was based on a university experiment, a report by Scharer (56) on prototyping for industrial and commerical software indicated very good successes.

Table 3-32 shows the impact of prototyping on large-system development. The systems used in the case study are assumed to be internally developed general ledger systems for medium-sized corporations, which total 100,000 COBOL source statements.

Project and personnel variables. Both the prototyped and conventionally specified versions of the systems are internal projects and are not intended for sale or lease. The programs within the system are interactive and are intended for utilization by nonprogrammers. The systems are centered around a large commercial database product and include a passive data dictionary.

The senior analysts and programmers in both cases are knowledgeable about general ledger products, although there is a mixture of new

Table 3-32 The impact of prototyping on large-system development

	Case 1: Conventional specifications	Case 2: High-speed prototyping
Size in lines (COBOL)	100,000	100,000
Schedules (calendar months)		
Requirements	6	4
Prototyping	0	5
Design	10	4
Coding	6	6
Testing	8	6
Total	30	25
Overlapped	20	19
Development effort (person-months)		
Requirements	50	30
Prototyping	0	50
Planning and business	60	60
Design	70	50
Internal documentation	75	65
External documentation	125	120
Coding	180	160
Testing	115	110
Defect repairs	300	200
Management	110	100
Total	1,085	945
5-year maintenance effort		
Delivery	100	100
Central maintenance	380	300
Field maintenance	0	0
Total	480	400
Project total	1,565	1,345
Staff size	54	50
Cost per month	$5,000	$5,000
Total cost	$7,825,000	$6,725,000
Cost per line	$78.25	$67.25
Lines per month	92	106

hires and novices. The projects are being done within single locations, and the finished systems will be used at those locations, so there is no travel at all. In both cases the comptroller has assigned senior personnel to serve as the interface with the systems development group, and the requirements have been worked out in joint planning meetings. After completion, maintenance of the systems will be carried out informally on an as-needed basis by systems development personnel.

Environmental variables. In both cases, the analysts and programmers have their own terminals and essentially unrestricted access to machine time. There are no major constraints on performance or memory usage of the finished programs.

Since a majority of the system users will be nonprogrammers who have little experience with computers, particular care is taken to make the HELP screens, menus, and user's guides clear and easy to understand. But for these internal systems, the user's guides are merely printed from a daisy wheel printer and are not typeset or bound into book form.

Data and code-structure variables. As full-scale integrated general ledger systems for medium-sized corporations, both versions have very complex data relationships and fairly complex functions. In both cases, the code itself is well-structured COBOL. Case 2, the prototyped version, used a commercial database system and language prior to starting COBOL development.

Table 3-32 reveals several surprising aspects of high-speed prototyping. Prototyping not only slightly reduces development schedules and significantly reduces development effort, but it also significantly reduces maintenance effort. The reason for this is that prototyping is successful in minimizing requirements and scope changes, and the prototype itself is a useful tool for defect prevention and defect removal.

Very few large or complex engineered products—automobiles, aircraft, military equipment—are ever constructed without careful prototypes. This common activity was long absent from software engineering, because first-, second-, and third-generation languages were often unsuited for high-speed prototyping. For example, prototyping the system shown in Table 3-32 in COBOL would certainly have taken between 25,000 and 50,000 source statements and many months of effort. While interpreted languages such as APL, BASIC, and FORTH have been used for prototyping, with some success, even with them the effort to finish a significant prototype is greater than desirable if the system is large and complex.

One of the most useful features of the new nonprocedural languages surrounding commercial database products is that not only can they be used to build systems themselves, but they facilitate prototyping of systems which may be very large and complex.

As of 1985, high-speed prototyping is starting to enter the mainstream of system development and is becoming a very successful technology.

THE IMPACT OF ORGANIZATION
STRUCTURES

A 1985 review of the software management literature has turned up an interesting phenomenon: Matrix management is usually cited as a source of trouble and confusion and is not often regarded by experienced software managers as a useful method for large systems. For example, in *The Mythical Man-Month*, Brooks points out, "The principle that no man can serve two masters dictates that the authority structure be tree-like." In "Organizing for Successful Software Development," Daly (57) observes, "Probably the major disadvantage to a matrix operation is that there is no single person responsible for the success of each project." In "Organizing for Project Management," Green (63) notes, "One source of problems within the matrix form of organization is the apparent conflict between the authority of the project manager and the authority of the functional manager." Matrix management is usually cited either as a negative factor or as a potentially useful method that needs a great deal of extra care for successful use.

Hierarchical organization, where all subordinate project managers and technical personnel report up the same chain of command, is usually the method that has the greatest pragmatic success on large projects. As a rule of thumb for large software projects (more than 50,000 source code statements), about 3 out of every 10 hierarchically managed projects will run into schedule delays and cost overruns, but perhaps 5 out of every 10 matrixed projects will encounter delays and overruns. Obviously problems outside the basic organization structure are significant, but the matrix organization seems less effective than the hierarchical in resolving them.

Table 3-33 discusses the same project developed in both hierarchical and matrix organizational forms. The systems used in the case study are assumed to be the same internally developed full-scale general ledger systems used in Table 3-32, which total 100,000 COBOL source statements. In Case 1, the hierarchical form, the project manager controls the entire project, and all subordinate managers and technical staff personnel are in the same reporting structure. That is, the personnel working on requirements, design, coding, documentation, integration, and testing are all part of the same organization and their functions reports to the senior project manager.

In Case 2, the matrix version, the design personnel report to a design functional manager, the coding personnel report to a coding functional manager, and so on; these managers are not in the chain of command leading to the project manager. Indeed, in the matrix form only a few planners and analysts report directly to the project manager, who must use negotiation and appeals to corporate management to resolve disputes with the functional managers.

Project and personnel variables. Both the hierarchical and matrix-managed versions of the systems are internal projects and are not intended for sale or lease. The programs within the system are interactive and are intended for utilization by nonprogrammers. The systems are centered around a large commercial database product and include a passive data dictionary.

The senior analysts and programmers in both cases are knowledgeable about general ledger products, although there is a mixture of new hires and novices. In Case 1, the hierarchical project, the analysts report upward to the project manager; in Case 2, the matrixed project, they report laterally to a functional design manager.

The projects are being done within single locations, and the finished systems will be used at those locations, so there is no travel at all.

In both cases the comptroller has assigned senior personnel to serve as the interface with the systems development group, and the requirements have been worked out in joint planning meetings.

Environmental variables. In both cases, the analysts and programmers have their own terminals and essentially unrestricted access to machine time. There are no major constraints on performance or memory usage of the finished programs.

Since a majority of the system users will be nonprogrammers who have little experience with computers, particular care is taken to make the HELP screens, menus, and user's guides clear and easy to understand. Since these are internal systems, the user's guides are merely printed from a daisy wheel printer and are not typeset or bound into book form.

Data and code-structure variables. As full-scale integrated general ledger systems for major corporations, both versions have very complex data relationships and fairly complex functions. In both cases, the code itself is well-structured COBOL. The prototyped version used a commercial database system and language prior to starting COBOL development.

As can be noted from Table 3-33, matrix management introduces a certain level of confusion and ambiguity into large software projects, which usually gets translated into longer schedules and somewhat higher costs for projects for the same kind of work that are managed in a conventional hierarchical fashion.

The span-of-control concept is based on the fact that as the number of people who must communicate about a common activity goes up arithmetically, from 2 to 3 to 4 and so on, the possible number of communication channels goes up geometrically, at a much faster rate. Since all possible combinations of staff communications can exist, an eight-person department has some 40,320 possible ways to communicate. While the real-life consequences are not as bad as the mathematics indicate, there is a certain communication confusion associated with large projects.

The hierarchical organization structure tends to minimize the mathematics of communication, while the matrix organization tends to amplify

Table 3-33 The impact of hierarchical and matrix management on large-system development

	Case 1: Hierarchical management	Case 2: Matrix management
Size in lines (COBOL)	100,000	100,000
Schedules (calendar months)		
Requirements	6	6
Design	10	12
Coding	6	8
Testing	8	6
Total	30	32
Overlapped	20	22
Development effort (person-months)		
Requirements	50	60
Planning and business	60	75
Design	70	80
Internal documentation	75	80
External documentation	125	125
Coding	180	190
Testing	115	120
Defect repairs	300	350
Management	110	150
Total	1,085	1,230
5-year maintenance effort		
Delivery	100	100
Central maintenance	380	400
Field maintenance	0	0
Total	480	500
Project total	1,565	1,730
Staff size	54	55
Cost per month	$ 5,000	$ 5,000
Total cost	$7,825,000	$8,650,000
Cost per line	$ 78.25	$ 86.50
Lines per month	92	81

the problem. The span-of-control concept is usually applied only to the number of workers who must report to a single manager. It is intended to limit the number of direct reports to a quantity within the capabilities of a normal supervisor; about eight direct reports appears to be the norm in the United States.

However, with matrix organizations, the number of managers who must communicate can reach significant levels. For really large systems, there may be 20 or 30 managers at the same level who must communicate plans and information back and forth, and sometimes these managers can spend more than 50% of their daily working time at meetings or in telephone conversations with their fellow managers. If even a dozen functional and project managers must communicate as peers, the number of possible communication channels is 4,790,016,000, and it is easy to see why aspects of the project may be forgotten or not handled effectively.

The span-of-control concept is seldom invoked to explore the impact of complex peer communication at the management level, but this is a mistake, since the problems are real and significant.

THE IMPACT OF TEAM MORALE AND STAFF COMPENSATION

Among the variables most recently quantified for software projects is the morale of project staff members and how they are compensated for their efforts; this can exert a significant impact on productivity and quality. A survey of large-system productivity by the International Data Corporation in 1982 (59) concluded that morale and the reward structures ranked among the most significant factors in affecting productivity.

It is also of interest that the enterprises which rank fairly high in overall software productivity, such as IBM tend to have dual compensation plans, under which technical staff members can achieve salary levels equal to those in managerial careers. Within IBM, for example, technical workers such as programmers, analysts, and quality assurance personnel can look forward to salary levels that ascend at least as high as those of third-line managers. If the prestigious "IBM Fellows" rank is considered, then selected technical workers can earn as much as senior IBM executives.

Conversely, enterprises which rank fairly low in overall productivity often have technical compensation plans which stop at or about the first-line management level, thus forcing technical employees to either get into management or leave the enterprise in order to achieve economic parity.

There is not always a correlation between high technical skills and managerial abilities, and it is a well known phenomenon that promotion to management is not always a suitable reward for technical professionals.

The other alternative, or having capable technical personnel leave the enterprise, has serious and negative consequences for the enterprise itself. Since the most qualified and expert technical personnel are in the greatest demand, they tend to leave in the greatest numbers. This results in the highest attrition rates for the most valuable technical workers, and a gradual decline in overall enterprise technical skills. After a few years, the average level of technical competence can hover around marginal, and since the enterprise will not have a particularly good reputation, it becomes increasingly difficult for it to attract new and innovative staff or return the skill level to a high plateau.

Table 3-34 shows the impact of morale and compensation on two

Table 3-34 The impact of morale and compensation on large-system development

	Case 1: High-morale environment	Case 2: Low-morale environment
Size in lines (COBOL)	100,000	100,000
Schedules (calendar months)		
Requirements	6	6
Design	10	12
Coding	6	10
Testing	8	8
Total	30	36
Overlapped	20	26
Development effort (person-months)		
Requirements	50	80
Planning and business	60	75
Design	70	100
Internal documentation	75	90
External documentation	125	150
Coding	180	220
Testing	115	130
Defect repairs	300	400
Management	110	160
Total	1,085	1,400
5-year maintenance effort		
Delivery	100	100
Central maintenance	380	460
Field maintenance	0	0
Total	480	560
Project total	1,565	1,945
Staff size	54	54
Cost per month	$ 5,500	$ 4,500
Total cost	$8,607,500	$8,725,500
Cost per line	$ 86.08	$ 86.25
Lines per month	92	71

identical projects using the same 100,000-COBOL-source-statement integrated general ledger system used in Tables 3-32 and 3-33.

Project and personnel variables. Both versions of the system are internal projects and are not intended for sale or lease. The programs within the system are interactive and are intended for utilization by nonprogrammers. The systems are centered around a large commercial database product and include a passive data dictionary.

In Case 1, the high-morale and effective-compensation example, the senior analysts and programmers are knowledgeable about general ledger products, although there are some new hires and novices.

In Case 2, the low-morale and ineffective-compensation example, there are no senior analysts and programmers, since they have either moved into management or left the company. The project is staffed by a majority of new hires, with a small number of relatively long-term but only average analysts and programmers.

The projects are being done within single locations, and the finished systems will be used at those locations, so there is no travel at all.

In both cases the comptroller has assigned senior personnel to serve as the interface with the systems development group, and the requirements have been worked out in joint planning meetings.

After completion, maintenance of the systems will be carried out informally on an as-needed basis by systems development personnel.

Environmental variables. In both cases, the analysts and programmers have their own terminals and essentially unrestricted access to machine time. There are no major constraints on performance or memory usage of the finished programs.

Since a majority of the system users will be nonprogrammers who have little experience with computers, particular care is taken to make the HELP screens, menus, and user's guides clear and easy to understand. For these internal systems, the user's guides are merely printed from a daisy wheel printer and are not typeset or bound into book form.

Data and code-structure variables. As full-scale integrated general ledger systems for medium-sized corporations, both versions have very complex data relationships and fairly complex functions. In both cases, the code itself is well-structured COBOL. The prototyped version used a commercial database system and report language prior to starting COBOL development.

In Table 3-34, note the average salary differential: $5500 a month (fully burdened) for Case 1, with senior-level staffing and an effective compensation plan, versus $4500 a month for Case 2, with the junior and average personnel. Yet in spite of the cost differential of $12,000 per person-year, the life-cycle cost for Case 1 was $118,000 less than for Case 2.

There is no question that experienced, skilled personnel are perhaps the most valuable assets that enterprises have. If they are well treated and properly rewarded, then they tend to do their best for the enterprise. Conversely, enterprises that do not treat their technical workers well or reward them properly tend to lose their best workers in relatively large numbers, thus lowering the average skill levels of the enterprise and lowering net productivity as well.

CONSOLIDATING THE VARIABLES OF SOFTWARE PRODUCTIVITY

Thus far Chapter 3 has dealt individually with the 20 primary variables for which a reasonable quantitative assessment can be made, and for which sufficient historical data exists to state their impacts on software projects.

However, in real life all 20 of the variables can change and interact simultaneously. Not only that, but there are many other variables, not yet fully quantified, which can affect productivity and quality as well.

It is of interest to conclude this chapter with a case study, presented in Table 3-35, in which all of the major variables change, to show the cumulative impacts of all of the individual factors as they might appear in real-life systems. To do this, let us consider the same system as it might be developed by two separate enterprises. One of the enterprises is at the leading edge in terms of tools, methods, and skill levels, and one of the enterprises is at the trailing edge. The system for this demonstration is assumed to be a large integrated order entry/inventory management/sales analysis system which totals 500,000 COBOL source statements.

At the leading-edge enterprise, a running prototype using a commercial database product and its associated query language is constructed soon after the requirements are discussed. The detailed design is constructed by modifying a standard design or blueprint, and about 40% of the code is taken from the enterprise library of standard reusable COBOL modules.

At the trailing-edge enterprise, this system is treated as an entirely new creation, and requirements and design are laboriously worked out from scratch. Although some included COBOL code will be used spontaneously by the programmers themselves, each programmer will do essentially private development of code and very little common code will be drawn from a corporate library—only calendar and date management routines, and a few staple subroutines.

Project and personnel variables. In both cases, the order entry/inventory management/sales analysis system is being developed as an internal product and is not aimed at being marketed commercially. Both versions are interactive and are aimed at allowing nonprogramming managers and staff personnel to handle incoming orders, query the status of orders, and trigger production; as well as providing both ad hoc queries and standard reports on sales volumes by product type, region, and customer.

In both cases, the application area is fairly well understood, and both

Table 3-35 Comparison of the results of trailing-edge and leading-edge methods for similar software systems (COBOL)

	Case 1: Trailing-edge methods	Case 2: Leading-edge methods
New code size	495,000	300,000
Reused code size	5,000	200,000
Total size	500,000	500,000
Schedules (calendar months)		
Requirements	10	3
Prototyping	0	3
Design	24	9
Coding	18	14
Testing	36	12
Total	88	41
Overlapped	60	30
Development effort (person-months)		
Requirements	250	50
Prototyping	0	50
Planning and business	175	100
Design	375	250
Internal documentation	200	100
External documentation	500	200
Coding	800	400
Testing	700	300
Defect repairs	900	300
Management	400	250
Total	4,300	2,000
5-year maintenance effort		
Delivery	0	0
Central maintenance	6,400	1,500
Field maintenance	0	0
Total	6,400	1,500
Project total	10,700	3,500
Staff size	72	67
Cost per month	$ 4,500	$ 5,000
Total cost	$47,250,000	$19,250,000
Cost per line	$ 94.50	$ 38.50
Lines per month	116	250

the leading-edge and trailing-edge enterprises have partial existing systems which automate some of the same functions; but these older systems are not integrated, do not share common data, and have become difficult to update and modify.

At the leading-edge enterprise, the systems staff has a rich mixture of senior and experienced personnel, due to the policy of having a dual compensation plan. At the trailing-edge enterprise, the staff members are either new or inexperienced, due to the high attrition rate among the more qualified employees.

In the leading-edge enterprise, the system requirements were worked out carefully between the user representatives and the systems personnel by means of intensive joint planning sessions. Within a few months, a running prototype demonstrating the major output screens and reports and input screens had been produced, and the user representatives were able to get actual experience with the prototype. This experimental stage lasted for approximately six weeks and resulted in the elimination of several reports and the simplification of a number of the input screens.

At the trailing-edge enterprise, the vice presidents of sales and manufacturing were requested by the systems director to write a text requirements specification, which the systems group would then review and respond to. The two executives assigned staff personnel to the task, but the result was two separate requirements specifications, of which one emphasized the sales requirements while the other emphasized the manufacturing and inventory management requirements. The systems director was essentially passive until both documents were received, whereupon he pointed out that the two requirements were mutually inconsistent. A compromise requirements specification was eventually produced.

The projects are being done at single locations, and there is no travel at all. When completed, maintenance will also be done at single locations.

Environmental variables. Following are the differences between the leading-edge and the trailing-edge enterprise in terms of environmental factors:

	Leading-edge enterprise	Trailing-edge enterprise
Ratio of terminals to staff members	1 to 1	1 to 4
Management tools	Automated estimating and project planning and tracking	Manual estimating and project planning and tracking
Requirements methodology	Joint workshops and prototypes	Text requests and responses
Design methodology	Standard designs, data analysis, on-line graphics	Text documents, informal design
Coding methodology	Reusable code library of 200 to 500 modules	Hand coding of modules

	Leading-edge enterprise	Trailing-edge enterprise
Library controls	Automated code library	Manual code library
Documentation	Document support tools and standard formats	No document support and no standard formats
Screen and menu development	Automated screen construction tools	Hand coding of screens
Defect removal	Prototypes, formal reviews, test specialists, and formal testing	Partial reviews and informal testing

Data and code-structure variables. In both cases, the data complexity of the system is very high. At the leading-edge enterprise, however, data analysis is a formal discipline performed by trained specialists, and the system's data requirements are considered in terms of long-range enterprise needs. In the trailing-edge enterprise, data analysis barely exists, and the analysts and designers carry out only local design for their particular programs or segments.

While the new code is nominally structured COBOL in both systems, the leading-edge enterprise is able to make use of several hundred standard reusable COBOL modules from the corporate library. Of the 500,000 COBOL source statements in the delivered system, only 300,000 had to be coded by hand, while 200,000 were merely reused from the standard library.

In the trailing-edge enterprise, there is no corporate library of standard reusable modules, although each programmer has a small private library of favorite routines and included code. Only calendar and date management routines are shared among all of the programmers of the system.

From a review of Table 3-35, it may be seen that although large-software system development is still a major undertaking, there are enormous differences between the enterprises that are at the leading edge and those at the trailing edge: Schedule reductions of 2 to 1, lifetime effort reductions of 3 to 1, and maintenance reductions of 4 to 1 are achievable in 1985, with even more significant gains likely to occur in the future.

Since lines of source code remains an unsatisfactory metric, especially for reusable code, Table 3-36 gives the productivity results for the trailing-edge and leading-edge projects in terms of the Albrecht function-point method.

Table 3-36 Comparison of the results of leading-edge and trailing-edge methods for similar software systems, using function points

	Case 1: Trailing edge	Case 2: Leading edge
Function points	4800	4800
Development cost per function point	$4031	$2291
Function points per month	1.1	2.4

To summarize the results of the quantified variables discussed in this chapter: Skilled professionals working with good tools in a well-managed environment can achieve very respectable overall productivity and quality rates.

The many claims in the commercial software press for order-of-magnitude or 10-to-1 software productivity gains must be viewed with caution. When examined closely, they seem to be based either on very small projects or only on coding, and they do not include requirements, planning, design, documentation, management, or integration and testing.

Yet development speed improvements of even 2 to 1, and life-cycle effort improvements of 3 to 1, are not trivial accomplishments. The leading-edge software-producing enterprises are starting to place software on a firm engineering basis. With each month that passes, more data becomes available, and more factors that affect productivity and quality are understood. Although software development is not yet a true science, the steps that have been taken in recent years are moving it in that direction.

REFERENCES

1. Albrecht, A.J. and Gaffney, J.E.; "Software Function, Source Lines of Code, and Development Effort Prediction"; *IEEE Transactions on Software Engineering*, Vol. SE-9, No. 6, November 1983; pp. 639-647.
2. Behrens, C.A.; "Measuring the Productivity of Computer Systems Development Activities with Function Points"; *IEEE Transactions on Software Engineering*, Vol. SE-9, No. 6, November 1983; pp. 648-651.
3. Jones, T.C.; "Measuring Programming Quality and Productivity"; *IBM Systems Journal*, Vol. 17, No. 1, 1978; pp. 39-63.
4. Brooks, F.P. Jr.; *The Mythical Man-Month*; Addison-Wesley; Reading, MA; 1982.
5. Jones, Capers; *Program Quality and Programmer Productivity*; TR 02.764; IBM Corporation, San Jose, CA; January 1977. (Also included in *Programming Productivity—Issues for the Eighties*; IEEE Press, Silver Spring, MD; Cat. No. EHO 186-7; 1981; pp. 130—161)
6. Boehm, B.W.; "Software and Its Impact—A Quantitative Assessment"; *Datamation*, May 1973; pp. 48—59.
7. Chrysler, E.; "Some Basic Determinants of Computer Programming Productivity"; *Communications of the ACM*, Vol. 21, No. 6, June 1878; pp. 472-483.
8. Boehm, B.W.; *Software Engineering Economics*; Prentice-Hall; Englewood Cliffs, NJ; 1981; pp. 427-444.

9. Sackman, H. et al; "Exploratory Experimental Studies Comparing On-Line and Off-Line Programming Performance"; *Communications of the ACM*, Vol. ll, No. 1, January 1968; pp. 3-11.

10. Curtis, B.; "Substantiating Programmer Variability"; *Proceedings of the IEEE*, Vol. 69, No. 7, July 1981. (Also included in *Human Factors in Software Development*; Curtis, B., ed.; IEEE Press, Silver Spring, MD; Cat. No. EHO 185-9; 1981; pp. 533-541.)

11. McCabe, T.J.; "A Complexity Measure"; *IEEE Transactions on Software Engineering*, May 1978; pp. 187-194.

12. Jones, Capers; *Program Quality and Programmer Productivity*; TR 02.764; IBM Corporation; San Jose, CA; January 1977. (Also included in *Programming Productivity, Issues for the Eighties*; Jones, T.C., ed.; pp. 130-161.)

13. Myers, G.J.; *Composite/Structured Design*; Van Nostrand Reinhold; New York; 1978.

14. Stevens, W.J.; *Using Structured Design*; Wiley; New York; 1981.

15. Constantine, L.L. and Yourdon, E.; *Structured Design*; Prentice-Hall; Englewood Cliffs, NJ; 1979.

16. Linger, R.C., Mills, H.D., and Witt, B.I.; *Structured Programming—Theory and Practice*; Addison-Wesley; Philippines; 1979.

17. Warnier, J.D.; *Logical Construction of Programs*; Martinus Nijoff; Boston; 1975.

18. Warnier, J.D.; *Logical Construction of Systems*; Van Nostrand Reinhold; New York; 1981.

19. Orr, K.; *Structured Systems Development*; Yourdon; New York; 1977.

20. Orr, K.; *Structured Requirements Definition*; Ken Orr & Associates; Topeka, KS; 1981.

21. Hansen, K.; *Data Structured Program Design*; Ken Orr & Associates; Topeka, KS; 1983.

22. Jackson, M.; *Principles of Program Design*; Academic; New York; 1975.

23. Yourdon, E.; *Techniques of Program Structure and Design*; Prentice-Hall; 1975.

24. Weinberg, G.M.; *The Psychology of Computer Programming*; Van Nostrand Reinhold; New York; 1971.

25. Dijkstra, E.; "GOTO Statements Considered Harmful"; *Communications of the ACM*, Vol. 11, No. 9, November 1968; pp. 147-148.

26. Bohm, C. and Jacopini, G.; "Flow Diagrams, Turing Machines, and Languages with Only Two Formation Rules"; *Communications of the ACM*, Vol. 9, No. 5, 1966; pp. 366-371.

27. Mills, H.D.; *Mathematical Foundations for Structured Programming*; IBM Corporation; Gaithersburg, MD; Technical Report FSC 72-6012; 1972.

28. Wirth, N.; *Algorithms + Data Structures = Programs*; Prentice-Hall, Englewood Cliffs, NJ; 1976.

29. Endres, A.; "An Analysis of Errors and their Causes in System Programs"; *IEEE Transactions on Software Engineering*, June 1975; pp 140—149. (Also included in *Programming Productivity—Issues for the Eighties*; pp. 86-95.)

30. Jones, T.C.; "Prevention and Removal of Programming Defects"; Electrical Communication—*The Technical Journal of ITT*, Vol. 57, No. 4, 1983; pp. 295-300.

31. Basili, V.; "Changes and Errors as Measures of Software Development"; in *Models and Metrics for Software Management and Engineering*; IEEE Press; Silver Spring, MD; Cat. No. EHO 167-7; 1980; pp. 62-64.

32. Walston, C.E. and Felix, C.P.; "A Method of Programming Measurement and Estimation"; *IBM Systems Journal*, Vol. 16, No. 1, 1977; pp. 54—73.

33. Brandon, D.H. and Segelstein, S.; *Data Processing Contracts*; Van Nostrand Reinhold; New York; 1976.

34. Remer, D.; *Legal Care for Your Software*; Addison-Wesley; Reading, MA; 1982.

35. Pooley, J.; *Trade Secrets*; Osborne/McGraw-Hill; Berkeley, CA; 1982.

36. *The Ada Programming Language Standard*; ANSI MIL-STD-1815A-1983; Stock No. 008-000-00394-8; U.S. Government Printing Office; Washington, D.C.; 1983.

37. Druffel, L.E., Redwine, S.T., and Riddle, W.E.; "The STARS Program: Overview and Rationale"; *IEEE Computer*, Vol. 16, No. 11, November 1983; pp. 21-29.
38. Plotkin, S.; *The Real Cost Workbook*; Stephen Plotkin; Glen Mills, PA; 1982.
39. Reifer, D.J. and Trattner, S.; "A Glossary of Software Tools and Techniques"; *IEEE Computer*, July 1977; pp. 52-60. (Also included in *Programming Productivity—Issues for the Eighties*; pp. 352-360.)
40. Wasserman, T.; "The Ecology of Software Development Environments"; *IEEE Press*; Silver Spring, MD. (Also included in *Programming Productivity—Issues for the Eighties*; pp. 380-384.)
41. "IEEE Workshop on Software Productivity Issues"; *Fifth International IEEE Symposium on Software Engineering*; San Diego, CA; March 1981.
42. Jones, T.C.; "Technical and Demographic Trends in the Computing Industry"; keynote presentation, *Proceedings of the 1983 Data Structured Systems Design Conference*; Ken Orr & Associates; Topeka, KA; 1983.
43. Kendall, R. and Lamb, E.C.; "Management Perspectives on Programs, Programming, and Productivity"; presented at GUIDE 45; Atlanta, GA; November 1977. (Also included in *Programming Productivity—Issues for the Eighties*; pp. 201-211.)
44. Jones, T.C.; "Programming Defect Removal"; presented at GUIDE 42; Miami, FL; May 1975.
45. Martin, J. and McClure, C.; *Software Maintenance*; Prentice-Hall; Englewood Cliffs, NJ; 1983.
46. Parikh, G. and Zvegintzov, N.; *Program Maintenance*; IEEE Press; Silver Spring, MD; Cat. No. ISBN 0-8186-0002-0; pp. 360.
47. Jones, T.C.; "Reusability in Programming—A Survey of the State of the Art"; *IEEE Transactions on Software Engineering*, Vol. SE-10, No. 5, September 1984.
48. Biggerstaff, T., Perlis, A., and Cheatham, T.E.; *Workshop on Reusability in Programming*; ITT Programming Technology Center; Stratford, CT; September 1983.
49. Biggerstaff, T., ed.; "Special Issue on Reusability in Programming"; *IEEE Transactions on Software Engineering*, Vol. SE-10, No. 5, September 1984.
50. Martin, J.; *Application Development Without Programmers*; Prentice-Hall; Englewood Cliffs, NJ; 1982.
51. Weiss, D.M.; "Evaluating Software Development by Error Analysis: The Data from the Architectural Research Facility"; *The Journal of Systems and Software*, Vol. 1, 1979; pp 57-70.
52. Gaffney, J.E. Jr.; "Estimating the Number of Faults in Code"; *IEEE Transactions on Software Engineering*, Vol. SE-10, No. 4, July 1984; pp. 459-463.
53. Fagan, M.E.; "Design and Code Inspections to Reduce Errors in Program Development"; *IBM Systems Journal*, Vol. 5, No. 13, 1976; pp. 219-248.
54. Jones, T.C.; "A Survey of Programming Design and Specification Techniques"; in *Programming Productivity—Issues for the Eighties*; Jones, T.C., ed.; IEEE Press; EHO 186-7, 1981; pp. 224-236.
55. Boehm, B.W., Gray, T.E., and Seewaldt, T.; "Prototyping Versus Specifying: A Multiproject Experiment"; *IEEE Transactions on Software Engineering*, Vol. SE-10, No. 3, May 1984.
56. Scharer, L.L.; "Prototyping in a Production Environment"; in proceedings of the ITT Conference on Programming Productivity, June 1983; Curtis, B., ed.; pp. 440-455.
57. Daly, E.B.; "Organizing for Successful Software Development"; *Datamation*, December 1979; pp. 107-116.
58. Green, L.H.; "Organizing for Project Management"; in *Systems Developemnt Management*; Hannan, J., ed.; Auerbach; New York, N.Y.; 1982; pp. 115-126.
59. *Systems Development Productivity*; International Data Corporation; Waltham, MA; January 1981; pp. 56-60.

CHAPTER
FOUR
EXPLORING THE INTANGIBLE SOFTWARE FACTORS

The factors discussed in Chapter 3 are regular and predictable in their impact; but there are also quite a few variable factors that either occur randomly or have not been quantified in enough depth to model them with high precision. For example, project redirections and restarts, when they occur, have a significant impact on productivity. But predicting the occurrence of restarts and direction changes is outside the scope of normal estimating, with the exception of the use of probabilistic techniques such as Monte Carlo simulations.

In this chapter, we discuss 25 factors which are considered to be significant determinants of productivity, but which are not readily quantified:

1. Schedule and resource constraints
2. Staff sizes
3. Total enterprise size
4. Attrition during development
5. Hiring and relocation during development
6. Unpaid overtime
7. Business systems and/or strategic planning
8. User participation in requirements and design
9. End-user development
10. Information centers
11. Development centers

12. Internal staff training and education
13. Standards and formal development methods
14. Canceled projects and software disasters
15. Project redirections and restarts
16. Project transfers from city to city
17. Response time and computer facilities
18. Physical facilities and office space
19. Acquiring and modifying purchased software
20. Restructuring and repairing aging systems
21. Internal politics and power struggles
22. Legal and statutory constraints
23. U.S. export license requirements
24. Measuring productivity and quality
25. Productivity and quality improvement programs

While all 25 variables seldom occur simultaneously on the same project, it is not uncommon for any given software project to be affected by from 4 to 10 of them. Because the data quantifying their impact is either scarce or ambiguous, all that can be said is that perhaps 30% of the productivity variations that occur on software projects result from these more or less intangible factors. Chapter 4 presents the current hypotheses regarding each of the 25 factors.

THE IMPACT OF SCHEDULE AND RESOURCE CONSTRAINTS

Of all the problems observed on contract software, and to a lesser degree on internal software, one stands out as the source of more major catastrophes than any other: making schedule and cost commitments that cannot be achieved, and are known to be impossible by the technical personnel.

What often happens with commercial contract software is that the marketing and sales personnel sign a contract calling for something like an 18-month delivery schedule for projects of such scope and magnitude that no similar systems have ever been developed in less than 36 months. In worst-case situations, what will occur is a fixed-price, fixed-delivery contract with penalties for nonperformance!

For internal projects, senior corporate management or user management often insists on a delivery date, and the data processing managers are ordered to meet that date. A frequent corollary is for the data processing manager to also be directed to meet the date with a staff that is too small for the work to be done, with the assumption that overtime can compensate for lack of adequate resources.

Schedule and resource constraints can have one of two significant effects:

1. *Tight but achievable constraints.* When the schedule or staff size constraints are tight but not actually unworkable, what often happens is that the staff work together as a happy, cohesive team, and the extra hours and weekends are regarded as unavoidable and necessary steps for completion. Those who work on projects that have tight delivery dates, but where the dates have a good chance of being met, often feel a kind of excitement that comes from overcoming shared challenges. The same kind of feeling sometimes happens to groups of mountain climbers or to boat crews: a feeling of teamwork develops that is actually enjoyable.
2. *Unachievable constraints.* When the schedule for a project is totally unreasonable and unrealistic, and no amount of overtime can allow it to be met, the project team becomes angry and frustrated. Senior management is viewed as incompetent and insensitive (probably a justified view), and morale drops to the bottom. In this situation, the employees with the most experience and skills tend to quit, leaving behind those who are not as experienced. The incoming people must be brought up to speed, and the whole project can get so out of control that it may be canceled.

The situation of constraints on schedules and resources is so common in industry that it deserves a serious look. Four widespread reasons exist for this phenomenon. The first reason is that management may make a deliberate attempt to keep employees busy and productive. Parkinson's law (1) holds that work expands to fill the time allotted to it, and this is probably a true observation. Therefore management tends to set schedules that are slightly difficult to achieve, in order to keep the organization at what is regarded as the peak of efficiency.

The second reason for constraints has to do with competitive bidding and software procurement. Any company that is competing with others for a software development contract is likely to have two schedules: the one that is in the proposal, which everyone knows to be optimistic and unlikely, but which is thought necessary to keep the company from looking worse than the competitors; and the true internal schedule, which is not revealed to customers initially, but which gradually becomes known once the contract is started.

The third reason for constraints is that the scope of the project may be expanded in the middle of development. In a set of 64 IBM cost estimates examined by the author in the early 1970s, the average size of the software when delivered was 44% larger than the initial estimate. Also, 35% of the delivered functions were not in the initial requirements, but came in later as afterthoughts by the clients. Yet in spite of the expanded scope of the work, the initial schedules were viewed as "real" and the development staffs were urged to meet them.

The fourth reason for constraints is inexperience or estimating error, where contracts and commitments are made by people who have no real knowledge of how long a program or system might take or of the true staffing required.

For whatever reasons, schedule pressures and staff sizes too small for the projects are endemic in the industry, and the impact of the situation is ambiguous. Really impossible demands for delivery long before realistic completion is technically feasible can lead to total disaster and failure of the project. Slightly tight schedules, on the other hand, can lead to a feeling of teamwork and high morale from overcoming shared problems.

THE IMPACT OF STAFF SIZES

Brooks, in his classic The Mythical Man-Month (2), put forth the intuitively appealing hypothesis that time and humans are not inter-changeable: For example, 2 people working for 12 months produce notably different results from 12 people working for 2 months, even though the total amount of effort expended is the same in both cases. Figure 4-1 gives a graphic picture of the Brooks hypothesis.

In a similar fashion, Putnam in *Software Cost Estimating and Life-Cycle Control: Getting the Software Numbers* (3) applied the mathematics developed by Lord Rayleigh to the equations of time and person-months, developing an estimating model which has an interesting characteristic: Attempts to shorten the time schedule to less than the "natural" time for the project will drive up the number of people needed to alarming proportions. Figure 4-2 gives two Putnam-derived Rayleigh curves, with the left showing the natural project schedule and human effort and the right showing a project where people were added to compress the schedule.

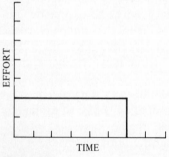

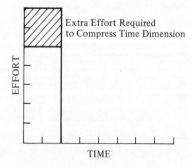

Extra Effort Required to Compress Time Dimension

Figure 4-1

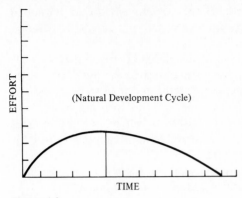

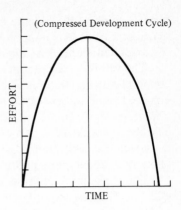

Figure 4-2

Both Brooks and Putnam feel that the reason for the dramatic increase in effort needed when time is compressed is that it is difficult to coordinate large numbers of workers who are trying to perform tasks in parallel.

This view was explored initially in the 19th century, by the pioneering organizational researcher Graicunias (4), whose work on military organization introduced squads and platoons into the U.S. Army.

Graicunias noted that as the number of workers who had to communicate increased arithmetically, from 1 to 2 to 3 to 4, and so on, the number of communication channels among them increased geometrically, and perhaps even combinatorially, so that four workers might have 24 different communication paths (although in real life the situation might not be so catastrophic). According to Graicunias, the upper limit of effective staff size for cooperative projects is about eight, and this is the origin of the current industrial and commercial dogma that department sizes should be limited to about eight workers per manager for professional tasks.

Although the Graicunias concept is intuitively appealing, it has not been actually verified in software organizations. In 1975, as a small, uncontrolled experiment, the author informally interviewed 15 IBM managers and their staffs. The managers had from 3 to 29 employees reporting to them (the manager with 29 was acting for two other managers at the time, while they were on special assignments). The interview consisted of asking a sample of the employees what projects they were working on and how they were doing and then asking the manager to describe the projects that the same employees were engaged in carrying out.

Somewhat surprisingly, the manager with 29 employees was among the top-ranked in knowing what the staff were doing, while the manager with only 3 employees was wrong about every worker (and within a year was removed from management). The study was not rigorous enough for formal conclusions, but the hypothesis that emerged was that individual managerial skill was a much more significant determinant than the span-of-control concept envisioned.

It appeared, based on the results of the interviews, that a more effective organization could be created by increasing the average span of control from 8 up to 16 and by giving the displaced managers training in important staff functions such as planning, scheduling, and estimating. The result would be a reorganized software laboratory with a few large departments, each having a full complement of staff support groups for tasks such as planning and documentation.

The traditional eight-person span of control has potentially harmful effects, which have not been properly explored or documented:

1. More than 12% of the effective work force are removed from direct technical work and put into management. A 12% reduction in direct technical workers is a major factor that should be explored in modern organizations, rather than taken on faith from 19th-century opinions.
2. Enormous possibilities for internal politics and interdepartment rivalries are opened up.
3. The small, eight-person departments almost never include trained support personnel for documentation, quality assurance, planning, integration, and so on.
4. Coordination and communication becomes a bigger problem when many, small departments work on a major project. Even though only eight employees may be reporting to a single manager, there may be dozens of departments that need to coordinate their work.
5. A very large number of managers or chief programmers are required when the span of control is limited to eight technical workers, and the demand for capable individuals for managerial jobs may well exceed the available supply. The result may be that a significant percentage of managers may be in the wrong kinds of work and incapable of managing effectively.

A reciprocal issue to the problem of selecting an appropriate staff size is that of selecting a natural scope of assignment; that is, what is the normal amount of code and documentation that a single experienced staff member can handle on a project without feeling that the assignment is excessive and should have been split up and given to more than one person?

As of 1985, there is no definitive answer to the scope-of-assignment question, but some provisional hypotheses can be stated on the basis of observations within various enterprises. Table 4-1 gives the ranges of assignments as a function of the programming source language:

Table 4-1 Ranges in sizes of coding assignments on large systems as a function of source language

Language	Low assignment size (lines)	High assignment size (lines)
Assembler	3,000	10,000
Macro Assembler	3,000	10,000
C	3,000	10,000
ALGOL	2,000	7,500
CHILL	2,000	7,500
COBOL	2,000	7,500
FORTRAN	2,000	7,500
JOVIAL	2,000	7,500
Pascal	2,000	7,500
RPG	1,500	6,000
PL/I	1,500	6,000
MODULA-2	1,500	6,000
Ada	1,500	6,000
PROLOG	1,000	5,000
LISP	1,000	5,000
FORTH	1,000	5,000
BASIC	1,000	5,000
LOGO	1,000	5,000
APL	500	3,000
SMALLTALK	500	3,000

It may be seen from Table 4-1 that the normal scope of assignment appears to be inversely proportional to the level of the language, or its power relative to Assembler language. Whether this observation is coincidental or significant is not clear in 1985. However, some interesting hypotheses can be made to explain the observation. One is that the normal scope of coding assignments is limited by the intellectual content of the programs, and that as language level goes up, a given number of source code statements will encompass a much broader range of intellectual and project-related issues. Hence a programmer working on 2000 source statements of COBOL must go to just as many meetings and have just as many discussions as a programmer working on 5000 source statements of Assembler language which perform the same functions. The act of coding itself may be accelerated by high-level languages, but the social and technical interactions among project members stay constant.

Since documentation, such as system specifications, user's guides, and test plans, is relatively independent of source language, a second hypothesis is that as the level of the source language goes up, documentation sizes are not affected. Hence the paperwork involved in software lowers the normal scope of assignment for high-level and very high-level languages.

THE IMPACT OF TOTAL ENTERPRISE SIZE

A very surprising observation on software productivity is that it tends to peak at the extreme ends of a spectrum: Private individuals who work at home comprise one end of the spectrum where productivity peaks, and very large enterprises with more than about 200 programmers in a single location comprise the other end.

Between these two extremes, productivity often sags. Whether this observation, which is based on visits to several hundred enterprises, is mere coincidence is not fully understood in 1985. However, the topic is of sufficient interest to make it at least worth formal exploration.

The individual home programmers with high productivity usually have microcomputer hardware and software whose total cost is in the range of $20,000 (i.e. maximum memory, hard disks, high-resolution graphics, and a full arsenal of utility and support software packages). They also tend to have small but well-stocked private libraries of the research materials used in their work. As might be expected from the fact that they have invested so much in their computer facilities, the individuals who work at home are very experienced and consider themselves senior professionals. The projects they handle, while sometimes large for individuals, usually are relatively small by corporate standards: 10,000 source statements or less.

At the other extreme, the large enterprises with high productivity usually have spent more than $60,000 per programmer/analyst on workstations and support tools. In addition, these high-productivity locations also tend to have good research libraries and good supporting services for the professional staffs. It may or may not be significant as a causative factor, but visits to high-productivity enterprises tend to reveal a number of repeating trends:

- Individual workstations for all programmer/analysts and sufficient floor space or office space to work without being crowded
- Deliberate policies of encouraging technical and professional growth by means of seminars, internal technical meetings, and external professional associations
- Specialization within the enterprise, such as having test specialists and maintenance specialists, professional documentation writers, data administration specialists, and network or telecommunications specialists
- Active technology exploration, with new tools and products being evaluated and piloted as the need arises
- Planning for, support of, and awareness of the importance of requirements and design, with automated graphics/text terminals and the usage of formal specification methods, prototyping, or both
- Deliberate usage of some kind of reusability, whether in the form of generators, libraries of standard functions, or database packages

• At least partial measurements of productivity and quality, so that both software and enterprise managers and staff have some quantified vision of what productivity and quality mean within the organization

Not all large enterprises, or even a majority, have high software productivity in 1985, but of those which do, the above list summarizes the salient observations. The large enterprises which are low in software productivity often tend to have ratios of workstations to programmers of 1 to 3 or worse, generally low levels of capital expenditures per staff member, no significant specialization, and no overall vision of what productivity or quality might be worth.

Small to medium-sized enterprises with perhaps 10 to 100 professional programmer/analysts tend in many cases to have lower levels of capital spending per staff person and to lack the specialization which is so often noted in large enterprises; that is, maintenance tends to be done informally by developers rather than by maintenance specialists, documentation is done informally by developers rather than by professional writers, and so forth.

There are small enterprises with high productivity, because they have good fortune in attracting very qualified staff, because they have enough discretionary funding to provide good tooling and support, or both. Often the small enterprises with high productivity are subsidiaries of larger enterprises and share in overall corporate policies and resources, such as libraries and technical conferences.

THE IMPACT OF ATTRITION DURING DEVELOPMENT

The software profession has been one of the most volatile occupations in world history in terms of mobility and job changing. Sociological studies, such as that of Cougar and Zawacki (5), indicate that programmers tend to be low in social needs and often more loyal to their profession than to any individual enterprise.

The U.S. average voluntary attrition of programmers per year has hovered around 12% (6). The author has observed individual enterprises with attrition rates of 65% for staff sizes in excess of 100 technical employees; that is, more than 60 out of every 100 employees were replacements, due to inept personnel and management decisions.

A few enterprises have had stable employment with near 0% attrition, and these are worth comment. From observations based on six low-attrition enterprises, the following factors seemed to be common:

• Generally benign treatment of employees, with features such as opinion surveys, "open-door" policies, executive or "skip-level" interviews, and other ways of letting staff members express their concerns to management in a way known not to bring reprisals for negative views

- Compensation plans that were fair and perceived as being based on rationality
- Interesting projects, which were perceived as being useful and worth doing
- Project managers and enterprise executives who were perceived as being capable and effective

From thoughtful analysis, it can be hypothesized that all of the above factors are related to the last one, and that enterprises which experience high attrition rates of professional staff members are perhaps being managed by executives of less than optimal skills and capabilities. Observations within enterprises that do have high attrition (more than 25%) tend to confirm this hypothesis.

Voluntary attrition has one other notable aspect, first studied within IBM, but not published externally. If departing technical personnel are grouped by their appraisal scores, the surprising finding is that the personnel with the highest scores tend to leave in the greatest numbers. For example, if an enterprise has a five-level appraisal system ranging from "excellent" through "not satisfactory," then a year's worth of voluntary resignations might have the following profile:

Appraisal score	Percentage of voluntary attritions
Excellent	30
Good	20
Average	15
Needs improvement	15
Not satisfactory	20

Although this profile has not been widely replicated and may be coincidental, it implies a very serious condition: If the most qualified people leave an organization in the greatest numbers (which can be expected, since they are obviously the most salable in the job market), then as time passes the average level of skill in an enterprise may decline to hazardous levels unless equally skilled replacements are found.

Moreover, it can be hypothesized that once such a trend starts, it will be difficult to reverse unless it is stopped almost immediately. Indeed, there may be some critical level at which the trend will become irreversable, and the enterprise acquires such a bad reputation that qualified people will not voluntarily work there (just as certain sailing ships in the 19th century acquired such bad reputations that staffing them with officers and crew was often difficult).

THE IMPACT OF HIRING AND RELOCATION
DURING DEVELOPMENT

As Plotkin points out in "The Real Cost of DP Professionals" (7), some very significant expenses occur even before a staff member joins the organization. For example, not only can advertising and personnel agency fees be in excess of $10,000 to fill any given position, but on-board managerial and technical personnel must participate in interviews and the selection process. Assuming an average of four candidates interviewed per offer given and accepted, then perhaps 2 weeks of staff time will be given over to interviews and associated activities.

If the position to be filled is a senior one—for which the benefits package includes moving costs, relocation expenses, real estate brokerage fees, and perhaps bridge loans, mortgage payment assistance, tax assistance, and so forth—then it is easy for an enterprise to pay $50,000 for each new senior staff member who joins the company from a distant location.

Moreover, a new staff member needs a period of learning about the company, its policies, and the projects for which he or she has been hired, prior to becoming fully effective. The combined costs of the on-board staff in bringing the newcomer up to speed, plus the salary for the new employee, can add another $50,000 very easily. Thus, in round numbers, it is not impossible for an enterprise to spend $100,000 to fill a senior position: half for moving costs and half for training costs.

Hiring and relocation costs are handled differently by different enterprises, but two very common approaches can be noted in the United States: entry-level recruiting and senior-level recruiting.

Entry-Level Recruiting

With entry-level recruiting, the majority of new hires are recruited directly from universities and colleges, and they are then given additional training within the company. Companies which feature entry-level recruiting usually have well-developed in-house educational facilities for staff personnel. Pragmatically, the benefits packages and relocation expenses for hiring young people directly from college are lower than for hiring senior employees with households and dependents: perhaps only $10,000 per employee.

Companies with entry-level recruiting also tend to have long-term, fairly loyal employees, with attrition rates often being less than 5%. Also, since they tend to promote managers and executives from within the corporation, there is often a feeling of shared goals and aspirations at all levels. On the whole, entry-level recruiting has been quite successful.

Senior-Level Recruiting

Companies which practice senior-level recruiting, including many aerospace companies, do so because they want to get experienced people with proven track records. The costs of senior-level recruiting are notably higher than with entry-level recruiting: $60,000 per staff member might be a good average. Also, since senior-level people brought in from outside have no particular investment in the new company's policies or history, the turnover rate in companies which practice senior-level recruiting is quite high. By actual observation within a large multinational corporation which practised senior-level recruiting, annual voluntary attrition among the corporate software staff was in excess of 20%. Although senior-level recruiting can sometimes produce good results on critical projects, it cannot be said that it appears to be a successful long-term strategy.

THE IMPACT OF UNPAID OVERTIME BY SOFTWARE PROFESSIONALS

The average programmer or analyst in the United States tends to work 46 to 50 hours per week, but since many programmers are exempt professionals and are not paid overtime, their extra time usually does not show up on project cost or schedule reports and may not even show up on time cards.

Unpaid, unrecorded overtime is one of the major fuzzy issues which make productivity and schedule estimating difficult, and which can even conceal substantial productivity gains.

A 50-hour workweek is 25% more than a normal 40-hour week. If a new tool or technology is installed that improves productivity by 25% in real life, which is not a trivial amount, it may result in nothing more than the personnel going home on time and not working Saturdays. While this is valuable in human terms, project management will see no perceptible cost or schedule reductions from the technology, since what was eliminated was unpaid overtime.

As surprising as it may seem when first considered, a tool or technology may have to yield more than a 30% increase in real productivity before its influence can even be measured, since a 20% or 25% gain may be absorbed merely by reduction of unpaid overtime!

THE IMPACT OF BUSINESS SYSTEMS AND/OR STRATEGIC PLANNING

Productivity in the sense of improving speed or lowering costs is a difficult but relatively straightforward topic. But another aspect of productivity is very difficult to come to grips with: Are the programs and systems which an enterprise develops actually useful to it, in terms of helping to meet its strategic and tactical needs? Obviously high-speed, low-cost development of a system with no utility to the enterprise is not very productive.

The commonest way for large enterprises to develop a rational basis for evaluating the potentials of new systems is to carry out what is called a "business systems plan," or a "strategic information plan." This is a fairly lengthy, fairly expensive study in which an enterprise maps out its long-range strategic goals and then evaluates both current and future systems in terms of how much they will help in achieving those goals. The data elements and database structures that will be the enterprise information repositories are also included.

A full-scale business systems plan in a major corporation can take about 3 calendar months, involve upward of 20 full-time participants, involve "guest appearances" by another 25 or so participants, trigger the arrival of 5 to 10 consultants or facilitators, and cost in the realm of $500,000.

Proponents of business systems planning state that they focus attention on the linkages between software activities and enterprise strategies and that the studies are quite valuable. Opponents of business sytems planning state that once the study is completed, little or no change may occur as a result, and so the whole exercise is of small tangible value.

Observations from 10 enterprises that have performed business systems planned indicated that the plans were perceived as useful in 7 of the enterprises and as interesting but ineffective in 3 enterprises. The reason for the perception of success was related to the fact that the planning exercise brought out fresh facts and caused the participants to examine operations from unusual perspectives. The reason for the perception of failure, perhaps, was that the industries where the plans were viewed as ineffective were declining and heavily beset by foreign competition.

THE IMPACT OF USER PARTICIPATION IN REQUIREMENTS AND DESIGN

The significance of user participation in requirements and design is sharply different for two major classes of software:

1. For internal systems within an enterprise, where the users are specific departments and the individuals within those departments, a high level of user involvement is almost always valuable.
2. For commercial software that may be marketed to hundreds or

thousands of customers, the significance of user involvement is somewhat lower, due to the dilution of any one person's requirements into the larger whole.

One of the classic problems of internal software production has been the expansion of a project and its unexpected growth in size due to last-minute changes in user requirements. In-depth user participation, it is claimed, will minimize those last-minute changes. In observations on some 20 internal projects that did change scope and grow in size, the following points were noted:

• The users themselves were relatively uncertain of what they actually wanted the system to do.
• The requirements were handled more or less remotely, as an exchange of documents and a few face-to-face meetings.
• There was no use of prototypes, nor was user involvement either continuous or extensive.
• The first hands-on experiences with the systems by users took place shortly before delivery rather than during early prototyping.

By contrast, these observations were taken from five internal projects that remained relatively stable throughout their development:

• Users and developers worked together in a more or less continuous series of meetings and joint sessions.
• The major screens and outputs were prototyped, and the users were able to gain some actual familiarity with what the systems might be like when finished.

For commercial software aimed at large numbers of external users, it is sometimes possible for users to try early designs and prototypes under special arrangements, but it is perhaps more common to simply develop the project with only "surrogate" users such as quality assurance or marketing personnel.

THE IMPACT OF END-USER DEVELOPMENT

Very few computing topics have stirred as much interest as the recent advent of microcomputers within large corporations. By means of spread-sheets, query languages, and the like, these are allowing many end users to carry out some of their own data processing needs, without resorting to professional programming assistance.

The perceived impact of end-user computing has ranged widely in the literature. Extreme claims are on the one hand that end users will start doing all development and on the other hand that end users will do little or

**Table 4-2 Estimated 1984 professional and end-user programming popula-
tions in the United States by industry segment**

Industry segment	Professional programmers	End users	Ratio of end users to programmers
Civilian government	215,500	452,550	1 to 2
Manufacturing	200,000	489,300	1 to 2.5
Computing/software	129,300	581,850	1 to 4.5
Retail/wholesale	101,950	356,825	1 to 3.5
Finance/insurance	85,400	384,300	1 to 4.5
Military	81,250	154,375	1 to 2
Energy/natural resources	74,200	222,600	1 to 3
Education	57,800	63,500	1 to 1.1
Services	45,800	91,600	1 to 2
Other	28,800	72,000	1 to 2.5
Average			1 to 2.8
Total	1,020,000	2,868,980	

no serious development and will be restricted primarily to getting
information out of databases via query languages, augmented by some
personal spreadsheet applications.

As part of a demographic and technical analysis of industry trends,
the author (8) attemped to estimate the total number of professional
programmers and end users who could perform at least some programming in the United States in 1984, by industry segment. Table 4-2 presents
the results of this study; the margin of error is fairly large, since the data
was extrapolated from observations within a single conglomerate.

The next stage in the demographic study of end-user trends was to
analyze the sizes of the applications being performed, by means of
estimating the probable number of COBOL source statements they would
have taken. Table 4-3 gives the results of this analysis.

**Table 4-3 1984 size ranges of applications developed by professionals and
end-users**

Application size	Percentage developed by professional staff	Percentage developed by end-user staff
Superlarge (>512 KLOC)	100	0
Large (64 to 512 KLOC)	100	0
Medium (16 to 64 KLOC)	100	0
Low medium (2 to 16 KLOC)	99	1
Small (.5 to 2 KLOC)	95	5
Very small (<.5 KLOC)	90	10

As of 1985, end-user development is still a comparative rarity and is still concentrated exclusively in the low end of the application size range. Since industrial and commercial software is characterized by very large volumes of very small applications, it can be hypothesized that end-user development will certainly become an increasingly important factor. However, it is highly unlikely that end users will develop large industrial and commercial systems, since even if the tools became available, it would take too long to accomplish. Therefore, it is unlikely that they would wish to do so. A probable scenario is for small special-purpose applications to migrate into the end-user domain, while the professional programming staffs continue to concentrate on large industrial systems.

THE IMPACT OF INFORMATION CENTERS

One of the quickest-growing phenomena to sweep through large commercial and industrial organizations has been the advent of "information centers," which are groups of professional programmers who are chartered to assist end users in getting started with microcomputers, database query languages, simple programming, and the like.

The rationale behind information centers is that having personal computers in the hands of untrained end users will not be very valuable and may even be detrimental. The information center concept was introduced to give training, advice, and assistance to corporate personnel as they begin to move into the microcomputing era.

Typical information center tasks include subsetting large corporate databases and making the subsets available to end users for spreadsheet analysis and smaller personal computer databases; assisting in evaluating word processing, spreadsheet, and other end-user tools; and answering questions and pleas for assistance.

Observations at more than 15 information centers in large corporations indicate that they seem to be generally beneficial. The only negative aspect observed is that if the ratio of end users to information center staff goes much beyond 100 to 1, the quality of service tends to degrade. In extreme cases, such as when the ratio of end users to center staff exceeds 200 to 1, even getting someone to answer the phone becomes difficult and the whole concept of the information center becomes frustrating for everyone.

THE IMPACT OF DEVELOPMENT CENTERS

In most large enterprises, technology transfer is painfully slow. An unpublished study by the the author within IBM (9) noted that technology transfer tended to take the shape of a Fibonacci series, and if the target population for a new technology was 1000 professionals, it would take a year to reach 15%, three years to reach 50%, and five years to reach 90%. By then, so many people would have quit that reaching 100% was unlikely.

The reasons for slow technology transfer are not hard to understand:

- There is a shortage of free time to learn about new methods.
- There are competing methods, and it is difficult to choose which ones to learn.
- There is a natural human tendency to do familiar things, rather than learn new things, until some strong external pressure intervenes.

Development centers are a recent attempt to overcome the problems of slow technology transfer within large enterprises, and speed things up a bit. The functions of a full-scale development center include many or most of the following:

1. Exploring new tools and methods of potential value
2. Teaching new tools and methods to software technical personnel
3. Providing a source of in-house expertise on technical subjects, such as networks, databases, local-area networks, telecommunications, and other rapidly changing technologies
4. Piloting new methods on small projects, to prove their effectiveness
5. Setting corporate policies and procedures on software tools, methods, and approaches

Whether or not development centers will be perceived as effective and useful depends upon several variables. One of the major ones is the expertise or the skill within the development center. In enterprises where development center personnel are in fact the top experts in their fields, the center concept seems to work fairly well. However, if development center personnel and management are not visible experts whose ideas are respected, then the development center concept can become a negative factor, with the entire group coming to be regarded as not living up to expectations.

Of the development centers within five large corporations, three were considered useful and successful. One was considered too academic and divorced from practical day-to-day problems, and another was disbanded after 2 years and the staff reabsorbed. In the case of the disbanded development center, the personnel were considered arrogant rather than capable and dictatorial rather than helpful.

THE IMPACT OF INTERNAL TRAINING AND EDUCATION

Internal training of professional employees ranges from a high of the Japanese average of 1 month per engineer per year (10), through the Bell Labs and IBM averages of 10 to 15 days per employee per year, through the many companies that have less than a week per employee per year, to the thousands of enterprises that have no internal training at all.

Which mode is most cost-effective? Lutz (11) reports that enterprises with internal training rates of 10 to 15 days per year tend to have higher productivity rates and lower attrition rates than enterprises which provide no training at all. Both Bell Labs and IBM are convinced that education is beneficial, and IBM has a pair of very well organized internal Systems Research Institutes, in New York City and in La Hulpe, Belgium, open to its software professionals, where students attend 10 weeks of graduate-level courses. These institutes are considered to be very successful by IBM management, and almost without exception the students who attend feel that the knowledge gained benefits their work when they return.

Indeed, the internal Systems Research Institutes proved to be so beneficial that an equivalent set of organizations was created for IBM's customers: the System Science Institutes in New York, Chicago, Los Angeles, and several European cities.

As a rule of thumb, successful major corporations place training and education fairly high on their lists of priorities. IBM and ITT both have internal faculties of more than 1000 instructors. The former chairman of ITT, Lyman Hamilton, once remarked informally to the author that ITT had a larger educational faculty than any U.S. university. Collectively, the U.S. Fortune 500 companies may have internal faculties and internal educational budgets that exceed those of the 500 largest universities and colleges in the United States.

THE IMPACT OF STANDARDS AND FORMAL DEVELOPMENT METHODS

Most large corporations have fairly massive internal standards programs. Most large corporations that produce software also have some kind of formal systems development methodology which often takes the form of a set of loose-leaf binders containing written procedures and directives aimed at defining the software development process and the utilization of standard practices.

Unfortunately, from observations of more than a hundred large enterprises in the United States and Europe, it would appear that the average manual of software standards and procedures is more than 500 pages in size and more than 3 years behind the actual state of the art. Very few contain any references to prototyping, fourth-generation languages, or any trends of the last few years.

In the late 1970s and early 1980s defining the life cycle was considered the ultimate weapon in achieving productivity and quality, and many enterprises devoted considerable efforts to putting out large binders filled with well-intentioned and sometimes useful information. Not only were internal efforts common, but a visit to a large bookstore in 1983 turned up some 50 volumes dealing with software development methods, standards, and practices.

The U.S. Department of Defense and the associated military services have carried the formalization of software standards and practices to its ultimate extreme, in the famous military specifications which govern so many aspects of software procurement and defense projects.

The fundamental question is: Are these standards and procedures actually useful? In a survey of some 50 large corporations, including 10 which did defense contracting, the following observations were noted:

- 100% stated that the standards were larger than necessary.
- 60% stated that the standards were used intermittently.
- 20% stated that the standards were used on all projects.
- 20% stated that the standards were no longer used at all.
- 25% stated that the standards were seldom updated.
- 20% stated that the standards were never updated.
- 55% stated that they did not know if the standards were updated or not.

Although the results were ambiguous, the weight of subjective evidence and personal opinions indicated that most people felt a certain comfort from the existence of standards and system development methodologies, even if they were only infrequently used. They were considered as being somewhat like rules of order: seldom needed, but useful from time to time to settle disputes.

A new generation of automated system development methodologies operating on microcomputers and mainframe computers is starting to appear. It should be technically achievable within a few years to merely "dial in" a description of the kind of system or program to be developed in order to have a fully automated system return all valid standards, policies, and even statutes which affect the project.

THE IMPACT OF CANCELED PROJECTS AND DISASTERS

In large corporations, a high percentage of projects are never finished or delivered to end users. Sometimes, as in the case of IBM, this can result from a deliberate policy of letting two or more competing projects get started, and then selecting the strongest for final delivery. Within the large-system divisions of IBM, the cancellation rate was about 25% betwen 1968 and 1979. In other cases, cancellations result from enormous cost and schedule overruns or from customer cancellation of the project.

Regardless of the reason for cancellation, canceled projects have a notable but often unmeasured impact on enterprise productivity. If productivity metrics are applied only to delivered systems, then a major cost element will be left out that can affect the total enterprise.

One useful "sanity check" is to consider productivity in terms of the total annual output of a software organization divided by the total number of staff that works there. This method, which absorbs canceled projects, temporary code, and other often unmeasured items, is very sobering to the enterprises which perform it: Annual rates of less than 200 lines of source code per employee are not uncommon, even for enterprises where completed projects may exceed 3000 to 4000 lines of code per employee-year.

THE IMPACT OF PROJECT REDIRECTIONS AND RESTARTS

It sometimes happens in mid-development that customer requirements change, that new hardware has to be considered, or some other significant event occurs that leads to partial redesign and redevelopment. For example, when IBM first introduced the HIPO design technique in the late 1960s, one of the first projects to use it had already completed perhaps 25% of its initial design with conventional flowcharts. While the HIPO method was useful, its imposition in mid-development caused a considerable amount of rework.

While such occurrences are normal parts of life and should not be viewed as unusual, they tend to affect the literature on software productivity in negative ways. Often the projects that have exceeded their schedules and budgets are the ones that had been redirected, but the redirection was not included in the final productivity analysis.

THE IMPACT OF PROJECT TRANSFERS FROM CITY TO CITY

Only fairly large multilocation enterprises encounter the problems of transferring projects from one site to another during mid-development. But when this occurs it always adds to the schedule and reduces productivity, since the new staff must be brought up to speed, and often personnel from the original site are transferred or get temporary assignments at the new location, adding to the overall dollar costs and person-months required for the project.

For projects within IBM, such as those transferred between laboratories, the author estimated about a 12% increase in total project costs and about a 3-month increase in overall schedules as a result of the transfers.

THE IMPACT OF RESPONSE TIME AND COMPUTER FACILITIES

Articles by Thadani (12) and Lambert (13) in the *IBM Systems Journal* elevated the topic of subsecond response time into a major productivity topic in 1984. The thesis of Thadani and Lambert, which has some experimental support, is that delay in response time on trivial tasks such as entering individual source code statements is psychologically disruptive and causes a longer delay than the actual elapsed time; usually for each second of delay, at least one more second of lost time will occur. Since a large programming system can have thousands of such trivial transactions, and very large systems can have millions, the cumulative lost time will amount to very significant proportions.

This line of reasoning may be sound, and indeed there is experimental evidence from outside the domain of programming, such as how speech is perceived, which indicates that too long a delay between items in a series slows down comprehension.

However, what the articles fail to mention is that subsecond response time is a very rare occurrence outside of a few large software engineering labs. In visits to over 50 major corporations in 1984, only two (IBM and one other) actually had achieved subsecond response time for trivial transactions.

The norm in the United States, at least among some of the larger corporations developing internal software, is for response times in the 2- to 5-second range, with occasional pauses out to 10 seconds. This may indeed be less than desirable, but since the phenomenon is so widespread it may not cause any competitive disadvantages.

Subsecond response time is starting to become a very significant factor in the marketing of powerful microcomputers and minicomputer-based workstations. Subsecond response times are much more easily achievable by offloading routine tasks to the smaller processors than by adding more capacity to the mainframes.

THE IMPACT OF PHYSICAL FACILITIES AND OFFICE SPACE

The software profession has been growing faster than almost any other occupational segment in the United States for the last 10 years; a problem throughout much of the world is where to put all of the programmers.

From observations in more than 100 U.S. and European companies, and a smaller number in Asia and the Middle East, it can be said that overcrowded physical facilities is a general way of life for software development in 1985. It is not uncommon to find office space totaling less than 50 square feet per programmer, with two to four programmers being jammed together around a common terminal. File cabinets, shelves for reference manuals, and storage space are luxuries beyond what many enterprises can offer.

Does this situation affect productivity? Because the situation is so widespread as to be almost the norm, it is difficult to arrive at an answer.

In the early 1970s, IBM began to explore the architectural requirements for a new office building to be aimed at software development. This building, when completed, became the Santa Teresa Programming Center in San Jose, California. The architect, Gerald McCue (14), had interviews carried out with several hundred programmers to find out what kinds of features they felt were necessary, and then built Santa Teresa in response.

Those who have seen the complex, and especially those who have worked there, are very favorably impressed. Each programmer has a private office, in a standard 10- by 10-foot configuration. Within the office the programmer has of course a terminal, and in addition almost 30 square feet of desk and table space for spreading out listings and documents. Each office has special bookshelves and cabinets for reference manuals, with lockable sections for items that need security precautions. The desks themselves have adequate drawer space, and additional file cabinets are also available. For every eight offices, a small conference room is available for reviews and group meetings. On the whole, the complex is one of the most comfortable and convenient office buildings within IBM, and each year it receives favorable comments on the annual opinion surveys.

But does this building improve productivity? In the opinion of one of IBM's vice presidents, when asked this question at a meeting, the facility was responsible for about an 11% productivity gain, compared to what had been accomplished by the same personnel in their old facility (15).

It would be interesting to have a similar statement about the effect of poor physicial conditions, to quantify the impact of being overcrowded. However, there are almost no studies on this topic in the productivity literature.

For the near future programming and software development will remain physically uncomfortable for many practitioners, for three main reasons:

1. Data processing and programming staffs have grown so rapidly that they have outpaced enterprise abilities to find adequate office space.

2. As of 1985, a majority of the world's programming population is employed in office buildings that were not planned for programming and hence were not constructed to meet software needs.
3. There is no quantified, hard evidence that work environments have a tangible impact on software productivity, although there is reason to suspect that the environment does have an impact.

It can be hypothesized that if IBM's excellent Santa Teresa complex is responsible for an 11% productivity gain, then the same projects and the same personnel trying to do the work in overcrowded, physically poor surroundings might have experienced a 10% or so productivity loss, compared to a normal environment of two persons sharing an office of reasonable size and a terminal. However, this conjecture is untested.

THE IMPACT OF ACQUIRING AND MODIFYING PURCHASED OR LEASED SOFTWARE

Surprisingly, the literature on the cost and productivity aspects of acquiring and using externally developed software is almost nonexistent, and that which does exist is usually not based on case studies, but only provides general advice. The major cost factors of software acquisition are:

1. Legal and contract negotiation. The cost can range from nothing for off-the-shelf packages to quite a large amount for custom contracts.
2. Evaluation and validation that the acquired program actually does what it is supposed to do. The decision can range from acceptance "as is" for a few well-developed programs to a decision to reject the package. One large development center in 1981 started to evaluate a commercial relational database package with a view to acquiring a corporate license, but the product turned out to be so immature and unready that after more than 18 months it was still not deemed really useful. The evaluation eventually totaled 24 calendar months and almost 9 person-months.
3. Customizing the product, if needed, to meet enterprise requirements. This is the weakest link in the software acquisition chain, and making substantial modifications to acquired packages can easily destroy the cost benefits.
4. Installing the new product on the computers where it will run, and linking it with any existing programs if needed. Here too the costs can range from nothing if it is a standalone program to quite a large amount if the new product must share data or interface with "alien" systems by other vendors.

5. Training of users in the new product. This can range from self-teaching for some of the new iconographic tools to almost undecipherable documentation for the worst-case examples.

As a rule of thumb, acquisition is a very cost-effective strategy if a commercial program has received good reviews in the software literature, if responses of existing customers are favorable at conferences and user groups, if the developer has a good reputation, and if the acquired program does not require heavy modification and customization.

Buying or leasing software is roughly analogous to buying a new home: Tract houses are readily available and often pretty good, but if your requirements are for custom architecture and innovative construction, you will have to build the home on your own.

In unpublished research, the author interviewed 15 programming managers and technical personnel to inquire what was the break-even point in modifying leased software. The general consensus was that almost any modification was hazardous, and the greater the modification, the greater the hazards. The following subjective recommendations were noted:

• If the vendor does not wish the code to be modified, it is generally dangerous to do it over these objections. At the very least, modifications will jeopardize service and warranty repairs.

• If the vendor will carry out the modifications with its own personnel under a contract or to complete the sale of the product, this is usually better than trying to perform the modifications after purchase.

• Once a purchased or leased software package is modified, all subsequent vendor enhancements or improvements must be applied with caution.

THE IMPACT OF RESTRUCTURING AND REPAIRING AGING SYSTEMS

Since the late 1970s, a new subindustry is starting to appear which may grow to major proportions before 1990. This new industry uses new tools and methods for analyzing and restructuring aging software systems, converting unstructured systems into relatively modern, structured ones.

As of 1985, several companies are offering either services or products that can restructure old code. In interviews, programming managers at five companies who have used one, or more than one, of these new concepts claimed the results were surprisingly good. The restructuring activity found many sources of error, and the new programs both seemed more reliable and in some cases seemed to outperform the previous versions.

Typically restructured programs averaged 10% or 15% larger size than the original versions. Performance was typically 10% to 20% slower than the original version measured at the microsecond level. But when monthly or quarterly throughput was considered, the restructured programs sometimes outperformed the original versions, because they did not fail or produce as many errors.

As of 1985, the commercial tools are aimed primarily at COBOL applications; this is a reasonable choice, considering the vast number of such programs.

The actual quantification of the costs and value of the restructuring process remains ambiguous, however. As a service, the fees range from less than $1 to perhaps $2 per source code statement. While the restructured programs are no doubt sounder and easier to maintain, it is not yet clear what the payback period is for the restructuring methodology.

THE IMPACT OF INTERNAL POLITICS AND POWER STRUGGLES

In today's large enterprises, terminations, transfers, and staff assignments have replaced the poison used in the court of the Borgias as the normal mode of eliminating rivals. Yet except for a few sociological studies, such as the excellent report by Keen on information systems and resistance to change (16), the topic of rivalry almost never surfaces in the productivity and quality literature.

The normal human mode in office environments is to have a circle of friends with whom one shares information and feels comfortable, a circle of neutral acquaintances with whom one occasionally deals, and a circle of enemies who may or may not be active opponents.

In several of the most chaotic and ill-planned systems which the author has observed first-hand, the personal dislikes among the project managers overshadowed the impact of tools and technologies. As a case in point, a major cost-estimating project ended up with no estimating capabilities at all, but only accounting features, because of the personal antagonisms between the manager handling the accounting portion and the manager developing a predictive estimating package. Indeed, three calendar years and over $500,000 were expended without any predictive capabilities at all being incorporated into the final system, as a result of territorial and political disagreement.

While anecdotal cases such as the above are very common, the topic of internal politics is usually not amenable to controlled study or to quantification, since most enterprises don't publically admit to the existence of the situation. However, from close observation within major corporations such as IBM and ITT, it can be hypothesized that perhaps 10% to 15% of the really catastrophic project failures are at least partly caused by personal human dislikes and political or territorial disputes.

IBM, under the policies originally established by T.J. Watson Sr., has one of the most effective ways of handling disruptive personal and political troubles. The normal IBM mode for dealing with those who are technically capable but find themselves in personal conflict situations is reassignment, since IBM is a very large corporation with hundreds of locations. In other corporations, the normal mode might be termination, which is not a good overall policy because the winning political groups tend to stock a location with people who think more or less alike.

THE IMPACT OF LEGAL, STATUTORY, AND WARRANTY CONSTRAINTS

As of 1985, legal, statutory, and warranty constraints on software are of only minor significance and probably affect only 5% or so of the programs in existence today. However, as time passes, the significance of these factors will become much greater.

Already programs that deal with sensitive financial or personal information are subject to various legal sanctions, as are programs dealing with aspects of stock transfers, commodity futures, and the like.

From a productivity standpoint, legal involvement is likely to stretch out schedules and raise costs. At the very least, it may cause legal services to become a new line item in software cost estimates. For one fairly small software product observed by the author, the schedule time for the legal reviews was twice as long as that for actually developing the product, and the attorneys' fees were greater than the software development costs.

Generally speaking, software vendors have not yet faced consequential damages due to errors in their software, but future generations may look back upon this time with longing. Doubtless within a few years a suit will be brought by someone losing valuable information or suffering property damage as a result of a software error, and if negligence or culpability is determined, then the future of software will be different forevermore.

Warranties are only emerging as a major topic in 1985, and most microcomputer software is notable for the fact that it clearly states that there are no warranties, either explicit or implied.

However, one of the emerging competitive factors in the software business will be the offering of money-back guarantees on microcomputer software products. This already occurs for some imported microcomputers, and it is likely to be an increasing trend.

THE IMPACT OF U.S. EXPORT LICENSE REQUIREMENTS

The U.S. Departments of Commerce and Defense are trying to slow down the migration of high-technology products and concepts to communist nations by requiring export licenses on the part of companies which sell software or computer components outside the United States.

From a productivity standpoint, this policy adds about 6 weeks and some new legal fees to internationally marketed products, and it tends to give a minor competitive advantage to companies large enough to have permanent legal staffs and Washington offices.

From a national standpoint, the policy seems to weaken the U.S. economy, since overseas customers may well prefer to buy high-technology products from Japan, Taiwan, Hungary, or wherever else the same classes of products can be acquired without such constraints.

The primary impact of this policy is to discourage American exports and to encourage international customers to buy from other high-technology countries.

THE IMPACT OF MEASURING PRODUCTIVITY AND QUALITY

While it is theoretically possible to improve both quality and productivity in real life without actually measuring the results, in practice it seldom happens that way. Generally, enterprises whose managers are serious about productivity want to know the results, and so some kind of measurement program is developed soon after, or often before, productivity and quality improvement programs are started.

Measuring software productivity and quality is not an easy task, as Chapters 1 and 2 pointed out. It is not a cheap task either. For example, in its large commercial software laboratories, IBM spends the equivalent of 5% of all development costs on measurement-related activities. However, IBM measures full life-cycle productivity and quality, from early design through the lifetime of the product, and makes use of the data to try to improve performance.

More typical corporate measurement programs run from 1.5% to 3% of the cost of developing software and measure only subsets of the kinds of information IBM would collect. More typical would be quality measurements that start at testing, rather than at design, and productivity measurements that cover only coding and testing. These partial measurements are useful, but obviously they focus attention on what is being measured, and tend to divert attention from some fairly important aspects that are not included.

The minimum set of practical measurements that can actually be used to help make improvements in software productivity and quality are these:

• Decide early whether you want to measure development productivity or delivery productivity. This is a major question with profound impact. The really sophisticated enterprises are moving beyond development productivity and are starting to concentrate on delivery. That is, they are measuring productivity in such a way that reusable modules, included code, and other high-productivity elements are included. While few enterprises can *develop* software at rates much in excess of 3000 source code statements per person-year, it is possible to *deliver* systems at output rates in excess of 30,000 source code statements per person-year by reusing standard elements.

• Measure the defect removal efficiencies of reviews, inspections, and testing by recording all of the defects which these activities find, and compare that to the number of defects reported during the first 2 years of actual production.

• Measure the distribution of defects through the modules and programs of large systems, to isolate and eliminate error-prone modules.

• Measure the total quantity of documents produced and the total number of screens and menus created. If the measures show that the number of English words is larger than 30 for every line of source code in the system, then use the measures to justify documentation improvements such as integrated graphics/text terminals.

• Measure productivity using both lines of source code and function points for the first few years. The reason for using both is to help in calibrating the ratio of source code statements to function points and to highlight any problem areas where function points are not fully effective, such as programs with heavy compute functions but only limited amounts of input and output.

• At the project level, have your productivity measurements include all of the key activities of development: Start with early planning and requirements, and move steadily through the development cycle, including design, document production, coding, reviews, inspections, integration, testing, and management. If your staff received training or education, include it. If you hired new staff for the project, include acquisition costs. If your project had high travel and communication costs, note it down. If your project has a quality assurance function, include their time and costs also.

• At the unit or enterprise level, a fairly effective way of approaching net productivity is to record the total number of function points and the total number of source code statements delivered to users and divide those quantities by the total number of employees of the unit in question.

That is, include all software-related staff, without leaving out anyone: secretaries, managers, project librarians, training personnel, quality assurance personnel and so forth. This method is not granular, but it focuses attention on enterprise productivity and it tends to be effective in comparing different organizations and even different companies.

The purpose of measurement is to answer questions about how much software costs, how much time is needed to deliver needed functions, and above all, why significant variations occur. Without knowing why the variations occurred, even exact knowledge of software costs and schedules will only be frustrating. Therefore it is important to assign measurement responsibilities to intelligent, active personnel who will not merely record numbers, but explore the process and project variables that caused the numbers to be what they were.

It is not uncommon in large enterprises, of say 1000 programmer/analysts, for the corporate software measurement function to be set up more or less as follows:

- A manager of programming metrics
- Two full-time statisticians
- Three analysts to work with project managers and collect the data
- Two data-entry clerks
- Two programmers, to develop the analysis and reporting routines to serve the measurement function

The output from such a group is often a large annual report of perhaps 100 pages on software quality and productivity, with smaller quarterly updates.

A fundamental question arises: Is a fairly large investment in measurement cost-justified or justified by tangible improvements? Within five large enterprises that had established permanent software measurement groups, all of the senior enterprise managers and a majority of the software managers thought that the measurement efforts had been worthwhile in eliminating vague and subjective claims and in giving all software projects known targets and common goals. No one was fully satisfied that measurement had solved major problems by itself, but most felt that the problems were much better understood.

When the SPQR tool described in Appendix A was used in the five enterprises with measurement departments, their projects appeared to have high productivity, compared to seven other enterprises that did not have measurements. The conclusion reached was that enterprises sophisticated enough to measure were sophisticated enough to solve other problems. The enterprises which were not measuring were not solving other problems, because sometimes they did not know the problems existed.

THE IMPACT OF PRODUCTIVITY AND QUALITY IMPROVEMENT PROGRAMS

Many enterprises have become interested in improving quality and productivity; the next stage is to try to make some progress toward accomplishing the improvements. The methods for doing this are numerous. Those chosen often depend on the overall size of the enterprise's software development and maintenance organizations, which of course reflect the overall size of the enterprise.

Productivity and Quality Improvements within Small Software Organizations of 1 to 10 Employees

Because small organizations tackle projects that are usually also small, productivity gains at smaller enterprises often occur from more capital investment in workstations and tools, which can make a significant impact on small projects in terms of schedule reduction. Obviously expending capital will drive up costs for the year. Similarly, choice of programming language can be significant, assuming that the staff knows more than one or two languages to choose from. In this size range, it is often helpful to carefully consider the use of packaged software, rather than in-house development, and to explore the use of spreadsheets for end users. For quality gains, small team reviews and inspections sometimes help, but the basic fact is that for very small projects the skills and abilities of the individual staff members tend to outweigh most other factors.

Productivity and Quality Improvements within Low-medium-sized Software Organizations of 10 to 50 Employees

Here too, project sizes tend to be rather small, and so capital investment in workstations and tools are effective in reducing schedules, although not in reducing costs. Organizations in this size range are usually too small for full specialization, but having a seasoning of programmers who are expert in selected topics such as networks, database products, and the like gives the effect of an impromptu "development center." In this size range, carefully considering the use of packaged software rather than in-house development and exploring the use of spreadsheets for end users are often helpful. Also, for internal projects, close relationships between the users and the development staffs can head off painful changes late in development, and prototyping before main development begins can be very effective for both quality and productivity improvements. Organizations in this size range are often candidates for database products, and if one is selected, then other productivity aids associated with the database environment can be used.

Productivity and Quality Improvements within Medium-sized Software Organizations of 50 to 200 Employees

Medium-sized organizations can tackle fairly sizable programs, for which documentation becomes expensive and defect removal very expensive, with many defects being traceable back to the original requirements and design. Also, medium-sized organizations are large enough to have some internal specialization, such as testing specialists, design specialists, and database specialists. Medium-sized companies often try to improve on the requirements and design of software by prototyping, by using formal design methods supported by graphics/text workstations, and by having close relationships with users during requirements. One fairly new approach is to have joint working sessions on requirements and design, in which the users and developers have intense planning sessions. Also frequently used are tools associated with database products, such as active data dictionaries, and application and program generators keyed to the database that the enterprise has selected. Also, adequate workstations and response times become significant factors. Pretest reviews, code inspections, and of course prototyping will be fairly effective in improving quality. Medium-sized organizations are starting to explore both development centers and information centers, with unquantified but subjectively positive results.

Productivity and Quality Improvements within Large Software Organizations of 200 to 1000 Employees

Large software organizations at the leading edge of productivity tend to make use of standard designs and standard reusable code modules. Developing a library of standard designs and reusable code can require several years and more than $1,000,000, so this technology tends to be found within large software centers. An effective approach outside of the domain of reusable code and standard designs is to concentrate on requirements rigor, prototyping, and solving design problems. Large organizations with high productivity usually have ratios of workstations to staff that approximate 1 to 1, and they have adopted good design methods supported by graphics/text terminals. Within large organizations, prototyping and full pretest reviews and code inspections are demonstrably effective for quality as well as productivity. Because large organizations are big enough for specialization, they have options such as establishing permanent test departments with skilled specialists and establishing permanent maintenance departments with full-time maintenance programmers. The impact of specialization on productivity and quality is still not quantified, but it seems to be a significant factor. Large organizations in 1985 tend to have formal development centers and formal information centers, with unquantified but subjectively positive results.

Productivity and Quality Improvements within Very Large Software Organizations of More than 1000 Employees

A demographic study by the author (8) indicated that in 1983 in the United States, there were perhaps 200 enterprises with more than 1000 software personnel at their locations. As might be expected, some of these are computer companies such as IBM, but others include banks, insurance companies, government installations, telecommunications companies, and a surprisingly rich variety of other enterprises.

Productivity in very large organizations is a special case. The very large organizations at the leading edge, which are using standard designs and reusable code as basic technologies, are very productive indeed: Delivery rates in excess of 30,000 source code statements per person-year have been noted. However, for projects that do not lend themselves to construction from standard elements, productivity within large organizations reverts to more normal ranges.

Very large enterprises with good conventional development productivity usually take extreme care with requirements and design. Indeed, many large organizations have developed internal, proprietary requirements and design tools that are superior to those available on the commercial market. This fact brings up a major point about very large organizations: They tend to make their own tools, to a much greater degree than smaller enterprises. Very few of the 200 organizations with more than 1000 programmers lack internal tool and support groups whose job it is to facilitate the work of application developers. Other kinds of specialization are also common, and very large enterprises often have full test departments, formal quality assurance departments, formal maintenance departments, data administration groups, and so forth. The concept is to highlight these areas and let staff members become expert in their intricacies.

Another point is also significant: The percentage of organizations with formal quality and productivity measurement programs is higher for very large than for smaller enterprises. Perhaps 25% of the very large organizations have formal measurement groups, while less than 10% of smaller enterprises have such groups.

Within this size range, a 1 to 1 parity of workstations to development personnel is found in the high-productivity enterprises.

Very large enterprises also share another interesting phenomenon: active technology exploration and technology transfer. Several very large enterprises have departments whose full-time work is to screen potentially interesting software packages and arrange corporate licenses for suitable ones. Also, many very large enterprises have sizable internal training and educational facilities and teach programmers and systems personnel their internal conventions and methods.

As might be expected, these ancillary functions result in high overhead rates as well. Nonetheless, as surprising as it may sound when first encountered, productivity rates within very large enterprises often exceed that of smaller groups, because of many factors:

• *Specialization* and the application of skilled personnel to defect removal, quality assurance, database design, network design, and several other esoteric domains where ordinary training is not always sufficient

• *Active technology exploration and technology transfer* by means of formal research groups, development centers, information centers, training groups, and so forth

• *Capital spending* and the provision of adequate tools and workstations for software personnel

• *Measurement* and the existence of formal measurement groups to collect, analyze, and report on measurement trends

SUMMARY AND CONCLUSIONS ON THE INTANGIBLE SOFTWARE FACTORS

Programming and software are still less than 40 years old. Our rate of progress in moving from an intuitive art form practiced in isolation to an engineering discipline is actually about as fast as that in any other science. A survey of chemical engineering 50 years ago, of geology 100 years ago, and of physics before 1910 revealed problems similar to those of ours, and it implies that software professionals are not yet members of a mature discipline but are certainly aware of deficiencies and trying to solve them.

The fundamental weakness of software, relative to the "hard" sciences, has been the lack of reliable metrics for either productivity or quality. Not only are lines-of-code metrics not reliable, but the paradoxical way they behave has tended to conceal real progress causing the first generation of software productivity researchers to come up with some erroneous conclusions.

Now that the essential mathematics of software productivity are no longer hidden behind the cloud of confusion associated with lines of source code, it becomes possible to explore factors which previously were not even recognized as significant.

As of 1985, the 25 factors discussed in this chapter are intangible and difficult to quantify. But it is not a law of nature that they will always be that way. For example, one of the assertions is that large enterprises tend to have higher productivity rates than smaller enterprises. These large enterprises are also more active in their use of high-level and fourth-generation languages than are smaller enterprises. So such an observation could not have been made using lines of source code as the productivity indicator, because the true productivity rates would have been lost in confusion. Now that the assertion has been made and can be verified by looking at function-point productivity records, within a few years it can be either confirmed or disproved.

Although software development is not yet a true science, the steps that are being taken are leading in that direction. By the end of the century, it is likely that software engineering will be just as solid a discipline as aeronautical engineering, mechanical engineering, or electrical engineering.

The shared goal of those of us in the software engineering community is to put our discipline beside the other sciences as a field of endeavor that gives pride to its practitioners and benefits humanity.

REFERENCES

1. Parkinson, C.N.; *Parkinson's Law and Other Stories in Administration*; Houghton Mifflin; Boston; 1962.
2. Brooks, F.P. Jr.; *The Mythical Man-Month*; Addison-Wesley; Reading, MA; 1982.
3. Putnam, L.; *Software Cost Estimating and Life-Cycle Control: Getting the Software Numbers*; IEEE Press; Silver Spring, Md; Cat. No. EHO 165-1; 1980.
4. Graicunias, I; "Program Quality and Programmer Productivity"; *IBM Corporation*; San Jose, CA; TR02.764; p. 4.
5. Cougar, J.D. and Zawacki, R.A.; "What Motivates DP Professionals"; *Datamation*, September 1978; pp. 116-123.
6. U.S. Bureau of Industrial Economics; Department of Commerce; 1984 U.S. Industrial Outlook for 200 Industries with Projections for 1989; U.S. Government Printing Office; Washington, D.C.; 1984; p. 550.
7. Plotkin, S.; "The Real Cost of DP Professionals"; Included in *The Real Cost Workbook*; Stephen Plotkin; Glen Mills, PA; 1982.
8. Jones, T.C.; "Technical and Demographic Trends in the Computing Industry"; *Proceedings of the 1983 Data Systems Structured Design Conference*; Ken Orr & Associates; Topeka, KS; October 1983; pp. 3-27.
9. Jones, T.C.; Unpublished internal correspondence within IBM on the rate of technology transfer; September 1973.
10. Passin, H.; *Society and Education in Japan*; Kodansha International; Tokyo; 1965.
11. Lutz, T.; Proceedings of the ITT Technology Planning Conference; Bolton, MA; June 1980; pp. 74-79.

12. Thadani, A.J.; "Factors Affecting Programmer Productivity During Application Development"; *IBM Systems Journal*, Vol. 23, No. 1, 1984; pp. 19-35.
13. Lambert, G.N.; "A Comparative Study of System Response Time on Programmer Development Productivity"; *IBM Systems Journal*, Vol. 23, No. 1, 1984; pp. 36-43.
14. McCue, G.M.; "IBM's Santa Teresa Laboratory—An Architectural Environment for Program Development"; *IBM Systems Journal*, Vol. 17, No. 1, 1978; pp. 4-25.
15. Quotation from IBM executives on the productivity impact of the Santa Teresa laboratory; included in *Programming Productivity—Issues for the Eighties*; IEEE Press; Silver Spring, MD; Cat. No. EHO 186-7; 1981; p. 318.
16. Keen, P.G.W.; "Information Systems and Organizational Change"; *Communications of the ACM*, Vol. 24, No. 1, January 1981; pp. 24-33.

APPENDIX
A

DESCRIPTION OF THE SOFTWARE PRODUCTIVITY, QUALITY, AND RELIABILITY MODEL (SPQR)

The SPQR estimating model used in the case studies within this book is a general-purpose estimating tool developed to allow the major factors which affect software projects to be studied both independently and in combination.

The SPQR tool consciously aims at the entire spectrum of all current software classes and types, rather than being restricted to a subset. Thus SPQR can perform productivity and quality predictions for the entire range of software classes and types currently being developed throughout the industry: batch application programs, interactive application programs, database programs, real-time systems, telecommunications systems, embedded systems, tool and support programs, operating systems, internal software, commercial software, military software, and many other kinds.

Further, because of the very high incidence of enhancement and maintenance work in the computing domain, the SPQR tool was developed to predict effort of adding code to existing systems, for both enhancements and maintenance. The tool was also aimed at predicting the maintenance that occurs on commercial software packages when the package is installed at the customer sites by vendor personnel and field service is provided, as well as central defect repairs.

The model has been calibrated against historical data from a broad spectrum of programs and systems and has generally come within plus or minus 15% of the observed results, except at the extreme ends of the model's operational range: that is, for programs of less than about 500 source statements, where individual human variance makes modeling uncertain, and for systems larger than about 15,000,000 source statements, where the time spans are so long and the data from successful projects is so sparse that accuracy is difficult to validate.

Matching historical data within plus or minus 15% does not actually imply an equivalent level of accuracy for a model. The probable error range and inaccuracy of the historical data itself may often be more than plus or minus 25%. Cases have been observed in which historical data was wrong by almost an order of magnitude; it was allegedly data for total development, but in fact it covered only coding through desk checking, omitting requirements, design, documentation, quality assurance, integration, and many other activities.

Although the SPQR tool contains a total of more than 175 variables, any particular estimate usually invokes and manipulates between 50 and 100 of them, depending upon whether the program is new or an enhancement; whether the project is internal, commercial, or military; whether reusable code is part of the project; and so forth. In other words, the SPQR tool is actually a composite of a number of different predictive formulas that deal with various classes and types of software, each of which can be invoked as required.

SPQR is a constructive "micro estimating" model, in that its mode of operation is to perform separate estimates for each activity that it predicts and then sum the results together to construct the final, overall estimate. This method tends to yield higher overall accuracies than the "macro estimating" technique, in which an overall project estimate is performed and then decomposed by means of ratios or algorithms into individual task, activity, and phase estimates.

SPQR is novel in its approach to software resource estimating: Its algorithms are based on the assumption that defect removal and paperwork are key factors in overall software costs and schedules, so SPQR begins by quantifying the volume of defects and the volume of paperwork that will affect a project and then uses those predictions as adjuncts to estimating coding schedules and costs.

Software estimating is an activity that attempts to predict the future, using both objective and subjective information. The objective information includes basic facts such as the starting date of the project, its size, and the number of locations that will be involved in development. The subjective information includes human opinions about topics such as skills, difficulty, and complexity. The need to utilize subjective information means that there is always a range of uncertainty in software estimating.

To minimize the impact of subjective information, the SPQR technique uses a set of questions in which the possible answers are displayed and ranked according to a 5-point scale. Thus all users of SPQR have access to the same basic information about every question. This technique does not by itself ensure consistency, but when different personnel working on the same project have filled out the questionnaire independently, without knowledge of one another's responses, their responses have tended to be homogeneous.

The questions which drive the SPQR model are a conscious attempt to capture all of the significant variables which affect a software project. Thus the questions by themselves, independent of the SPQR tool, provide a useful checklist of the factors which can affect software projects.

When using the questions without the SPQR tool itself, note that a score of 1 or 2 indicates a positive or beneficial effect, 3 is intended to be average, and 4 or 5 mean potential troubles from the variable.

Since a 5-point scale is not really sufficient to capture all of the possibilities, SPQR uses decimal values as well as integers. That is, to indicate that an answer lies somewhere between 3 and 4, it is acceptable to use 3.5 or any other decimal value.

INPUT QUESTIONNAIRE FOR THE SOFTWARE PRODUCTIVITY, QUALITY, AND RELIABILITY ESTIMATOR

(SPQR/100)

DEVELOPMENT, ENHANCEMENT, AND MAINTENANCE PROJECTS

Version 1.1—May 28, 1985

Security Level: _____

Organization: _____

Standard Industry Classification (SIC): _____

Location: _____

Project: _____

Manager: _____

Estimator: _____

Date of Estimate: _____

Time of Estimate: _____

Comments: _____

TABLE OF CONTENTS

ESTIMATE TYPE AND PROJECT CONSTRAINTS

ESTIMATE TYPE?:   _____
   1) New program development
   2) Functional enhancement/new features to existing program
   3) Maintenance change or defect repair to existing program
   4) Analysis and restructuring of an existing program
   5) Software package evaluation or acquisition

ESTIMATE SCOPE?:   _____
   1) Prototype: for demonstration purposes
   2) Prototype: to evolve into delivered program
   3) Module or subelement of a program
   4) Complete standalone program
   5) Component or program within a system
   6) System: multiple linked programs or components
   7) Release: current version of an evolving system

ESTIMATE GOALS?:   _____
   1) Quick sizing
   2) Find the normal average of schedule, effort, and quality
   3) Find the shortest development schedule
   4) Find the lowest development effort or cost
   5) Find the smallest average development staff
   6) Find the highest product quality and reliability
   7) Find the shortest schedule with very high reliability
   8) Find the optimum tools or methods for project
   9) Find the optimum language, tools, or methods for project
  10) Match the following project constraints:

MAJOR PROJECT CONSTRAINTS (OPTIONAL)

   1) Maximum development schedule (months)?:   _____

   2) Maximum development effort (person-months)?:   _____

   3) Maximum development cost (dollars)?:   _____

   4) Maximum development staff size (personnel)?:   _____

   5) Maximum defects at delivery (defects/KLOC)?:   _____

PROJECT FINANCIAL INPUTS (OPTIONAL)

Average monthly salary level (fully burdened)?:   _____

Project hiring and relocation costs?:   _____

Project capital equipment costs?:   _____

Other project costs, fees, services?:   _____

DEVELOPMENT PROJECT AND PERSONNEL VARIABLES

CURRENT PROJECT PHASE?:   _____
   1) Planning or proposal
   2) Requirements
   3) Prototyping
   4) Design
   5) Coding
   6) Integration and testing
   7) Installation or production
   8) Hybrid: parts of project in different phases
   9) Restart: project making major scope or direction change

PROJECT CLASS?:   _____
   1) Personal program
   2) Internal program, not for outside marketing
   3) Internal program, intended for reuse or commonality
   4) Internal program, with functions marketed as a service
   5) External program, to be put in public domain
   6) External program, leased to users
   7) External program, bundled with hardware
   8) External program, unbundled and marketed commercially
   9) External program, developed under commercial contract
   10) External program, developed under government contract
   11) External program, developed under military contract

PROJECT TYPE?:   _____
   1) Nonprocedural (generated, query, spreadsheet, etc.)
   2) Batch applications program
   3) Interactive applications program
   4) Batch database applications program
   5) Interactive database applications program
   6) Scientific or mathematical program

7) Systems or support program
8) Communications or telecommunications program
9) Embedded or real-time program
10) Graphics, animation, or image processing program
11) Artificial intelligence program
12) Hybrid project: multiple types

PROJECT NOVELTY?: _____
   1) Conversion or functional repeat of a well-known program
   2) Functional repeat, but with some new features
   3) Even mixture of repeated and new features
   4) Novel program, but with some well-understood features
   5) Novel program, of a type never before attempted

DEVELOPMENT PERSONNEL EXPERIENCE?: _____
   1) All experts in the type of program being developed
   2) Majority of experts, but some new hires or novices
   3) Even mixture of experts, new hires, and novices
   4) Majority of new hires and novices, with few experts
   5) All personnel are new to this kind of program

PERSONNEL EMPLOYMENT CLASS?: _____
   1) All permanent employees of enterprise
   2) Majority are permanent employees, with some contractors
   3) Even mixture of permanent and contracting personnel
   4) Majority of contract personnel
   5) All employees are contract personnel

USER EXPERIENCE?: _____
   1) User experience with project is not a major factor
   2) Users have significant experience with similar projects
   3) Users have some experience with similar projects
   4) Users have little or no experience with similar projects
   5) User experience with similar projects is not known

USER INVOLVEMENT DURING DEVELOPMENT?: _____
   1) User involvement is not a major factor for the project
   2) Users are heavily involved during requirements/design
   3) Users are somewhat involved during requirements/design
   4) Users are seldom involved during requirements/design
   5) User involvement is not currently known

USER DOCUMENTATION TYPE?: _____
   1) Primarily on-line iconographic documentation
   2) Primarily on-line menu-driven or text documentation

3) Mixed high-quality printed documents and on-line HELP
4) High-quality printed documents
5) Informal printed documents, with or without HELP

USER EDUCATION?:

1) Program is embedded and needs no explicit training
2) Program is self-teaching and needs no other training
3) Program can be learned from documents and HELP
4) Program requires minor instruction before usage
5) Program requires careful instruction before usage

PERFORMANCE AND MEMORY RESTRICTIONS?:

1) No memory or performance restrictions
2) Restrictions on performance, but not on memory
3) Restrictions on memory, but not on performance
4) Some memory and performance restrictions
5) Severe memory and performance restrictions

DEVELOPMENT GEOGRAPHY?:

1) Single-department, single-site development project
2) Multiple departments within single site
3) Multiple development sites or multicompany project
4) International development within same company
5) International multicompany development

NUMBER OF DEVELOPMENT LOCATIONS?:

MANAGEMENT PROJECT AND PERSONNEL VARIABLES

LEGAL AND STATUTORY IMPACTS?:

1) No known legal or statutory constraints
2) Export license required for non-U.S. distribution
3) Statutes or government regulations affect project
4) Security regulations or military security affect project
5) Stringent security or government regulations on project

PROJECT FUNDING SOURCE?:

1) Overhead funding or internal budget
2) Project charged back to users
3) Time and materials contract
4) Fixed-price, fixed-delivery-schedule contract
5) Venture capital or start-up funding

PROJECT JUSTIFICATION OR VALUE ANALYSIS?: _____
1) Strategic, technical, or market needs of the enterprise
2) Tangible and intangible benefits considered
3) Tangible benefits considered
4) Cost reduction is primary justification considered
5) Ambiguous or uncertain justifications

STAFFING AND HIRING?: _____
1) Personnel can be hired as needed
2) Personnel can be hired as justified
3) Personnel for project are already on board
4) Personnel hiring is difficult
5) Personnel hiring is frozen

TOOLS, EQUIPMENT, AND SUPPLIES?: _____
1) Tools and equipment can be acquired as needed
2) Tools and equipment can be acquired as justified
3) Tools and equipment for project are already in use
4) Tools and equipment acquisition is difficult
5) Tools and equipment acquisition is frozen

JUSTIFICATION FOR NEW STAFF OR EQUIPMENT?: _____
1) Technical needs of project
2) Schedule, cost, quality, or ease of use improvement
3) Schedule, cost, or quality improvement
4) Tangible cost saving is primary justification
5) Varying or ambiguous justifications

PROJECT PLANNING AND ESTIMATING?: _____
1) Fully automated planning and estimating tools
2) Partially automated planning and estimating tools
3) Formal manual planning and estimating methods
4) Informal manual planning and estimating methods
5) Schedules and costs set by directive

MILESTONE AND PROGRESS TRACKING?: _____
1) Automated and convenient milestone and progress tracking
2) Automated but cumbersome milestone and progress tracking
3) Formal manual milestone and progress tracking
4) Informal manual milestone and progress tracking
5) Little or no milestone and progress tracking

BUDGETING AND COST ACCOUNTING?: _____
1) Automated and convenient budget and accounting systems
2) Automated but cumbersome budget and accounting systems

3) Formal manual budget and accounting systems
4) Informal manual budget and accounting systems
5) Projects not covered by budget and accounting systems

PRODUCTIVITY MEASUREMENTS?:   _____
    1) Automated life-cycle productivity measures
    2) Manual life-cycle productivity measures
    3) Partial productivity measures during development
    4) Informal partial productivity measures
    5) No productivity measures

QUALITY MEASUREMENTS?:   _____
    1) Automated quality measures from design forward
    2) Automated quality measures from testing forward
    3) Manual quality measures from design forward
    4) Manual quality measures from testing forward
    5) No quality measures

SYSTEM DEVELOPMENT METHODOLOGY?:   _____
    1) Automated and effective system development methodology
    2) Automated but cumbersome system development methodology
    3) Manual and effective system development methodology
    4) Manual but cumbersome system development methodology
    5) No formal system development methodology in current use

STANDARDS AND POLICIES?:   _____
    1) Effective and well-understood standards and policies
    2) Project follows military or DOD standards and policies
    3) Well-understood but cumbersome standards and policies
    4) New or ambiguous standards and policies
    5) No formal standards or policies

STAFF OVERTIME?:   _____
    1) Overtime seldom or never occurs
    2) Overtime seldom occurs but is recorded when it does
    3) Overtime seldom occurs and is not usually recorded
    4) Overtime often occurs but is recorded when it does
    5) Overtime often occurs and is not usually recorded

STAFF COMPENSATION PLAN?:   _____
    1) Dual plan for technical and management to director level
    2) Dual plan for technical and management to 3rd-line level
    3) Dual plan for technical and management to 2nd-line level
    4) Technical salaries stop at 1st-line management level
    5) Technical salaries stop below 1st-line management level

STAFF PERFORMANCE AWARD METHODS?: _____
1) Merit appraisal system plus incentive bonuses
2) Merit appraisal system
3) Merit/longevity appraisal system plus incentive bonus
4) Merit/longevity appraisal system
5) Ambiguous or uncertain performance award system

STAFF MORALE INDICATORS?: _____
1) Open-door policy, opinion survey, & executive interviews
2) Open-door policy and planned executive interviews
3) Planned, scheduled executive interviews
4) Informal executive interviews
5) Ambiguous or uncertain morale indicators

STAFF PROMOTIONAL OPPORTUNITIES?: _____
1) Career planning and internal promotions are supported
2) Career planning and internal promotions sometimes occur
3) Career planning and internal promotions are exceptions
4) Career planning and internal promotions seldom occur
5) Ambiguous or uncertain internal opportunities

PROJECT ORGANIZATIONAL STRUCTURE?: _____
1) Individual project or very small team
2) Small team project
3) Conventional departments and hierarchical organization
4) Conventional departments and matrix organization
5) Ambiguous or uncertain project organization structure

PROJECT MANAGERIAL AND
TECHNICAL COHESIVENESS?: _____
1) Full agreement on project goals, schedules, methods
2) Partial agreement on project goals, schedules, methods
3) Some disagreement on project goals, schedules, methods
4) Sharp disagreement on project goals, schedules, methods
5) Uncertain or ambiguous goals, schedules, methods

LOCATION SOFTWARE PROFESSIONAL
STAFF SIZE?: _____
1) Fewer than 10 software employees at location
2) From 10 to 50 software employees at location
3) From 50 to 100 software employees at location
4) From 100 to 1000 software employees at location
5) More than 1000 software employees at location

PACKAGE EVALUATION AND ACQUISITION VARIABLES

PACKAGE CLASS BEING EVALUATED?: _____
  1) Software only
  2) Software and documentation
  3) Software, documentation, and training
  4) Software and hardware combination
  5) Software, hardware, documentation, and training

PACKAGE TYPE BEING EVALUATED?: _____

  1) End-user utility (Spreadsheet, wordprocessor, etc.)
  2) Batch applications program
  3) Interactive applications program
  4) CAI or educational support program
  5) Batch database applications program
  6) Interactive database applications program
  7) Decision support program
  8) Graphics support program
  9) CAD/CAE support program
  10) Scientific or mathematical program
  11) Systems program (operating system, utility, etc.)
  12) Compiler or assembler
  13) Program or application generator
  14) Process control program
  15) Communications or telecommunications program
  16) Embedded program
  17) Real-time program
  18) Robotics program
  19) Artificial intelligence program
  20) Military or defense system
  21) Hybrid: multiple types being evaluated

NUMBER OF PACKAGES TO BE EVALUATED FOR
THIS PROJECT?: _____
  1) Only 1
  2) From 2 to 5
  3) From 6 to 10
  4) From 11 to 20
  5) More than 20

PACKAGE VENDOR TYPES CONSIDERED?: _____
  1) Another location or unit of this enterprise
  2) A public domain source (university, government, etc.)
  3) A retail computer or software outlet

4) An established software or hardware company
5) An enterprise marketing a package developed for its use

PRIMARY EVALUATION METHODOLOGY?: _____

1) Review of published articles and critiques
2) Contacts with current package users
3) Documentation review with some on-site testing
4) Full on-site evaluation
5) Evaluation methodology is currently undefined

EVALUATION PERSONNEL CLASS?: _____

1) All experts in type of package being evaluated
2) Majority of experts, but some new hires or novices
3) Even mixture of experts, new hires, or novices
4) Majority of new hires or novices; few experts
5) All personnel are new to this type of package

STATUS OF EVALUATION BENCHMARKS?: _____

1) Completed and operational
2) Nearing completion
3) Defined and being developed
4) Currently under definition
5) Ambiguous or uncertain benchmarks for package evaluation

LICENSE OR ACQUISITION TYPE PLANNED?: _____

1) Outright purchase of all rights to program
2) Single-location, single-user license
3) Multilocation, multiuser license
4) Multilocation license, with rights to remarket
5) License type is currently not defined

MODIFICATIONS PLANNED AFTER ACQUISITION?: _____

1) No planned modifications
2) Minor changes only
3) Some customization for local requirements
4) Significant customization for local requirements
5) Modifications after acquisition are currently undefined

MODIFICATION PERFORMANCE?: _____

1) All modifications will be performed by vendor personnel
2) Most modifications will be performed by vendor personnel
3) Internal staff and vendor modifications
4) All modifications will be performed by internal staff
5) Modification performance is currently undefined

PACKAGE OPERATIONAL COMPATIBILITY?: _____
    1) Package operates with current hardware and software
    2) Package may require some new hardware or peripherals
    3) Package may require new hardware and software
    4) Package may require substantial hardware/software changes
    5) Package will require major hardware/software changes

ENVIRONMENTAL VARIABLES

REQUIREMENTS ENVIRONMENT?: _____
    1) Program developers are also the users of the program
    2) Working model or prototype, plus clear user requirements
    3) Fairly clear user requirements
    4) Incomplete or ambiguous user requirements
    5) User requirements are frequently changing and uncertain

PROTOTYPING ENVIRONMENT?: _____
    1) Prototyping of all major outputs, inputs, and functions
    2) Prototyping of some outputs, inputs, and functions
    3) Prototyping of major outputs and inputs
    4) Prototyping of a few outputs and inputs
    5) No prototyping at all

ANALYSIS ENVIRONMENT?: _____
    1) "Pattern matching" data and function analysis
    2) Structured data analysis and function analysis
    3) Informal or partial data and function analysis
    4) Minimal data or function analysis
    5) No data or function analysis

DESIGN AUTOMATION ENVIRONMENT?: _____
    1) Design-to-code automation with reusable code library
    2) Formal design methods & automated text/graphics support
    3) Semiformal design with some text/graphics support
    4) Semiformal design with text automation only
    5) Informal design with no automation

DATA ADMINISTRATION ENVIRONMENT?: _____
    1) Data administration or data dictionary not needed
    2) Data administration & active data dictionary available
    3) Data administration & passive data dictionary available

4) Data administration or data dictionary available
5) No data administration or data dictionary available

USER AND MAINTENANCE DOCUMENT PRODUCTION ENVIRONMENT?: _____

1) Professional staff; screen, text & graphics tools
2) Professional staff; screen & text tools; manual graphics
3) Programming or user staff; screen, text & graphics tools
4) Programming or user staff; screen & text tools only
5) Programming or user staff; no automated document support

DOCUMENTATION REPRODUCTION AND DISTRIBUTION ENVIRONMENT?: _____

1) Documentation reproduction/distribution is very minor
2) Automated documentation reproduction/distribution
3) Reproduction/distribution center with adequate capacity
4) Reproduction/distribution center sometimes overloaded
5) Reproduction/distribution of documents is a bottleneck

DEVELOPMENT HARDWARE ENVIRONMENT?: _____

1) Microcomputer
2) Minicomputer
3) Mainframe computer
4) Embedded or special-purpose computer
5) Hybrid development environment: multiple hardware types

WORKSTATION ENVIRONMENT?: _____

1) Individual office workstations and portable terminals
2) Individual office workstations
3) Shared workstations (two employees per workstation)
4) Shared workstations (three or more employees per station)
5) Batch development, with few or no workstations

RESPONSE TIME ENVIRONMENT?: _____

1) Response time is not a factor for this project
2) Subsecond response time is the norm
3) One- to five-second response time is the norm
4) Five- to 10-second response time is the norm
5) More than 10-second response time is the norm

PROJECT LIBRARY CONTROL ENVIRONMENT?: _____

1) Full project library with automated support
2) Program library with partly automated support
3) Partly automated source code and update support

4) Manual source code, update, and document controls
5) No formal source code, update, or document controls

VOICE AND DOCUMENT COMMUNICATION ENVIRONMENT?: _____

1) Project requires no remote communication capabilities
2) Teleconferencing, voice mail, and electronic mail
3) Voice mail and easy-to-use electronic mail
4) Partial or cumbersome electronic mail
5) No automated communication facilities

COMPUTER, DATA, AND PROGRAM COMMUNICATION ENVIRONMENT?: _____

1) All project personnel use the same computer system
2) Full network linking computers, data, and programs
3) Full network linking data and programs
4) Bulk data transfer
5) Limited or no computer, program, and data transfer

STAFF EDUCATION ENVIRONMENT?: _____

1) Education or staff training not needed on project
2) Technical education is readily available
3) Technical education is available if needed
4) Technical education is limited
5) Technical education is seldom available or is discouraged

STAFF INFORMATION RESOURCE ENVIRONMENT?: _____

1) Reference materials or library not needed for project
2) Full library and on-line information available
3) Some library and reference services available at site
4) Some technical reference materials available if needed
5) Little or no technical reference material available

TECHNOLOGY EXPLORATION ENVIRONMENT?: _____

1) Technology exploration not needed for this project
2) Development center, information center, or formal support
3) Informal but active technology exploration
4) Journal screening or casual technology exploration
5) Little or no technology exploration

INTERNAL TECHNOLOGY COMMUNICATION ENVIRONMENT?: _____

1) Enterprise technical journals, reports, and conferences
2) Enterprise technical reports and conferences

3) Occasional enterprise technical reports, or conferences
4) Some internal technical interchange or meetings
5) Little or no internal technical interchange

EXTERNAL TECHNOLOGY COMMUNICATION
ENVIRONMENT?: _____
1) Staff encouraged to publish or attend technical symposia
2) Staff encouraged to publish in some technical journals
3) Staff publishing or symposium attendance is voluntary
4) Staff publishing or symposium attendance seldom occurs
5) Staff publishing or symposium attendance is discouraged

PROGRAMMING OFFICE ENVIRONMENT?: _____
1) Private offices and adequate facilities
2) Doubled offices and adequate facilities
3) Multiemployee shared offices and storage facilities
4) Cramped, shared offices and insufficient facilities
5) No offices and insufficient facilities

SUPPORT SOFTWARE NOVELTY ENVIRONMENT?: _____
1) Tools, languages, and compilers are familiar and reliable
2) Some tools or languages are new to team
3) Some tools or languages are new and have minor problems
4) Most tools or languages are new and have minor problems
5) Most tools or languages are unfamiliar and unsuitable

HARDWARE NOVELTY ENVIRONMENT?: _____
1) All development hardware is generally familiar to team
2) Most development hardware is familiar to most of team
3) Most development hardware is familiar to some of team
4) Most development hardware is new to entire team
5) All development hardware is new to entire team

DEFECT REMOVAL EXPERIENCE AND METHODS VARIABLES

PRE-TEST DEFECT REMOVAL EXPERIENCE?: _____
1) All personnel experienced in reviews and inspections
2) Most personnel experienced in reviews and inspections
3) Even mixture of experienced and inexperienced personnel
4) Most personnel inexperienced in reviews and inspections
5) All personnel inexperienced in reviews and inspections

TESTING DEFECT REMOVAL EXPERIENCE?: _____

    1) All personnel experienced in software test methods
    2) Most personnel experienced in software test methods
    3) Even mixture of experienced and inexperienced personnel
    4) Majority of personnel inexperienced in test methods
    5) All personnel inexperienced in software test methods

PROGRAM DEBUGGING TOOLS?: _____

    1) Full screen editor, traces, cross-references, etc.
    2) Full screen editor, traces, but little else
    3) Full screen editor, but no trace or other flow aids
    4) Line editor, with some trace and flow aids
    5) No editing, tracing, or debugging aids of any real help

TESTING FUNCTION?: _____

    1) Formal test department, plus development and user tests
    2) Formal test department, plus development testing
    3) Formal testing with results compared to known criteria
    4) Informal testing with no predefined goals or criteria
    5) Hasty or casual testing due to schedule pressures

QUALITY ASSURANCE FUNCTION?: _____

    1) Formal QA group or IV&V, with adequate resources
    2) Formal QA group, but understaffed (<1 to 15 ratio)
    3) QA role is assigned to development personnel
    4) QA role is performed informally
    5) No QA function exists for the project

PROJECT AUDITING FUNCTION?: _____

    1) Formal audit group with adequate resources
    2) Formal audit group, but understaffed
    3) Project or process auditing is assigned as needed
    4) Audit function is performed seldom or informally
    5) Audit function does not exist for the project

PROJECT QUALITY AND RELIABILITY TARGETS?: _____

    1) No quality or reliability targets are needed for project
    2) Stringent targets set for project defect or failure rates
    3) Average targets set for defect rates and failure rates
    4) Informal targets set for defect rates and failure rates
    5) Project defect and failure targets are undefined

DEFECT REMOVAL ACTIVITIES FOR PROJECT

Business and Legal Reviews	**Full**		**Part**		**None**
1) Formal "make or buy" reviews	1	2	3	4	5
2) Proposal or bid reviews	1	2	3	4	5
3) Business phase reviews	1	2	3	4	5
3) Project value analysis reviews	1	2	3	4	5
5) Patent or legal reviews	1	2	3	4	5
6) Import/export license reviews	1	2	3	4	5

Pretest Defect Removal	**Full**		**Part**		**None**
1) Requirements review	1	2	3	4	5
2) Function design review	1	2	3	4	5
3) Prototyping	1	2	3	4	5
4) Module design review	1	2	3	4	5
5) Data structure design review	1	2	3	4	5
6) User/maintenance documentation review	1	2	3	4	5
7) Code review/inspection	1	2	3	4	5
8) Quality assurance review	1	2	3	4	5
9) Proofs of correctness	1	2	3	4	5
10) Independent verification & validation	1	2	3	4	5

Testing	**Full**		**Part**		**None**
1) Unit testing	1	2	3	4	5
2) New function testing	1	2	3	4	5
3) Regression testing	1	2	3	4	5
4) Stress or performance testing	1	2	3	4	5
5) System testing	1	2	3	4	5
6) User acceptance testing	1	2	3	4	5
7) Field testing at user location(s)	1	2	3	4	5
8) Independent testing organization	1	2	3	4	5

Postrelease Defect Removal	**Full**		**Part**		**None**
1) Postrelease project review	1	2	3	4	5
2) User satisfaction survey	1	2	3	4	5
3) User groups or user meetings	1	2	3	4	5
4) Error-prone module analysis	1	2	3	4	5
5) Automated restructuring	1	2	3	4	5

MAINTENANCE PROJECT AND PERSONNEL VARIABLES

SOFTWARE WARRANTY COVERAGE?: _____
1) No explicit or implicit warranties on software
2) Limited explicit warranties
3) Limited warranty, but additional support for good will
4) Limited warranty, with substantial guarantees
5) Limited warranty, with penalties for nonperformance

MAINTENANCE FUNDING?: _____
1) Maintenance is funded from overhead or enterprise funds
2) Maintenance is covered by informal contract or agreement
3) Hybrid: partial overhead and partial charge-out funding
4) Maintenance is charged out to users
5) Maintenance funding is currently undefined

MAINTENANCE PERFORMANCE?: _____
1) Maintenance is performed by customer personnel
2) Maintenance is performed by developers as needed
3) Maintenance is performed by formal maintenance group
4) Maintenance is performed by third-party contract
5) Maintenance performance is currently undefined

DELIVERY SUPPORT?: _____
1) No on-site customer support at delivery
2) On-site support during field test only
3) On-site support for early customers
4) On-site support for special cases
5) On-site support for all deliveries

CENTRAL MAINTENANCE?: _____
1) No central maintenance for project
2) On-line communication between users and maintenance
3) Informal defect repairs and update distribution
4) Formal defect repairs and update distribution
5) Formal defect repairs with 24-hour staffing

FIELD MAINTENANCE?: _____
1) No field maintenance for project
2) On-line communication between users and maintenance
3) Field maintenance for special and rare situations
4) Field maintenance at customer request
5) Permanent on-site field maintenance personnel

MAINTENANCE PERSONNEL CLASS?: _____
1) All experts in system being maintained
2) Majority of experts, but some new hires or novices
3) Even mixture of experts, new hires, and novices
4) Majority of new hires, with few experts
5) All maintenance personnel are new to the system

MAINTENANCE PERSONNEL EDUCATION?: _____
1) Maintenance training is not required for the project
2) Adequate training in projects and tools is available
3) Some training in projects and tools is available
4) Some training in projects to be maintained is available
5) Little or no training in projects or tools

REPLACEMENT AND ENHANCEMENT PLANNING?: _____
1) Automated code analysis and restructuring tools
2) Automated restructuring service from outside vendor
3) Replacement strategy for aging systems and programs
4) Enhancement strategy for aging systems and programs
5) No formal replacement or enhancement strategy

MAINTENANCE TRACKING TOOLS AND SUPPORT?: _____
1) Automated analysis, fault reporting, and fault tracking
2) Partly automated analysis tools and repair tracking
3) Formal manual fault reporting and repair tracking
4) Informal maintenance tools and control of fault reports
5) Maintenance tools or support are not currently defined

LONG-RANGE PROGRAM STABILITY?: _____
1) Few or no changes to code, data, or to new hardware
2) New functions and new data types will sometimes occur
3) New functions, data types, and hardware may occur
4) Frequent changes in functions and data types
5) Frequent changes in functions, data types, and hardware

PROGRAM EXECUTION FREQUENCY?: _____
1) Quarterly or annual runs
2) Monthly or weekly runs
3) Daily or hourly runs
4) Continuous runs or available continuously
5) Run frequency is not defined

MAINTENANCE RELEASE FREQUENCY?: _____
1) Maintenance releases will be distributed as needed
2) Maintenance releases will be quarterly or oftener

3) Maintenance releases will be annually
4) Maintenance releases will be longer than annual
5) Maintenance releases are currently not defined

INSTALLATION AND PRODUCTION GEOGRAPHY?: _____
  1) Single production site in a single city
  2) Multiple production sites in a single city
  3) Multiple production sites in multiple cities
  4) International installation and production
  5) Installation and production not defined

NUMBER OF SYSTEM INSTALLATION SITES?: _____

NUMBER OF SYSTEM MAINTENANCE SITES?: _____

ANTICIPATED YEARS OF SYSTEM'S USEFUL LIFE?: _____

NEW CODE VARIABLES (FOR ENTIRELY NEW PROGRAMS)

NEW CODE STRUCTURE?: _____
  1) Nonprocedural (generated, database, query, etc.)
  2) Built with program skeletons and reusable modules
  3) Well structured (small modules and simple paths)
  4) Fair structure, but some complex paths or modules
  5) Poor structure, with many complex modules and paths

NEW CODE DATA COMPLEXITY?: _____
  1) Simple data with few variables and little complexity
  2) Several data elements, but simple data relationships
  3) Multiple files, switches, and data interactions
  4) Complex data elements and complex data interactions
  5) Very complex data elements and data interactions

NEW CODE LANGUAGE(S)?: _____

NEW CODE LANGUAGE LEVEL?: _____

NEW CODE SIZE (KLOC)?: _____

FUNCTION-POINT ANALYSIS (OPTIONAL)

NUMBER OF INPUTS?: _____

NUMBER OF OUTPUTS?: _____

NUMBER OF INQUIRIES?: _____

NUMBER OF DATA FILES?:   _____

NUMBER OF INTERFACES?:   _____

REUSABLE CODE SIZING (OPTIONAL)

REUSABLE CODE LANGUAGE(S)?:   _____

REUSABLE LANGUAGE LEVEL?:   _____

REUSABLE CODE SIZE (KLOC)?:   _____

**BASE CODE VARIABLES (FOR MAINTENANCE
AND ENHANCEMENTS)**

BASE CODE ORIGIN?:   _____
1) Base code developed internally by location
2) Base code acquired from another enterprise location
3) Base code developed under custom contract
4) Base code acquired from an outside vendor
5) Hybrid: base code comes from mixed sources

BASE CODE AGE?:   _____
1) New or less than one year
2) Installed in 1980 or after
3) Installed in 1970—1979
4) Installed in or before 1970
5) Hybrid system with mixed ages for different parts

BASE CODE MAINTENANCE RESPONSIBILITY?:   _____
1) Base/reusable code is formally & externally maintained
2) Base/reusable code is informally & externally maintained
3) Project maintains any base/reusable code that is updated
4) Project maintains any base/reusable code that is included
5) Project maintains all base/reusable code in system

BASE CODE STATUS?:   _____
1) Stable system (<0.5 defects per KLOC per year)
2) Stabilizing system (<3.0 defects per KLOC per year)
3) Unstable system (>3.0 defects per KLOC per year)
4) Error-prone system (>6.0 defects per KLOC per year)
5) Hazardous system (>10.0 defects per KLOC per year)

BASE CODE ANALYSIS AND RESTRUCTURING?: _____

    1) Automated analysis and restructure of all base code
    2) Automated analysis and restructure of error-prone modules
    3) Analysis and restructure using outside vendor or service
    4) Manual analysis and restructure of error-prone modules
    5) Little or no analysis or restructure of base code

BASE CODE STRUCTURE?: _____

    1) Nonprocedural (generated, database, query, etc.)
    2) Constructed from standard reusable modules
    3) Well-structured, with small discrete functional modules
    4) Average structure, with some complex modules
    5) Complex structure, with some very complex modules

BASE CODE DATA COMPLEXITY?: _____

    1) Simple data with few variables and little complexity
    2) Several data elements, but simple data relationships
    3) Multiple files, switches, and data interactions
    4) Complex data elements and complex data interactions
    5) Very complex data elements and data interactions

BASE CODE LANGUAGE(S)?: _____

BASE CODE LANGUAGE LEVEL?: _____

BASE CODE SIZE (KLOC)?: _____

BASE CODE FUNCTION-POINT ANALYSIS (OPTIONAL)

NUMBER OF INPUTS?: _____

NUMBER OF OUTPUTS?: _____

NUMBER OF INQUIRIES?: _____

NUMBER OF DATA FILES?: _____

NUMBER OF INTERFACES?: _____

BASE CODE COMPONENT AND CODE SIZING (OPTIONAL)

COMPONENTS IN BASE?: _____

COMPONENTS TO BE CHANGED?: _____

DELTA CODE VARIABLES (FOR MAINTENANCE AND ENHANCEMENTS)

DELTA CODE STRUCTURE?: _____
   1) Nonprocedural (generated, database, query, etc.)
   2) Standard reusable modules, plus some scattered changes
   3) Delta code will be new components or new modules only
   4) Some new modules/components, plus scattered changes
   5) Delta code will be primarily scattered changes

DELTA CODE DATA COMPLEXITY?: _____
   1) Delta code has simple data elements and relationships
   2) Delta code shares the base system's data complexity
   3) Delta code adds some new data elements to base system
   4) Delta code adds significant new data complexity
   5) Delta code adds major new data elements and complexity

DELTA CODE LANGUAGE(S)?: _____

DELTA CODE LANGUAGE LEVEL?: _____

DELTA CODE SIZE (KLOC)?: _____

DELTA FUNCTION-POINT ANALYSIS (OPTIONAL)

NUMBER OF INPUTS?: _____

NUMBER OF OUTPUTS?: _____

NUMBER OF INQUIRIES?: _____

NUMBER OF DATA FILES?: _____

NUMBER OF INTERFACES?: _____

REUSABLE CODE SIZING (OPTIONAL)

REUSABLE CODE LANGUAGE(S)?: _____

REUSABLE LANGUAGE LEVEL?: _____

REUSABLE CODE SIZE (KLOC)?: _____

DESCRIPTIVE MATERIALS AND COMMENTS

DEVELOPMENT COMPUTER(S)?: _____

PRODUCTION COMPUTER(S)?: _____

DEVELOPMENT OPERATING SYSTEM(S)?: _____

PRODUCTION OPERATING SYSTEM(S)?: _____

MANAGEMENT TOOLS?: _____

_____

DEVELOPMENT TOOLS?: _____

_____

MAINTENANCE TOOLS?: _____

_____

DATABASE (OPTIONAL)?: _____

DATA DICTIONARY (OPTIONAL)?: _____

DATA COMMUNICATION (OPTIONAL)?: _____

COMMENTS AND ADDITIONAL EXPLANATIONS

_____

_____

_____

_____

_____

_____

_____

_____

SPQR LANGUAGES AND LANGUAGE LEVELS

LANGUAGE	DEFAULT LEVEL
01) Basic Assembler language	1
02) Macro Assembler language	1.5
03) C	2.5
04) ALGOL	3
05) CHILL	3
06) COBOL	3
07) FORTRAN	3
08) JOVIAL	3
09) Mixed languages (default value)	3
10) Other languages (default value)	3
11) Pascal	3.5
12) RPG	4
13) PL/I	4
14) MODULA-2	4
15) Ada	4.5
16) PROLOG	5
17) LISP	5
18) FORTH	5
19) BASIC	5
20) LOGO	5
21) English-based languages (INTELLECT, etc.)	6
22) Database languages (FOCUS, IDEAL, RAMIS)	8
23) Decision support languages (IFPS, EXPRESS)	8
24) STRATEGEM	9
25) APL	10
26) OBJECTIVE-C	12
27) SMALLTALK 80	15

28) Menu-driven generators   20

29) Database query languages   25

30) Spreadsheet languages (VisiCalc, LOTUS)   50

NOTE: The level of a language is its approximate power relative to assembler language. It can be considered the average number of statements it would take in assembler language to create the same function that one statement would produce in the target language.

INDEX